Israel and the Clash of Civilisations

Also by Jonathan Cook

Blood and Religion
The Unmasking of the Jewish and Democratic State

'Jonathan Cook's timely and important book on the Palestinians in Israel is by far the most penetrating and comprehensive on the subject to date. ... This work should be required reading for policymakers and for everyone concerned with the magnitude of the tasks confronting the two parties and the international community.'

– Dr Nur Masalha, Senior Lecturer and Director of Holy Land Studies; Programme Director of MA in Religion and Conflict, St Mary's College, University of Surrey, and author of *A Land Without a People* and *The Politics of Denial*

Israel and the Clash of Civilisations

Iraq, Iran and the Plan to Remake the Middle East

JONATHAN COOK

PLUTO PRESS
www.plutobooks.com

First published 2008 by Pluto Press
345 Archway Road, London N6 5AA

www.plutobooks.com

Copyright © Jonathan Cook 2008

The right of Jonathan Cook to be identified as the author of this work
has been asserted by him in accordance with the Copyright, Designs
and Patents Act 1988.

British Library Cataloguing in Publication Data
A catalogue record for this book is available from the British Library

ISBN   978 0 7453 2755 6 hardback
ISBN   978 0 7453 2754 9 paperback

Library of Congress Cataloging in Publication Data applied for

10 9 8 7 6 5 4 3 2

Designed and produced for Pluto Press by
Chase Publishing Services Ltd, Fortescue, Sidmouth, EX10 9QG, England
Typeset from disk by Stanford DTP Services, Northampton
Printed and bound in the European Union by
CPI Antony Rowe, Chippenham and Eastbourne

For my parents, Keith and Elena

CONTENTS

Preface   x

1 Regime Overthrow in Iraq   1

The body count keeps growing – A war for oil – US policy
in the Gulf – Containing Saddam – The neocon vision of
the Middle East – Finding a pretext to invade – Israel's role
behind the scenes

2 The Long Campaign Against Iran   36

The propaganda war – Israel's fear of a nuclear rival –
US readies for a military strike – Turning the clock back
20 years in Lebanon – Evidence the war was planned
– Syria was supposed to be next – A power struggle in
Washington – Ahmadinejad: the new Hitler

3 End of the Strongmen   79

Who controls American foreign policy? – The dog and
tail wag each other – Israel's relations with its patrons
– Sharon's doctrine of empire – Making the Middle
East collapse

4 Remaking the Middle East   116

Neocon motives in backing Israel's vision – The occupied
territories as a laboratory – Over the precipice and into
civil war – Iraq: a model for the region?

Notes   150
Select Bibliography   186
Index   189

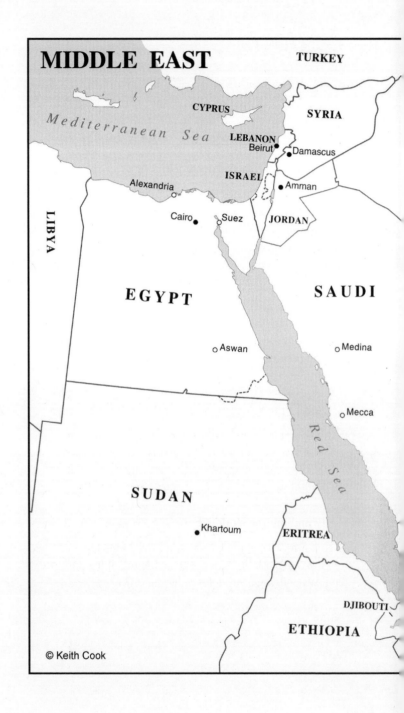

MIDDLE EAST

TURKEY

CYPRUS

SYRIA

Mediterranean Sea

LEBANON
Beirut • • Damascus

Alexandria o

ISRAEL

• Amman

LIBYA

Cairo • o Suez

JORDAN

EGYPT

SAUDI

o Aswan

o Medina

o Mecca

Red Sea

SUDAN

• Khartoum

ERITREA

DJIBOUTI

ETHIOPIA

© Keith Cook

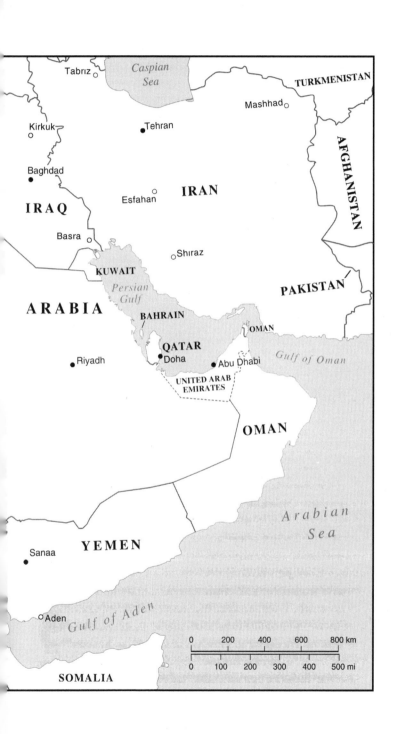

PREFACE

In summer 2007, Ghaith Abdul Ahad of the *Guardian* and Rajiv Chandrasekaran of the *Washington Post*, two young journalists who had recently won awards for their coverage of the US occupation of Iraq, sat down to discuss the disaster unfolding there. In particular, Abdul Ahad, an Iraqi who had spent years on the run from Saddam Hussein's army, could claim an intimate familiarity with Iraqi society not possible for his Western colleagues. Also unlike them, he did not live in the Green Zone, a sealed-off area of Baghdad from which Western journalists rarely ventured, and when on assignment he never 'embedded' with US soldiers. The two journalists agreed that Iraq, a country where more than 650,000 people had probably been killed since the US invasion, would continue to be 'bloody and dark and chaotic' for years to come. They also noted that before the US invasion, no one had been able to tell whether a neighbourhood was Sunni or Shia, two branches of Islam whose rivalry was at the root of a sectarian war engulfing the country. Under Saddam, Iraq had had the highest rate of Sunni and Shia intermarriage of any Arab or Muslim country, they pointed out. Abdul Ahad observed:

> Now we can draw a sectarian map of Baghdad right down to tiny alleyways and streets and houses. Everything has changed. As an Iraqi I go anywhere (not only in Iraq, but also in the Middle East), [and] the first thing people ask me is: 'Are you a Sunni or a Shia?' ... I think the problem we have now on the ground is a civil war. Call it whatever you want, it is a civil war.

Four million of Iraq's 27 million inhabitants had already fled the country or become internal refugees, exiled from their homes. Was partition of Iraq between the three main communities there – the Sunni, Shia and Kurds – inevitable? Chandrasekaran thought so: 'People are already voting with their feet. They're dividing

themselves on their own, people are moving from one community
to another, one neighbourhood to another in Baghdad. In some
cases they're leaving Iraq outright. This is the direction things are
headed.' Abdul Ahad, clearly upset by the thought of his country
breaking apart, nevertheless had to agree that communal division
was happening:

> I see a de facto split in the country, I see a de facto cantonisation between
> Sunnis and Shia. To enshrine this in some form of process will be messy,
> it'll be bloody. The main issue is for the Americans to recognise they don't
> have an Iraqi partner.

So who was responsible for the civil war and the humanitarian
catastrophe? Chandrasekaran answered: 'I wouldn't blame
the US for the civil war in Iraq, but I certainly think an awful
lot of decisions made by Ambassador [Paul] Bremer, the first
American viceroy to Iraq, have helped to fuel the instability we
see today.'[1]

In this book, I argue that this prevalent view of Iraq's fate
– that its civil war was a terrible unforeseen consequence of the
US invasion and a series of bad decisions made by the occupation
regime – is profoundly mistaken. Rather, civil war and partition
were the intended outcomes of the invasion and seen as beneficial
to American interests, or at least they were by a small group of
ultra-hawks known as the neoconservatives who came to dominate
the White House under President George W. Bush. The neoconservatives' understanding of American interests in the Middle East
was little different from that of previous administrations: securing
control of oil in the Persian Gulf. But what distinguished Bush's
invasion of Iraq from similar US attempts at regime change was
the strategy used to achieve this goal.

In his recent book *Overthrow*, Stephen Kinzer, a former *New
York Times* correspondent, argues that Iraq was only the most
recent of several examples over the past century when the US
government directly intervened to depose a foreign ruler. Kinzer
admits that this kind of 'regime change' is the exception: more
usually the US resorts to threatening uncooperative foreign

governments to make them do American bidding, or it supports
coups and revolutions carried out by others. Kinzer cites twelve
other examples of US-implemented regime change that preceded
the Bush Administration's Middle East adventures in Iraq and
Afghanistan. One thing is notable about his list: most of the
invasions, starting with Hawaii and Cuba in the 1890s and
including Puerto Rica, Honduras, Nicaragua, Guatemala, Grenada
and Panama, targeted small, largely defenceless countries, mostly
in America's 'backyard' of Central America and the Caribbean,
that could be attacked, or even occupied, by the US with relative
impunity. In the handful of more significant examples – Iran
(1953), South Vietnam (1964–75) and Chile (1973) – it is clear
that the US had in mind whom it was planning to assist or install
and how it hoped to effect regime change, even if in Vietnam,
for example, US planners failed miserably to achieve their goal.
However, in the case of Iraq – and Afghanistan – not only is
it impossible to identify the new strongman Washington hoped
would replace the old one, but the actions of the Bush Administration post-invasion deliberately ensured that no new strongman
would emerge. Iraq, unlike Kinzer's other significant cases, seems
to be a genuine example of regime overthrow rather than regime
change. Brutal military occupation appears to have been the goal
of the invasion rather than a brief transition phase while a new
leader was installed.

Kinzer notes that in most of his examples US interference created
'whirlpools of instability from which undreamed-of threats arose
years later',[2] or what is sometimes referred to as 'blowback'.
But again Iraq was different: the threats arose immediately and
were predictable – and readily predicted by many analysts of the
region.[3] Also, unlike Vietnam, it looked impossible for the US
to contemplate a withdrawal from Iraq. In the case of Vietnam,
south-east Asia could to be taught a painful lesson for its defiance,
by bombing its inhabitants into the dark age, but in Iraq the US
had either to remain in place as the occupier or find a suitable
alternative way of controlling the country's huge oil reserves
for its own benefit. Noam Chomsky has made much the same

point, observing that comparisons between Iraq and Vietnam
are misleading:

> In Vietnam, Washington planners could fulfill their primary war aims by
> destroying the virus [local nationalism] and inoculating the region, then
> withdrawing, leaving the wreckage to enjoy its sovereignty. The situation
> in Iraq is radically different. Iraq cannot be destroyed and abandoned ...
> Iraq must be kept under control, if not in the manner anticipated by Bush
> planners, at least somehow.[4]

This distinctive new strategy for regime overthrow adopted
by the White House originated far from Washington, and was
apparently opposed by most of the country's senior military
command and by the State Department under Colin Powell. In
the early 1980s Israel's security establishment had developed ideas
about dissolving the other states of the Middle East to encourage
ethnic and religious discord (Chapter 3). This was in essence a
reimagining of the regional power structure that had existed under
the Ottomans – before the arrival of the European colonialists
and their forced reordering of the Middle East into nation states
– but with Israel replacing the Turks as the local imperial power.
In this way, hoped Israel and the neocons, large and potentially
powerful states such as Iraq and Iran could be partitioned between
their rival ethnic and sectarian communities.

For Israel, this outcome was seen as having four main beneficial
consequences, all of which would contribute towards the related
goals of strengthening Israel against its regional challengers and
weakening the ability of the Palestinians under occupation to
resist Israel's long-standing plan to ethnically cleanse them from
within its expanded, 1967 borders. First, the 'Ottomanisation' of
the Middle East would bolster the influence of other minorities in
the region – such as the Kurds, Druze and Christians, all of which
had been marginalised and weakened by the existing system of
European-imposed nation states – against a more dominant Islam,
in both its Sunni and Shia varieties. Israel would be able to make
and exploit alliances with these minorities, as well as provoking
conflict between the Sunni and Shia, and thereby prevent the

emergence of the biggest threat facing Israel: a secular Arab nationalism. Second, by destroying the integrity of other Middle Eastern states, and leaving their former inhabitants feuding and weak, Israel could more easily dominate the region militarily and maintain its privileged alliance with Washington. Its role as the region's policeman, though one spreading discord rather than order, would be assured. Third, it was hoped that instability in the region – particularly in Iraq and Iran – would lead to the break-up of the Saudi-dominated oil cartel OPEC, undermining Saudi Arabia's influence in Washington and its muscle to finance Islamic extremists and Palestinian resistance movements. And fourth, with the Middle East in chaos, and much of the Palestinian resistance already dispersed to refugee camps in neighbouring states, Israel's hand would be freed to carry on with, and complete, the ethnic cleansing of the Palestinians from the occupied territories, and possibly from inside Israel too (for more on this last ambition see my earlier book, *Blood and Religion*).

Israel's moment arrived with the attacks of 9/11 and the rise of the neocons, who persuaded the rest of the Bush Administration that this policy would be beneficial not only to Israel but to American interests too. Control of oil could be secured on the same terms as Israeli regional hegemony: by spreading instability across the Middle East. That was why the US broke with its traditional policy of rewarding and punishing strongmen, and resorted instead in Iraq to regime overthrow and direct occupation, as described in Chapter 1. Notably, this policy was opposed by both the oil industry and the US State Department, which wanted a dictator in place in Iraq after Saddam Hussein's removal, assuring the safe passage of oil to the West. Divisions within Washington that surfaced during Bush's second term can be attributed to differing views on the wisdom of the neocon strategy. Whether the same model would be applied to Iran, despite a determination by Israel and the neocons to continue the experiment, was unclear at the time of writing. However, the build-up to an attack on Tehran, including the related assault on Lebanon in 2006 and a planned strike against Syria afterwards, is documented in Chapter 2.

Finally, it should be noted that the model of discord Israel and the neocons are pursuing was tested in the laboratory of the occupied Palestinian territories over several decades (Chapter 4). Interestingly, a possible lesson that might have been learnt from that 'experiment' was ignored: that in seeking to destroy Palestinian nationalism, and hopes of meaningful statehood, Israel encouraged a greater Islamic fundamentalism among some Palestinians that offered a new and different kind of threat. Similar developments can be detected in the deepening of Islamic extremism in areas of the Middle East, and particularly in the growing popularity of the Shia militia Hizbullah, even among Sunni Arabs, after its resolute engagement with the Israeli army's 2006 assault on Lebanon.

Nonetheless, Israel and the neocons may have believed that there were benefits to be derived from the growth of Islamic radicalism too. With the rise of Hamas in the occupied territories, Israel was further able to exploit Western fears of Islam as a 'global threat'. The question of what to do with the Palestinians has increasingly been tied to the question of what the West should do about Islamic extremism. Israel has therefore been nurturing a view of itself as on the frontiers of the West in an epoch-changing clash of civilisations. In particular, Israel and the neocons have seized the opportunity presented by the 'war on terror' to reshape the Middle East in their own interests. It is no coincidence that, today, many features of the US occupation of Iraq echo features of Israel's occupation of the Palestinians. It is also not entirely accidental that in dragging the US into a direct occupation of Iraq that mirrors Israel's own much longer occupation of the Palestinian territories, Israel has ensured that the legitimacy of both stands or falls together.

*　*　*

Three points about language. In general, I have avoided littering the text with qualifiers denouncing regimes as aggressive, undemocratic, oppressive, militaristic, unpleasant and so on. This is not because I do not believe most of the regimes discussed here cannot be described in these terms; it is because such adjectives too often become lazy shorthand to indicate which side an author is taking and to suggest which regimes or groups should be approved of and which not. Thus, most observers usually feel the need to append negative qualifiers to regimes like Syria or Iran that are seen as anti-Western, but not to regimes like Saudi Arabia, Egypt or Jordan that are seen as pro-Western. Such moral judgments are rarely as simple as we would like to believe. There is no doubt that Saddam Hussein was a brutal dictator whose regime used terror and fear to ensure his rule was not challenged, and that he waged vicious wars against his neighbours, but he also presided for many years over one of the most impressive and generous welfare systems to be found in the Arab Middle East. Such contradictions do not apply only to Arab states. The US government can be considered largely democratic and accountable inside its own borders, but in foreign policy it is a relentlessly aggressive state – even a rogue state, in the view of some – that has recently waged an illegal, pre-emptive war in Iraq and for decades has been subverting numerous other regimes, including democratic ones, through covert action and proxies.[5] It is now occupying a sovereign nation, Iraq, and making systematic threats to overthrow another regime, Iran, whose mainly theocratic government has at least some democratic features (more than can be said of most of its neighbours) and has so far shown no signs of wanting to attack other states. Of Israel we can raise similar doubts: is it less militaristic than Syria, or less aggressive than Hizbullah? Such judgments are not, in my view, straight-forward and, as they are not the subject of this work, they have been avoided in the main. Instead I have tried to illuminate the changing dynamics of power politics in the Middle East. Rather than making easy judgments about the nature or character of regimes, I have concentrated on their behaviour in relation to their neighbours, allies and enemies.

There was some confusion, even apparently in the Bush Administration, about whether the US attacks on Afghanistan and Iraq were being conducted under a doctrine of pre-emptive or preventive war. Both are wars of aggression, the 'supreme international crime', according to the 1950 principles established by the Nuremberg war crimes tribunal. It is debatable whether wars classified as pre-emptive are ever a valid application of force under international law, but it might be possible to justify them if the threat from another state is immediate, plausible and severe. It could be argued that the attack on Afghanistan, given 9/11 and the Taliban's harbouring of al-Qaeda, fell within this category. The use of force against the prospective and speculative threat posed by Iraq should almost certainly be classified as preventive war and therefore as a clear violation of international law. However, the Administration muddied the waters by creating a fictitious and largely implausible scenario that Iraq was holding and intending to use weapons of mass destruction against the West. Reluctantly, but for the sake of simplicity, I have given the benefit of the doubt to the White House and referred to its wars as 'pre-emptive' throughout the book. That should not, however, been seen as explicit or implicit condonement of these wars. I have also referred to the organised attacks on US and British troops occupying Iraq as part of an 'insurgency', the usual characterisation in the Western media. But they could equally be described, as they are in much of the Arab world, as a national resistance against occupation.[6]

Transliteration from Arabic is always problematic and particularly, it seems, in relation to the Lebanese Shia militia whose name means 'Party of God' and which has almost as many variations of spelling in English as fighters in Lebanon. I have chosen 'Hizbullah' throughout, but the reader should appreciate that the same organisation is being referred to when a different spelling appears within quotations. I have also used 'Shia' in the text to refer to the Islamic sect, but in quotations it sometimes appears as 'Shiite' or 'Shi'ite'. Similarly, 'Shebaa Farms' may be found spelt as 'Shaba' and 'Sheba'. There are doubtless a few other examples.

* * *

I never met the late Israeli human rights activist and scholar Israel Shahak, but I wish to acknowledge the debt I owe him, especially in shaping my thoughts in certain sections of the book. In particular, I have been influenced by the method he uses in his most comprehensive book on Israeli foreign policy, *Open Secrets*, of drawing back the veil of secrecy covering Israeli policy by piecing together and analysing the trail of evidence left by Israeli officialdom. For a society usually considered open and democratic, Israel's government, military and bureaucracy have a well-developed talent for remaining tight-lipped about their true intentions and goals. In the 1990s Shahak exploited the one weakness of the system: feeling cocooned from scrutiny because they were communicating in Hebrew, a language few outsiders understood, Israel's leaders spoke relatively freely and honestly. Shahak therefore made it his priority to translate newspaper articles, giving non-Israelis a window on the chauvinistic and racist worldview of the Israeli leadership. Today, when most Israeli media are readily available in English and preserved on the internet, the country's officials are usually more cautious about what they say in public. However, ego and the need to have a permanent record of their moment in the sun mean that many still find it hard not to let slip what was intended rather than what was claimed.

There are too many other people to thank individually but I hope each knows how much I value their support. In addition to those I named in the acknowledgments of *Blood and Religion*, I would like to mention: Nick Dermody and Shaun Briley, two good friends who shared the most intellectually formative periods of my life; Raneen Bisharat, Nidal Bisharat and Elias Khoury, Marie and Hamoudi Badarne, and Katie Ramadan and Nasser Rego for enriching my time in Nazareth; Asim Rafiqui, for showing me, through his photographs, my new city in a different light; David Cromwell and David Edwards, editors of the magnificent Media Lens website, which helped me make sense of my own profession's profound failures in covering the Israeli-Palestinian conflict; John Haines for his gifted selection of articles and his generous and timely donation of George and Douglas Ball's *The Passionate Attachment*; and my editor at Pluto, Roger van Zwanenberg, for his advice and vision, and for suggesting that I expand my short essay 'End of the Strongmen' to book length.

Special thanks go again to my family – my mother, my father, Clea, Richard, Sue, Aliona and Joe – and to my wife, Sally Azzam, whose patience and support are the soil in which my ideas take root.

Jonathan Cook
Nazareth
July 2007

1

REGIME OVERTHROW IN IRAQ

The official justification for the US-led invasion of Iraq in March 2003 had been the need to disarm Iraq's unstable dictator, Saddam Hussein. It was assumed that for more than two decades he had been amassing weapons of mass destruction (WMD), developing an advanced biological and chemical weapons programme and making repeated attempts at acquiring nuclear warheads. When the West began a campaign to disarm him from 1991, enforced through United Nations inspections, many reasons were cited for why he might try to evade the inspectors and hold on to his WMD. One was his undoubted need to use coercion to hold together a state that embraced three large, rival communities – an Islamic Shia majority of about 60 per cent, alongside two minorities of roughly equal size, the Islamic Sunnis and the ethnic Kurds.[1] A Sunni leader, Saddam needed to instil fear among the Shia and Kurdish populations to prevent them from rising up against him, and had proved in the past his readiness to do so, most notoriously in 1988 when he used poison gas against the Kurdish town of Halabja, killing 5,000 inhabitants.[2] In addition, Saddam feared the power of the neighbouring state of Iran, ruled since 1979 by Shia clerics who he worried might make an alliance with his own Shia population to overthrow his regime. Iraq fought a bloody eight-year war through the 1980s in which Saddam used chemical weapons against Iranian soldiers, possibly believing that this contributed to the defeat of his neighbour's larger forces.[3] He was also believed to harbour an ambition to become the unquestioned leader of the wider Arab world, and may have believed that nuclear weapons, in particular, were the key. Then there was his bitter experience of dealing with the West, which had nurtured him as a brutal dictator – including helping to arm him with the chemical weapons used against the Kurds – only to attack him militarily a few years later when he invaded the small oil-rich Gulf state of Kuwait, which was safely within the Western sphere of control. And finally, there was the widespread assumption that Saddam, who was vociferous in espousing the cause of the Palestinians, wanted to use his weapons to destroy Israel. 'With nuclear weapons he would feel able to confront Israel in a spectacular way', argued William Shawcross, a board member of an independent and highly respected organisation dealing with conflict resolution, the International Crisis Group, a month before the invasion.[4]

As became apparent soon after the US attack, however, Saddam had been effectively disarmed following the Gulf War of 1991 by a savage sanctions regime justified in the West by the need to force Iraq to submit to the UN inspections. The Iraqi leader, it seemed, had secretly disposed of his WMD and then played a game of cat and mouse with the inspectors to conceal from his own public and from Iran both his humiliation at the hands of the West and his new state of defencelessness. Saddam was aware that his continuing rule of Iraq was dependent on his *appearing* invincible. Nonetheless, there was much evidence available to the Bush Administration that he had been effectively disarmed since the early 1990s, though US officials worked strenuously to ensure that the information was either suppressed or contradicted. A series of UN reports into Iraq's suspected nuclear programme showed that the threat had been 'neutralized' and that 'there were no unresolved disarmament issues'. UN inspectors hunting for biological and chemical weapons issued more circumspect reports but still found no evidence of such WMD, and argued for more time to complete their searches.[5] Also, the highest-profile defector from Saddam's regime, his son-in-law, Hussein Kamel, who had run the WMD programme through the 1980s and into the early 1990s, had told the Central Intelligence Agency back in 1995 that 'Iraq destroyed all its chemical and biological weapons stocks and the missiles to deliver them'. The story, which was leaked to *Newsweek* eight years later, made no impression on the public debate as it was published only days before the invasion of Iraq.[6] Similarly, some of those involved in the inspection process, including Scott Ritter, who had headed the UN inspectors in Iraq for a time, concluded before the invasion that Saddam was as good as disarmed, though they made almost no impression on the public debate. In 2002 Ritter wrote: 'While we [the UN inspectors] were never able to provide 100 per cent certainty regarding the disposition of Iraq's proscribed weaponry, we did ascertain a 90–95 per cent level of verified disarmament.'[7] Ritter was proved right in the aftermath of the invasion, in 2004, when a US survey team concluded: 'Iraq unilaterally destroyed its undeclared chemical weapons stockpile in 1991.' The report added that the team could find 'no credible indications that Baghdad resumed production'.[8]

Given both the lack of plausible evidence that Iraq possessed WMD, or that it intended to use them against the West, few experts believed a 'pre-emptive' attack on Iraq could be justified in international law.[9] But even before the official reason for the invasion had been discredited, the White House offered a secondary justification for its military occupation. US forces, claimed President George W. Bush, were there to liberate the Iraqi people from Saddam's rule, which was believed to have resulted in the deaths of hundreds of thousands of Iraqis over more than two decades – though Bush and others avoided mentioning that many of those deaths were caused by the West's strict sanctions regime. In Saddam's place, the US army would create an environment in which democracy could flourish. In February 2003, shortly before the invasion, President Bush predicted: 'A new regime in Iraq would serve as a dramatic and inspiring example of freedom for other nations in the region.'[10] Soon the attack on Iraq was being portrayed as the main thrust of a wider US plan to spread democracy through the Middle East. Iraq's invasion, noted one commentator in the *Washington Post*, 'may be the most idealistic war fought in modern times – a war whose only coherent rationale, for all the misleading hype about weapons of mass destruction and al Qaeda terrorists, is that it toppled a tyrant and created the possibility of a democratic future'.[11]

But in the wake of the invasion, the White House's moral jus-
tifications for overthrowing the Iraqi dictator raised two obvious
questions: was freedom really flourishing under the occupation
and were Iraqis now better off than under Saddam? A simple
measure by which the strength of the White House's claims could
be judged was whether the suffering of Iraqis was being brought
to an end by the occupation. Although the US media had largely
abided by the wishes of the White House in shielding American
audiences from the sight of bodybags returning from the Middle
East, the numbers of US dead were at least known. By summer
2007, more than four years after the invasion, the death toll
among American soldiers had passed the 3,500 mark, and more
than seven times that number were officially injured. The month
of May had seen 127 American deaths, making it one of the
deadliest faced by the US army since the invasion, with more than
four soldiers being killed on average each day.[12] Some 150 British
soldiers had died over the four years of occupation,[13] as had a
further 900 contractors, out of a total of some 180,000 working
for the US government, more than a quarter of them believed to
be mercenaries.[14]

THE BODY COUNT KEEPS GROWING

Assessing the casualties among Iraqis, however, was far harder.
In December 2005, President Bush admitted that several tens
of thousands of Iraqi civilians might have paid with their lives:
'How many Iraqi citizens have died in this war? I would say
30,000, more or less, have died as a result of the initial incursion
and the ongoing violence against Iraqis.'[15] He appeared to be
basing his estimate on the work of a British group of academics
calling themselves the Iraq Body Count who regularly updated
the total number of Iraqi deaths reported by 'reliable' sources,
mainly the Western media. By summer 2007, the Iraq Body
Count's figure had reached about 70,000 Iraqi dead.[16] However,
there were strong reasons for believing that these statistics were
in fact a gross under-estimation. With most foreign correspondents consigned to a sealed-off area of Baghdad known as the

Green Zone – under heavy protection from US troops – there was little coverage of Iraqi deaths apart from those killed in newsworthy events such as suicide bombings, often reported by Iraqi stringers working on behalf of the foreign media. Drive-by shootings, atrocities happening in remoter parts of Iraq, and the deaths that resulted from the rapid deterioration in sanitation, access to water and electricity, and the closure of hospitals, were not normally reported by the Western media. Even in the case of large-scale bombings, there were grounds for suspecting that the reported casualty figures under-estimated the fatalities. As one internet pundit pointed out:

In the news today, [it was reported that] a car bomb in Baghdad killed 23 people and injured 68 others, while later, a second killed 17 people and wounded 55 others. Will you ever hear what happened to those 123 injured people (or the others who were injured in incidents where the numbers of dead didn't reach double-digits, and weren't even 'newsworthy' by the standards of American reporting on Iraq)? Not a chance. Will some, maybe even the majority, die later today in the hospital, or tomorrow, or next week? Quite likely. But according to the Western press (and those such as Iraq Body Count), 40 people died in those two incidents, a number which will never change.[17]

A more plausible, though less quoted, figure had been produced by the Bloomberg School of Public Health at Johns Hopkins University, and published in the eminent British medical journal *The Lancet* in October 2006. Using the standard methodology for estimating deaths in conflict zones, its survey of Iraqi households showed that the most likely number of extra deaths among Iraqi civilians as a result of the US occupation stood at 655,000. This figure was widely rubbished by British and US government officials, though it later emerged that the British Defence Ministry's chief scientific adviser, Sir Roy Anderson, had privately supported the methods used by the survey and the reliability of the findings.[18] If the *Lancet* figures were right, nearly 200,000 Iraqis had been killed each year since the US invasion. In addition, other sources reported that some two million Iraqis out of a population of some 27 million had fled Iraq and a similar number had been displaced to other parts of the country in what was becoming a slow process of ethnic cleansing.[19] A report compiled by 80 aid agencies in summer 2007 showed that eight million Iraqis – or nearly a third of the population – were in need of emergency aid, 70 per cent had inadequate access to water, 80 per cent were without effective sanitation, more than 800,000 children had dropped out of school and there was rampant malnutrition among the young.[20] In every sense, the White House's decision to topple the Iraqi dictator had created a humanitarian catastrophe for the country's people, producing suffering on a greater scale than had been experienced even under Saddam himself.

The dramatic increase in the deaths of ordinary Iraqis could be easily explained. They found themselves caught in the crossfire of a vicious insurgency to oust the US occupying forces and a relentless campaign of violence unleashed by American soldiers (and a large force of unaccountable mercenaries) to subdue all resistance. US troops and Iraqis who collaborated with them, particularly those joining the new security forces, were the main targets of the insurgency. One of its leaders told a British newspaper: 'Our position is that there are two kinds of people in Iraq: not Sunni and Shia, Kurdish and Arab, Muslim and Christian, but those who are with the occupation and those who are against it.'[21] In an attempt to crush the resistance and reduce the number of US casualties, the army admitted that it was resorting to hi-tech firepower, particularly airpower, that was taking a large toll on the civilian population. Eldon Bargewell, a general who investigated a massacre of 24 Iraqi civilians committed by US soldiers at Haditha, assessed the army's philosophy in Iraq in the following terms: 'Iraqi civilian lives are not as important as US lives, their deaths are just the cost of doing business, ... the Marines need to get "the job done" no matter what it takes.'[22]

In addition, a growing sectarian war between the country's two main rival Islamic constituencies, the majority Shia population and the former ruling Sunni community, was claiming an ever larger number of civilian lives. The civil war was filling the power vacuum left by the overthrow of Saddam Hussein's regime. One independent analyst observed in his testimony to the US Senate Foreign Relations Committee on Iraq in early 2007:

> The origins of the civil war lie in the complete collapse of administrative and coercive capacity of the state. The Iraqi state, its ministries, civil servants, police force and army, ceased to exist in any meaningful way in the aftermath of regime change. It is the inability of the US to reconstruct them that lies at heart of the problem.[23]

The White House tried to deflect attention from both its failure to restore order in Iraq and its refusal to end the country's occupation by claiming that the insurgency was not locally organised but being engineered by infiltrators bent on undermining American attempts to bring democracy to Iraq. Both militant Islamic fundamentalists (jihadis) associated with al-Qaeda and the neighbouring Shia-dominated state of Iran were put in the frame. However, neither seemed to be the chief culprit. According to a report by the Iraq Study Group, a cross-party Congressional group led by James Baker, a former Secretary of State in the Administration of George Bush's father:

> Most attacks on Americans still come from the Sunni Arab insurgency. The insurgency comprises former elements of the Saddam Hussein regime, disaffected Sunni Arab Iraqis, and common criminals. It has significant support within the Sunni Arab community ... Al Qaeda is responsible for a small portion of the violence in Iraq, but that includes some of the more spectacular acts: suicide attacks, large truck bombs, and attacks on significant religious or political targets.[24]

A respected Middle East analyst, Hussein Agha, suggested instead that Iraq's own paramilitary groups had much to gain from the Americans staying, at least for the time being. As long as the US troops were there to impose a loose order, the groups could arm, build their forces and reinforce wider regional alliances for the moment when American troops were forced to leave.

> Inside Iraq, this is a period of consolidation for most political groups. They are building up their political and military capabilities, cultivating and forging alliances, clarifying political objectives and preparing for

impending challenges. It is not the moment for all-out confrontation. No group has the confidence or capacity decisively to confront rivals within its own community or across communal lines. Equally, no party is genuinely interested in a serious process of national reconciliation when they feel they can improve their position later on.[25]

A Palestinian academic, Karma Nabulsi, pointed out the similarities in the futures being created for both Iraqis and the Palestinians of the West Bank and Gaza, the latter under a much longer Israeli occupation that seemed to be the template for the new US one in Iraq. Under occupation, the two peoples were living in 'a Hobbesian vision of an anarchic society: truncated, violent, powerless, destroyed, cowed, ruled by disparate militias, gangs, religious ideologues and extremists, broken up into ethnic and religious tribalism and co-opted collaborationists'.[26]

While Bush described the continuing US occupation in terms of bringing democracy to Iraq, he seemed unconcerned by the express wishes of the local population. In poll after poll, it was clear that Iraqis wanted liberation from US forces and profoundly mistrusted the motives behind the invasion. A survey conducted in summer 2006 by the US State Department showed 65 per cent of those living in Baghdad favoured an immediate withdrawal of US forces, while a poll by the University of Maryland found that 71 per cent of Iraqis wanted foreign soldiers to depart within a year. Nonetheless, 77 per cent of Iraqis also believed that the US intended to stay permanently.[27] They were clear about the reasons why. A 2003 Gallup poll found that 43 per cent of Iraqis believed US and British forces had invaded mainly 'to rob Iraq's oil'; only 5 per cent believed the invasion was designed 'to assist the Iraqi people' and 1 per cent believed it was to establish democracy.[28] A later survey, in early 2006, discovered that 80 per cent of Iraqis believed that the US government planned to station permanent military bases in Iraq.[29] Possibly as a consequence, another poll found that 61 per cent of Iraqis approved of 'attacks on US-led forces', including 92 per cent of Sunnis and 62 per cent of Shia (the overall figure was reduced by the opposition of the third main group in Iraq, the Kurds, who backed the US occupation, hoping it would lead to partition of the country and eventual statehood for them).[30]

A WAR FOR OIL

The grounds for Iraqis' suspicions of US motives for remaining in their country proved more than justified. In January 2007, despite pressure from critics in Washington to find an exit strategy from Iraq, Bush announced a surge of 30,000 additional troops to crush the insurgency and secure Baghdad, bringing the total number of US soldiers in Iraq to 160,000.[31] In a further indication that a withdrawal was far from the thoughts of the White House, the American Defense Secretary, Robert Gates, announced in May 2007 that the US was looking for a 'long and enduring presence' in Iraq under an arrangement with its government. Iraq would not be another Vietnam, he said, with the US forced to leave. 'The Korea model is one, the security relationship we have with Japan is another', he said,[32] referring to the stationing of US troops in South Korea since the Korean war of the early 1950s, and the establishment of US military bases in Japan since 1945. At about the same time the White House spokesman, Tony Snow, confirmed that President Bush wanted a permanent troop presence in Iraq. 'The situation in Iraq, and indeed, the larger war on terror, are things that are going to take a long time.'[33] As the veteran Middle East commentator Patrick Seale noted: 'Seen in this light, the US enterprise – for all the talk of democracy – is an unmistakable neo-colonial or imperial project such as the region suffered at the hands of Britain and France in an earlier age.'[34] As critics of the invasion had originally claimed, it looked like the occupation was about securing and permanently controlling Iraq and its huge oil reserves, widely believed to be the largest after Saudi Arabia's.

Control of oil, as Noam Chomsky and others have pointed out, has been the guiding concern of US foreign policy since the Second World War. In 1945, US foreign policy planners recognized that the Gulf's energy resources were 'a stupendous source of strategic power, and one of the greatest material prizes in world history'.[35]

As Chomsky notes, most of the Gulf's oil was not needed for US consumption, which was satisfied by domestic production and exports from Venezuela. Rather,

> Control over Gulf energy reserves provides 'veto power' over the actions of rivals, as the leading planner George Kennan pointed out half a century ago. Europe and Asia understand [this] very well, and have long been seeking independent access to energy resources. Much of the jockeying for power in the Middle East and Central Asia has to do with these issues. The populations of the region are regarded as incidental, as long as they are passive and obedient.[36]

In September 1978 a Joint Chiefs of Staff memorandum listed three strategic objectives for the US in the Middle East: 'to assure continuous access to petroleum resources, to prevent an inimical power or combination of powers from establishing hegemony and to assure the survival of Israel as an independent state in a stable relationship with contiguous Arab states'. Kenneth Pollack, President Clinton's adviser in the National Security Council on policy towards Iraq, has written that these goals 'have guided US policy ever since'.[37]

Although the 'inimical power' was generally presented as the threat of Soviet dominance of the Middle East, the Soviet Union never seriously challenged US control of the region. In 1979, official US estimates assessed the Soviets as influencing 'only 6% of the world population and 5% of the world GNP' outside its borders.[38] Nonetheless, as Samuel Huntington, a Harvard professor and later populariser of the 'clash of civilisations' thesis, noted in 1981, 'selling' intervention abroad might require creating 'the misimpression that it is the Soviet Union you are fighting'.[39] In reality, US planners were more concerned with curbing and crushing any expression of Arab or Iranian nationalism that might inspire Middle Eastern states or their peoples to claim the benefits of local resources as their own. 'The most serious threats [to US power] may emanate from internal changes in the gulf states', observed a Congressional report in 1977.[40] This thinking derived from the familiar 'Domino Theory', the idea, as Noam Chomsky has characterised it, that 'successful independent development and steps towards democracy, out of US control, might well have a domino effect, inspiring others who face similar problems to pursue the same course, thus eroding the global system of [US] domination'.[41]

For those with a long memory, the US interest in Iraq's oil had strong echoes of an earlier time, in 1918, when the British forces took control of the region following the collapse of the Ottoman empire. Britain installed in Iraq a loyal ruler, King Faisal, who signed a concession agreement with the British-dominated Iraqi Petroleum Company, turning over all rights in the country's oil to the foreign firm on terms that assigned minimum royalties to the Iraqi state. The Iraqi Petroleum Company succeeded in resisting attempts to change the terms of the agreement, even after Iraqi independence in 1958, until a nationalisation of some of the country's oilfields in 1961, followed by full nationalisation in 1972. The US first responded to Iraq's defiance in 1963, according to Roger Morris, a former National Security Council staffer, by carrying out 'regime change ... in collaboration with Saddam Hussein' and his socialist Ba'ath party. Using lists of 'Communists' supplied by the CIA, Iraq's 'Ba'athists systematically murdered untold numbers of Iraq's educated elite'.[42] The coup was overturned by the Iraqi army within a few months. A more successful coup, organised by the Ba'ath party and renegade factions of the army, and again backed by the CIA, took place in 1968, bringing Saddam Hussein to prominence, first as vice-president and finally as president in 1979.

In putting the oil industry under state ownership, Iraq joined its major oil-producing neighbours – Saudi Arabia, Iran and Kuwait – all of which controlled their own oil resources. Other, lesser oil states, such as Oman, Qatar and the United Arab Emirates, have only partially privatised their oil operations, with ultimate control resting in state hands. By late 2006, however, it was clear that Iraq was under strong pressure from Washington to hand over effective control of its oil wealth to foreign firms, as had been the case under the British Mandate. In doing so, Iraq was breaking with the model of all other oil-producing states in the region.

At the heart of the US plan was an Oil Law secretly drafted by Iraqi officials under the watch of American government and oil industry experts.[43] A State Department spokesman commented in April 2007: 'Our guys are helping the Iraqis write their law and pass their law.'[44] The law locked Iraq into offering extravagantly generous terms to foreign oil firms for decades under 'production-sharing agreements' (PSAs). Although PSAs had been used in deals between the oil industry and states such as Jordan and Algeria, they were usually resorted to only when returns on exploration were unpredictable; typically, PSAs were seen as rewarding oil companies for exploring new fields when it was unclear if there were substantial reserves waiting to be exploited. In Iraq's case, everyone was agreed that there were enormous reserves, possibly as much as 200 billion barrels, and that – apart from the dangers associated with the insurgency – exploration was a straightforward matter. Analysts believed that the PSAs being demanded by the White House could potentially drain tens of billions of dollars in oil revenues from the state's coffers. As the country depended on oil for 70 per cent of its gross domestic product, the agreements threatened to destroy any hope of reconstructing Iraq. The country's main unions issued a statement in December 2006: 'Iraqi public opinion strictly opposes the handing of authority and control over the oil to foreign companies that aim to make big profits at the expense of the people and to rob Iraq's national wealth by virtue of unfair, long-term oil contracts that undermine the sovereignty of the state and the dignity of the Iraqi people.'[45] By summer 2007, as the unions began mobilising popular opinion against the Oil Law, the Iraqi government revived legislation from the Saddam era to outlaw them from commenting on the draft.[46]

To avoid growing domestic protest against the Oil Law, the draft version considered by the Iraqi government of Nuri al-Maliki dropped the term PSAs in favour of 'exploration risk contract'. There were other sleights of hand that suggested the US was not acting in best faith. The Bush Administration promoted the law as an important 'benchmark', one that would create the conditions for 'reconciliation' by allowing Iraq's sectarian and ethnic communities to share the country's oil revenues on a fair basis. However, just one of the draft law's 43 articles mentioned revenue-sharing, and then only in the context that a separate law, yet to be considered by Iraqi legislators, would decide the method of distribution.[47] Furthermore, according to an independent Iraqi political analyst, unseen appendices would later 'decide which oil fields will be allocated to the Iraqi National Oil Company (INOC) and which of the existing fields will be allocated to the IOCs [international oil companies]. The appendices will determine if 10% or possibly up to 80% of these major oil fields will be given to the IOCs.'[48] The Iraqi cabinet passed the law in February 2007 after huge pressure had been exerted by the International Monetary Fund, on behalf of the US. The IMF used as leverage Iraq's gigantic debts of $120 billion, demanded by the West as reparations for Saddam Hussein's invasion of Kuwait and the Gulf War that followed. The IMF promised the Iraqi government that a portion of the debt would be forgiven – as it should have been under international law when Saddam Hussein was toppled – if it signed up for sweeping free-market reforms, including of the oil industry. After the cabinet passed the law, it moved to the parliament for ratification, as US officials watched impatiently from the sidelines. In April 2007 Defense Secretary Robert Gates pushed al-Maliki to make quick progress on passing the law, observing that 'the clock is ticking'.[49]

In sum, the law presented to the parliament stripped Iraq's national oil company of control of a large swath of the country's oilfields; new deposits not yet tapped, which constitute most of Iraq's reserves, would be set aside for foreign development and exploitation; long-term contracts would ensure the plunder was legal for decades to come; foreign companies would have no obligations to hire local workers, respect union rights, or share the new technologies they used; and the division of what was left of the oil profits could be split according to any principle that suited the White House, including rewarding those communities that remained obedient or that assisted in the country's occupation. Such a deal left the Iraqi parliament caught between a rock and a hard place: it could accept the Oil Law and have the country's wealth looted by the West or it could reject the law and face its oil revenues being diverted abroad to pay off Saddam's debts. By summer 2007, the path of the Oil Law was still blocked by the Iraqi parliament, which, much to the fury of the White House, was refusing to sign it. After a speech by Bush on the law, a rare critic in the US Congress, Dennis Kucinich, issued a statement observing that Bush and his Vice-President, Dick Cheney, 'have consistently misled the Congress on this matter, attempting variously to mask the privatization scheme as "equitable revenue sharing" and as a means toward "reconciliation." This is a grand deception.'[50]

US POLICY IN THE GULF

The ousting of Saddam Hussein and the subsequent direct occupation by American forces to secure Iraq's oil were a decisive break with traditional US policy in the region. It was also a dramatic departure from the experience of European colonial rule in the Middle East, where Britain and France had preferred to install a strongman who would do their bidding, usually to ensure their uninterrupted exploitation of local resources such as oil. If the local ruler defied the colonial power, he was replaced with another strongman – in what today would be called 'regime change'. That was why Iraq's King Faisal had little choice but to sign the concession with the Iraqi Petroleum Company in the 1920s. It was also why for many years neighbouring Iran had been ruled by a series of monarchs, the Shahs, who signed similar oil deals with European and Soviet companies. After a nationalist prime minister, Mohammed Mossadeq, nationalised Iran's oil industry in 1951, a prolonged power struggle between Mossadeq and the Shah ended with the latter fleeing into exile in 1953. Within days the CIA had engineered a coup to restore the Shah to power. One of the Shah's first acts after his return was to sign a new oil concession with an international consortium, led by American companies. The West also began helping him to develop a nuclear energy programme, possibly to silence domestic demands for the renationalisation of the oil industry. The Shah was overthrown in an Islamic Revolution in 1979, a blow to

Western control of the country that consecutive US Administrations have never forgiven.

American dealings with the region's other major oil state, Saudi Arabia, were murkier still. In the early twentieth century, a powerful Sunni family, the Sauds, had unified various Gulf provinces, ruling them as a monarchy with Western backing. The Sauds had signed an oil concession with an American firm in the 1930s and the two countries rapidly developed close ties. As early as 1943 President Franklin D. Roosevelt remarked that 'the defense of Saudi Arabia is vital to the defense of the United States'.[51] Saudi Arabia's key place in US Middle East policy, however, only emerged in the early 1960s with the establishment of an oil cartel, OPEC, over which the kingdom had decisive control. The point of OPEC – which grew to include eleven nations – was to ensure that oil prices remained above production costs to maximise profits for both the oil-producing countries and Big Oil, based in the US. Under anti-trust legislation, the cartel could have been challenged as illegal had it been formed by the corporations themselves, but the oil nations had a freer hand.[52] OPEC came into its own in the 1970s as the main oil countries nationalised their industries.[53] Its first, and only, real show of strength was to protest American intervention in the 1973 'Yom Kippur War' – when President Richard Nixon airlifted arms to Israel to prevent its defeat by its Arab neighbours – by cutting off oil supplies and dramatically raising global prices. Following the death of King Faisal al-Saud two years later, the new Saudi monarch, Fahd, entrenched the 'special relationship' with Washington and effectively eroded the strength of OPEC. Instead, Saudi Arabia promised stability in oil prices and profits on condition that the US protected the regime against the threat from powerful neighbours like Iraq and Iran and from its own home-grown Islamic militants. For this reason, the Saudi regime has been consistently, and misleadingly, labelled as 'moderate' in the West. The Sauds have also reliably invested hundreds of billions of dollars of their oil profits in Western economies and bought the latest US military hardware, much of it needed to protect their regime from the rise of radical Islamic groups in the region.

The long-standing and intimate relations between the Saudi rulers and key figures in the American political and economic establishment, including the Bush family and the veteran statesman James Baker, may go some way to explaining the enduring US indulgence of this unpleasant, though consistently obliging, regime. The House of Saud has managed to contain, even if barely, the explosive tensions created by the US demand following the 1991 Gulf War to station thousands of troops on Saudi territory. The presence of foreign soldiers in the same country as Islam's two holiest sites, Mecca and Medina, became a symbol for the radical Islamists of the way the West had humiliated and desecrated the Arab world. The Sauds' deep ties to the US establishment may also explain the otherwise baffling decision by the White House to ignore the established links between Saudi Arabia and the terror attacks of 11 September 2001 on the World Trade Center in New York and the Pentagon in Washington. Fifteen of the 19 men who hijacked the planes used in the attacks were Saudi nationals. The refusal by the Bush Administration to publish a section of a Congressional report into Saudi Arabia's links with the hijackers was explained by a US official: 'It's really damning. What it says is that not only Saudi entities or nationals are implicated in 9/11, but the [Saudi] government.'[54] Instead the US pursued Iraq's Saddam Hussein, even though he had no known connection to the attacks.

Describing British colonial dealings with Middle Eastern states, Mark Curtis, a former research fellow at the Royal Institute of International Affairs, noted:

> British policy in the Middle East is based on propping up repressive elites that support the West's business and military interests ... Repressive Middle Eastern elites understand these priorities, and also that their role in this system helps keep them in power locally; the West could withdraw its support for them if they got any wayward ideas ... London and Washington have throughout the postwar period connived with Middle Eastern elites to undermine popular, secular and nationalist groups which have offered the prospect of addressing the key issues in the region – the appalling levels of poverty and undemocratic political structures.[55]

When Britain's influence in the region waned after the Second World War, Washington took over, adopting similar methods for dominating the region – as its interventions in Iran, for example, proved. But, as Curtis points out, this traditional approach was beginning to backfire and 'helping to fan the flames of religious extremism that is often the only alternative available to those being repressed'. In US military jargon this would later come to be called 'blowback'. The outcome in Iran was an Islamic Revolution in 1979 that replaced the Western-backed Shah. But there were many other examples of blowback: it explained the emergence of Shia militias, including Hizbullah, in Lebanon that drove out US forces in 1983 and nearly two decades later ended Israel's occupation of the country's south; it accounted for the success of the Taliban fundamentalists, nurtured in the madrasas of Pakistan with CIA funding, who not only ousted the Soviet army from Afghanistan but then went on to take over the country, offering a base to Islamic militants from across the region; and it could be blamed for the rise of the Sunni jihadi movements that were conveniently labelled al-Qaeda and expressed a destructive longing for Islamic self-sufficiency and revolt against Western interference in the region.

Two doctrines – those of Presidents Truman and Eisenhower – were at the heart of US plans during the Cold War to contain the supposed threat of Soviet influence in the Middle East. The Truman Doctrine of the early 1950s stipulated that the US would send military aid to countries threatened by Soviet communism, with the security of Iran and Saudi Arabia considered priorities. The Eisenhower Doctrine of 1957 stated that the US would consider using its armed forces to prevent imminent or actual aggression against its own territory, and that countries opposed to communism would be given aid. Later doctrines projected American military might more specifically into the Middle East to combat the twin threats of Soviet influence and Arab nationalism. The Nixon Doctrine of 1969 grew out of the significant losses of US soldiers during the Vietnam War, and proposed finding local proxies, or client states, to fight on behalf of US interests and as a way to damp down protests back home. President Richard Nixon outlined the new policy in a speech: 'We shall furnish military and economic assistance when requested ... But we shall look to the nation directly threatened to assume the primary responsibility of providing the manpower for its defense.'[56] In the Middle East, Israel, the Shah's Iran, Turkey and Saudi Arabia were considered natural proxies. This policy was quickly put into effect in the Persian Gulf, where it was seen as the best way to protect the weak but loyal monarchy of Saudi Arabia, and the oil cartel it controlled, from the potential threats posed by its oil-rich neighbours of Iraq and Iran. Neither of these countries was reliably under the thumb of Western control: Iraq's leadership espoused a secular socialist Ba'athist philosophy and had ambitions to lead an Arab nationalism that posed the biggest threat to conservative Arab monarchies like the Sauds and to Israel; and Iran's nationalists, who had proved their popular base of support in the early 1950s by removing the Shah, drew on a blend of Persian nationalism and socialism that was seen in Washington as a threat similar to that of Arab nationalism.

In the case of Iran, the Nixon Doctrine meant propping up the Shah, who was encouraged to use the country's oil wealth to buy advanced American weapons, while thousands of American and Israeli agents advised his regime. Two events in 1979, however, suggested to Washington that it needed a new model for dealing with the Middle East: the Shah's overthrow by the Islamic Revolution, and the Soviet invasion of Afghanistan. In response, President Jimmy Carter proclaimed: 'Let our position be absolutely clear: An attempt by any outside force to gain control of the Persian Gulf region will be regarded as an assault on the vital interests of the United States of America, and such an assault will be repelled by any means necessary, including military force.'[57] The Carter Doctrine presumed a pressing Soviet threat to US interests in the Persian Gulf and recognised the limits of relying on unstable surrogates. Instead it proposed that the US should intervene directly through a Rapid Deployment Force, later called Centcom, which required Saudi Arabia's agreement to buy a sophisticated US communications system and package of advanced weaponry. In addition, it was hoped to locate US military bases on Saudi soil. At the centre of the arrangement was the sale to the Saudis in 1981 of AWACS, an elaborate airborne radar system that would allow US forces to be deployed quickly in the Gulf against 'outlaw states' in such overwhelming numbers that casualties would be low and protests back home minimal. This approach was field-tested in the 1991 Gulf War against Iraq. President Bill Clinton's first National Security Adviser, Anthony Lake, argued that, in the same way that the US had taken the lead in containing the Soviet threat, it must now bear a 'special responsibility' to 'neutralize' and 'contain' rogue states in the Middle East, including Iran, Iraq, Libya and Sudan.[58]

These doctrines variously guided US responses to the events that unfolded after the Islamic Revolution of 1979. In the early 1980s, Washington began secretly arming both Iran and Iraq, encouraging these deeply hostile states to wage war in what the US may have believed would bring about their mutual destruction.[59] A savage eight-year war beginning in 1980 exhausted the two countries, costing at least half a million lives and damaging both countries' oil production and economic infrastructure. In parallel, the US also tried to develop contacts with the Iranian army in the hope of engineering a military coup to bring down the Shia clerics running the country. But, as that policy failed to bear fruit, Washington increasingly favoured Saddam Hussein's regime with military and intelligence assistance.[60] As well as receiving US aid, Iraq was supported by other Arab regimes, including Saudi Arabia and Jordan, which regarded it as representing the Sunni-dominated Arab world against the threat posed by the non-Arab Shia regime of Iran. Contrary to US interests, Iraq emerged from its long war with Iran clearly the most powerful state in the region after Israel.

CONTAINING SADDAM

In summer 1990 a victorious Saddam Hussein, believing himself to be the protector of the Arab world, switched his attention to another oil-rich neighbour, the tiny state of Kuwait. The Iraqi leader complained to the Arab League about the fall in oil prices caused by a glut of crude produced by Kuwait and the United

Arab Emirates, which he claimed had cost Iraq $1 billion in lost revenues at a time when the country desperately needed reconstruction. As he massed 100,000 troops along the border with Kuwait, Saddam also demanded that the small kingdom write off large debts accumulated during the Iran–Iraq War and lease part of its territory to Baghdad. In August 1990 he invaded. The attack had been predicted two years earlier by the CIA, which warned that Saddam might target the Kuwaiti islands of Bubiyan and Warba to expand Iraq's 'narrow access to the Gulf', but the full-scale invasion of Kuwait caught Washington unprepared. Kenneth Pollack, a CIA analyst who would become one of Clinton's key advisers, later wrote that the US Administration of the time feared that, if Iraq captured Kuwait's oilfields, it could rival Saudi Arabia in oil production and so control the price of crude, bypassing OPEC.[61] Saddam turned from being considered a friend of the West into its number one enemy.

There is strong evidence that Saddam's invasion could have been rapidly reversed without resort to war. That was the view of Arab League officials, who believed a compromise could quickly be reached between Iraq and Kuwait that would have led to Saddam withdrawing his troops. However, the US Administration had other ideas. It warned Saudi Arabia that it was facing imminent attack from Iraqi soldiers in Kuwait, though no evidence was produced to support this claim. Saudi Arabia accepted an offer from the US to defend the kingdom against Iraq's supposed territorial ambitions by stationing large numbers of American troops on Saudi soil. In the meantime, the US did little to pursue a peaceful resolution, rejecting peace plans from France, Russia and Yemen, and instead cornered Baghdad with demands for a series of humiliating climbdowns. One Middle East analyst, Stephen Zunes, assessed Washington's policy as follows: 'The U.S. position was that, without a war, Saddam Hussein's regime would remain with its military assets intact, free to sell its oil, popular among some segments of the Arab world's population and still able to threaten its neighbours. This was considered unacceptable.'[62]

In other words, in the 1980s Washington had indulged Saddam Hussein because it needed him strong to confront, punish and weaken Iran. Now he was seen in a different light, as a challenge to the two main US allies in the region. His army might threaten the Saudis' control of the Middle East's oil cartel, and his widespread popularity in the Arab world combined with his vocal support for the Palestinian cause made him a nuisance to Israel, which was planning, with tacit American approval, to annex as much of the occupied territories as possible. In addition, across much of the Arab world Saddam was seen as a hero, a new Gamal Abdel Nasser, the Egyptian leader who had infused Arab nationalism with a romantic appeal through much of the 1950s and 1960s. President George H.W. Bush called Saddam 'another Hitler',[63] before launching Operation Desert Storm in January 1991. Within six weeks, a ferocious US air campaign and a coalition force of half a million troops had brought Iraq to its knees, killing some 100,000 Iraqi soldiers, many of them Kurdish and Shia conscripts whose fate Saddam was doubtless none too concerned by. The bombing raids targeted much of Iraq, destroying its infrastructure and economy in what Secretary of State James Baker boasted would return Iraq 'to the pre-industrial age'.[64]

In contrast to the invasion of Iraq to effect regime overthrow that his son, President George W. Bush, would launch twelve years later, Bush Snr pulled back from invading Baghdad and toppling Saddam. The White House even abandoned the Kurds and Shia when they followed Bush's advice and mounted insurrections against Saddam to remove him from power. Tens of thousands were killed as the Iraqi president crushed the rebellion. The reason for Washington's reticence, it seems, was a fear that success by Iraq's Kurds and demands for partition post-Saddam might fuel a rebellion among the restive Kurdish population in neighbouring Turkey, a close US ally in the region. Instead, the White House, first under Bush Snr and then Bill Clinton, pursued a policy of containment, keeping Saddam weak, with the hope that in the long run an Iraqi rival would come to power by engineering a coup against him. The goal was explained by the then chief diplomatic correspondent of the *New York Times*, Thomas Friedman. He observed that Washington was hoping to induce Iraqi generals to topple Saddam Hussein, 'and then

Washington would have the best of all worlds: an iron-fisted Iraqi junta without Saddam Hussein'.[65]

Containment was achieved through a dual policy of 'no-fly zones' in the country's north and south, which allowed the US and British air forces to box Saddam's army into the centre of the country, and a system of swingeing UN sanctions that deprived the Iraqi population of most essentials, including supplies of food and medicines. The decade of sanctions, in particular, led to terrible suffering among ordinary Iraqis that has been estimated to have cost the lives of as many as one million, many of them children. Unicef, the United Nations Children's Fund, concluded in 1999 that 4,000 children under the age of five were dying each month from the sanctions – or half a million children dead in the eight years covered by the report. Before the Gulf War of 1991, contrary to the impression in the West, Iraq had the most advanced welfare system in the Arab world. An average annual income of $4,000 in 1980 had fallen to $500 by 2003.[66] On the eve of invasion, *Time* magazine reported: 'Industry has ceased to exist and unemployment may be as high as 50 percent. The agricultural sector is in complete disarray, leaving more than 60 percent of the population to rely on the UN Oil for Food program [covering basic needs]. About 40 percent of the nation's children are suffering from malnutrition.'[67] Shortly after the 1999 Unicef report was published, Anupama Rao Singh, the fund's senior representative in Iraq, observed:

> The change in 10 years is unparalleled, in my experience. In 1989, the literacy rate was 95%; and 93% of the population had free access to modern health facilities. Parents were fined for failing to send their children to school. The phenomenon of street children or children begging was unheard of. Iraq had reached a stage where the basic indicators we use to measure the overall well-being of human beings, including children, were some of the best in the world. Now it is among the bottom 20%. In 10 years, child mortality has gone from one of the lowest in the world, to the highest.[68]

In 1998, a year before the report was published, Denis Halliday, Assistant Secretary-General of the United Nations and its coordinator of humanitarian relief to Iraq, resigned his post. He told the investigative journalist John Pilger: 'I had been instructed to implement a policy that satisfies the definition of genocide: a deliberate policy that has effectively killed well over a million individuals, children and adults.'[69] Two years later, Halliday's successor, Hans von Sponeck, resigned, quickly followed by Jutta Burghardt, head of the World Food Programme in Iraq. In 1999, 70 members of the US Congress took the unprecedented step of signing a petition to President Clinton appealing to him to end 'infanticide masquerading as policy'.[70]

THE NEOCON VISION OF THE MIDDLE EAST

The policy of containing Iraq came to end with the election of President George W. Bush in 2000. In a speech in 1997, President Clinton's Secretary of State, Madeleine Albright, had made clear that regime change was the goal of containment, saying that the US would support sanctions 'as long as it takes' to usher in 'a successor regime'.[71] However, the sanctions, rather than weakening Saddam Hussein, were simply entrenching his rule. Removing Saddam by other means was a priority for everyone in the Bush Administration but became the particular obsession of a group of ultra-hawkish advisers known as the neoconservatives, or 'neocons' for short. While many of them, though far from all, are American Jews, the group was most obviously distinguished by its ideological sympathy for the Israeli right.[72] Many neocons had forged their political careers heading various rightwing think-tanks, such as the American Enterprise Institute, the Jewish Institute for National Security Affairs, the Project for the New American Century, and the Center for Security Policy. They also enjoyed close, verging on incestuous, relations with Washington's muscular pro-Israel lobby groups, particularly the American Israel Public Affairs Committee (AIPAC) and the Conference of Presidents of Major American Jewish Organizations.

A brief survey of the backgrounds of some of the key neocons gives a flavour of their 'special relationship' to Israel. According to investigative journalist Seymour Hersh in his account of the Nixon presidency, Secretary of State Henry Kissinger discovered that

Richard Perle, one of the figureheads of the neocon movement, had been passing classified material from the National Security Council to the Israeli embassy.[73] A Bush neocon, Douglas Feith, who became Under-Secretary of Defense, had, according to the *Washington Post*, 'written prolifically on Israeli–Arab issues for years, arguing that Israel has as legitimate a claim to the West Bank territories seized after the Six Day War as it has to the land that was part of the U.N.-mandated Israel created in 1948'.[74] Elliott Abrams, Bush's neocon director of Mideast affairs for the National Security Council, had made an impressive political comeback after his conviction on two counts of lying as a State Department official in the Reagan Administration over the Iran-Contra scandal, when the White House sold arms to Iran to pay the Contra rebels who were trying to overthrow the democratically elected Nicaraguan government. Abrams had written in October 2000: 'The Palestinian leadership does not want peace with Israel, and there will be no peace.'[75] On the question of Jewish identity in the Diaspora, he observed that Jews outside Israel should 'stand apart from the nation in which they live'.[76] Meyrav Wurmser, an ally in the neocon think-tank the Hudson Institute, noted: 'Elliott's appointment is a signal that the hardliners in the administration are playing a more central role in shaping policy.'[77] Years later John Wolfensohn, a former head of the World Bank and the Quartet's Middle East envoy in the period immediately before and after the Gaza disengagement, would claim that Abrams had almost singlehandedly 'undermined' him as well as an agreement on Gaza's border terminals that, in his view, destroyed the Palestinian economy.[78]

The wider neocon philosophy of power was neatly encapsulated in a comment made by an anonymous senior Bush adviser: 'We're an empire now, and when we act, we create our own reality.'[79] Or as one Washington observer, Anatol Lieven, summed up neo-conservative thinking: 'The basic and generally agreed plan is unilateral world domination through absolute military superiority, and this has been consistently advocated and worked on by the group of intellectuals close to Dick Cheney and Richard Perle since the collapse of the Soviet Union in the early 1990s.'[80] Lieven also noted that at the heart of neoconservatism was the idea of pre-emptive war to defeat any state that might be considered a potential threat to US global dominance in the future. The neocons had been impressed by President Ronald Reagan's uncompromisingly hostile stance towards the Soviet Union in the 1980s, which they credited with bringing about its demise.

The neocons had a strong presence in Washington well before the election of President Bush in 2000. Perle had served as an Assistant Defense Secretary in Reagan's administration, and afterwards spent many years on the Defense Policy Board. Bush's first Defense Secretary, Donald Rumsfeld, and his Vice-President, Dick Cheney, had brought young neocons on to their staffs when they held senior positions in previous Republican administrations. But under Clinton's presidency, the neocons remained mostly on the margins of power, using those fallow years cooped up in their think-tanks to begin reimagining an imperial role for the US in the post-Soviet era. The Middle East, with its huge oil wealth, was at the heart of their designs, and Israel – as Washington's closest ally in the region – was, in their view, the key to American success. The neocons positioned Israel at the centre of a remade Middle East. In the new reality, American global dominance (and its control of oil) would be inseparable from Israel's regional dominance (and the security they believed would follow for Israel from its annexation of Palestinian land). Israel's unassailable strength in the Middle East would derive from its sole possession of nuclear weapons, which it had developed half a century earlier in cooperation with Europe and the US and which were entirely unmonitored because Israel had never admitted to their existence and had therefore not signed the Nuclear Non-Proliferation Treaty.[81] As far as the neocons were concerned, whatever Israel wanted, it should get.

It was no surprise that Perle was one of the main authors of a report published in 1996 by yet another neocon think-tank, the Institute for Advanced Strategic and Political Studies, that was submitted to the newly elected Israeli prime minister, Binyamin Netanyahu. It urged him to abandon the peace process of Oslo and its formula of 'land for peace', while advising him on ways to cement his country's special relationship with the US in the new imperial project. Other key authors included Douglas Feith and David Wurmser, later to be Vice-President Dick Cheney's adviser on the Middle East. Called *A Clean Break: A New Strategy for Securing the Realm*, the report proposed 'rebuilding Zionism' by 'weakening, containing, and even rolling back Syria' and 'removing Saddam Hussein from power in Iraq', as well as finding ways to 'wean the south Lebanese Shia away from Hizballah, Iran, and Syria' and 'cultivate alternatives to Arafat's base of power' in the occupied Palestinian territories. In metaphysical prose typical of the neocons, the authors proposed that 'Israel will not only contain its foes; it will transcend them.' In addition, the neocons had ideas about how Israel might overcome expected resistance to this aggressive new Middle East strategy in the less sympathetic Washington of the time: 'To anticipate US reactions and plan ways to manage and constrain those reactions, Prime Minister Netanyahu can formulate the policies and stress themes he favors in language familiar to the Americans by tapping into themes of American administrations during the Cold War which apply well to Israel.'[82] Though it would be another five years till the 11 September 2001 attacks on the World Trade Center, the neocons were already proposing, in embryo, selling Israel's central place in a coming 'clash of civilisations' between the Judeo-Christian West and the Islamic East.

Two years later, in January 1998, several key neocons wrote a letter to President Bill Clinton arguing that American policy towards Iraq was failing, and that 'we may face a threat in the Middle East more serious than any we have known since the end of the Cold War'.[83] The letter was signed by, among others, Richard Perle, and several figures who would soon become significant in the Bush Administration, including Donald Rumsfeld, Paul Wolfowitz, Elliott Abrams and John Bolton. A few months later the same group wrote to the Speaker of the House of Representatives, Newt Gingrich, and the Senate Majority Leader, Trent Lott, to express their belief that the policy of 'containment' of Saddam Hussein had proven unsuccessful and to recommend 'the removal of Saddam and his regime from power'.[84]

Another important neocon document, *Rebuilding America's Defenses*, published in September 2000 by the Project for the New American Century, was widely seen as the blueprint for the Bush Administration's foreign policy.[85] The report's authors admitted drawing heavily on a previous classified defence document, written in early 1992 for the then Defense Secretary, Dick Cheney, by a group of Pentagon staffers that included two neocons, Lewis 'Scooter' Libby and Paul Wolfowitz, who would become under Bush respectively the chief of staff to Vice-President Cheney and the Deputy Defense Secretary.[86] In the 1992 document, Cheney's aides had called for the US to assume the position of lone superpower and act pre-emptively to prevent the emergence of any regional competitors. 'In the Middle East and Southwest Asia, our overall objective is to remain the predominant outside power in the region and preserve US and Western access to the region's oil.' Although the 1992 paper was disowned by the then White House, Dick Cheney reportedly told the authors: 'You've discovered a new rationale for our role in the world.'[87] The updated 2000 report continued in much the same vein. New technologies, it noted,

> are creating a dynamic that may threaten America's ability to exercise its dominant military power. Potential rivals such as China are anxious to exploit these transformational technologies broadly, while adversaries like Iran, Iraq and North Korea are rushing to develop ballistic missiles and nuclear weapons as a deterrent to American intervention in regions they seek to dominate ... Over the long term, Iran may well prove as large a threat to US interests in the Gulf as Iraq has. And even should US-Iranian relations improve, retaining forward-based forces in the region would still be an essential element in US security strategy given the long-standing American interests in the region.

These neocon visions, as will become clear over the next three chapters, closely reflected positions developed by the Israeli security establishment nearly two decades earlier. To prevent Middle Eastern states from accreting military strength that might rival Israel's, and in particular to stop them developing nuclear weapons, the Israeli army and its intelligence services had formulated a strategy that, they believed, would guarantee Israel an imperial role in the Middle East to complement the American global one. This could best be achieved, they argued, with the dissolution of rival Arab and Muslim states through the spread of ethnic and sectarian strife across the region – in a particularly sophisticated version of the familiar colonial practice of 'divide and rule'. The US-led invasion of Iraq in 2003, Israel's attack on Lebanon in summer 2006, the endless threats against Iran, and the seeming revival in late 2006 of US policies to fund militant Sunni fundamentalist groups against the new 'Shia arc of extremism' (ignoring the lessons of 'blowback' from a similar exercise during the 1980s in supporting jihadis against the Soviet army in Afghanistan) suggested that Israel's strategy had seduced the neocons and, in turn, the Bush Administration. This is a story we shall return to in much greater detail in subsequent chapters.

FINDING A PRETEXT TO INVADE

The neocons' chance to create their own reality in the Middle East – and one more suited to both the US and Israel – came with the 9/11 attacks. The Administration's first task was to exploit the resulting deaths to create a new political and ideological climate in which a 'war on terror' would become the alibi for a neocon-inspired US foreign policy, justifying 'pre-emptive' wars to remake the Middle East. As part of that goal, the White House went after the most likely culprits for 9/11, 'smoking out', as President Bush phrased it, the jihadis of al-Qaeda in Afghanistan.[88] Plausible as the war on terror looked at this stage to many observers, for the neocons the real battle was yet to begin.[89] An indication of their priorities came with a speech by Bush in January 2002 in which he identified as an 'axis of evil' the rogue nuclear state of North Korea – a potential Far Eastern ally of America's only global challenger, China – along with Israel's two large, regional rivals, Iraq and Iran.[90]

With the neocons occupying many of the key positions in a Defense Department headed by Rumsfeld,[91] and supported by neocon journalists in senior posts in the US media,[92] they pushed very publicly for an invasion of Iraq as the next step in the war on terror. As we have already seen, they promoted not only erroneous information about Iraq's supposed stockpiles of WMD,[93] but also the improbable possibility that the secular Ba'athist regime was offering sanctuary to al-Qaeda.[94] The evidence for quite how desperate the neocons had grown to find a pretext for attacking Iraq was revealed five years later by a Pentagon investigation into the build-up to war. Included in its final report was a memo from Deputy Defense Secretary Wolfowitz, one of the most influential neocons in the Administration, to Douglas Feith, who was then head of the Pentagon's 'Office of Special Plans' and whose job it was to pave the way for an assault on Baghdad. Dated 22 January 2002, the memo from Wolfowitz states: 'We don't seem to be making much progress pulling together intelligence on links between Iraq and Al Qaeda. We owe SecDef [Rumsfeld] some analysis of this subject.'[95] The Pentagon inquiry concluded that Feith's Office had 'developed, produced and then disseminated alternative intelligence assessments on the Iraq and al-Qaeda relationship', including 'conclusions that were inconsistent with the consensus of the Intelligence Community'.[96] In other words, Feith had manufactured lies to justify the coming attack.[97]

According to the journalist Bob Woodward, who was given unrivalled access to Administration officials for his book *Bush at War*, the Pentagon had been working months before 9/11 on 'developing a military option for Iraq'. When the World Trade Center and Pentagon were attacked, Rumsfeld was ready to raise 'the possibility that they could take advantage of the opportunity offered by the terrorist attacks to go after Saddam immediately'. Wolfowitz too favoured invading Iraq in response to 9/11. According to Woodward: 'Rumsfeld raised the question of Iraq. Why shouldn't we go against Iraq, not just al Qaeda? He asked. Rumsfeld was speaking not only for himself when he raised the question. His deputy, Paul D. Wolfowitz, was committed to a policy that would make Iraq a principal target of the first round in the war on terrorism.'[98] Woodward's account is corroborated by an early passage in the memoirs of the head of the CIA at the time, George Tenet. The day after 9/11, Tenet reports passing

Richard Perle in the corridors of the White House's West Wing. Perle turned to Tenet and said: 'Iraq has to pay a price for what happened yesterday. They bear responsibility.' Tenet recalled:

> I was stunned but said nothing ... At the Secret Service security checkpoint, I looked back at Perle and thought: What the hell is he talking about? Moments later, a second thought came to me: Who has Richard Perle been meeting with in the White House so early in the morning on today of all days? I never learned the answer to that question.[99]

The neocons were not alone in wanting Saddam Hussein removed. In January 2004, the former US Treasury Secretary, Paul O'Neill, went public that there had been a memorandum preparing for 'regime change' in Iraq almost from 'day one' of the Bush Administration – and well before the September 11 attacks.[100] Meetings on Iraq were held in January and February 2001 by the National Security Council, part of the State Department, which O'Neill attended and at which an invasion of Iraq was discussed. 'It was all about finding a way to do it. That was the tone of it. The president saying "Go find me a way to do this".' By March 2001 a secretive Energy Task Force under Cheney had accumulated several documents on Iraq, including one entitled *Foreign Suitors For Iraqi Oilfield Contracts*, discussing ways to carve up Iraq's crude reserves between Western oil companies.[101]

According to the investigations of an American journalist, Greg Palast, the oil industry was also deeply involved in plotting Saddam's overthrow. Palast reports that three weeks after Bush's election, a confidential meeting took place at Walnut Creek, near San Francisco, at the instigation of the State Department and to which the oil industry was invited. Under discussion was a plan for a rapid invasion of Iraq to topple Saddam Hussein. His removal was wanted by the industry because he was considered unpredictable and the country's chaotic oil output was creating fluctuations in the price of crude and damaging markets. Also, the continuing sanctions regime was handicapping US oil firms, preventing them but not their counterparts in Europe, China, Russia and India, from signing exploration contracts for the moment the sanctions were lifted.[102] The *Suitors* document listed

Royal Dutch Shell, Russia's Lukoil and Total Elf Aquitaine of France as among the firms lined up for 'production-sharing contracts' with Iraq since the late 1990s. The Council on Foreign Relations, whose corporate members include most of the big oil companies, concluded that Saddam was a 'destabilising influence ... to the flow of oil to international markets'.[103] The plan envisaged a US-backed coup by a Ba'athist army general; the new strongman would be transformed into a democratic leader by elections held within three months. 'Bring him in right away and say that Iraq is being liberated – and everybody stay in office ... *everything as is*', recalled Falah Aljibury, an Iraqi exile, friend of the Bush family and the man called on by the State Department to plot the coup.[104] In other words, the State Department wanted regime change and the briefest possible occupation by US soldiers.

The plan, however, was hijacked and redirected by the neocons ensconsed in the Pentagon, led by Rumsfeld and Wolfowitz (with another neocon, Elliott Abrams in the National Security Council, possibly acting as an informant on the discussions taking place in the State Department). The neocons wanted a lengthy occupation as Iraq's assets, especially its oil, were sold off to foreign companies. The costs to the US could be offset by Iraq's increased oil revenues – 'between $50 and $100 million over the next two to three years', Wolfowitz promised Congress.[105] The invasion of spring 2003 followed the neocon script, with the White House installing Paul Bremer, a former official of Henry Kissinger and Ronald Reagan, as the head of the Coalition Provisional Authority, an occupation regime that notably resisted installing a new strongman to replace Saddam Hussein, as Big Oil had envisioned. Instead Bremer appointed an Iraqi 'governing council' led by Ahmed Chalabi, an Iraqi exile and convicted conman who had cultivated the neocons in the Pentagon. The US, instead of installing a new dictator to replace the unreliable old one, was now pursuing a policy that was deeply, and possibly permanently, miring it in Iraq.

What was the basis of the difference in vision of Iraq's future between Big Oil and the neocons? The oil industry favoured the creation of an Iraqi state-owned company that would restrict production, staying within quotas and shoring up Saudi Arabia's control of OPEC. Big Oil would oversee production, ensure oil prices remained stable, and rake off large profits for foreign companies. The neocons, on the other hand, wanted the Iraqi oil industry privatised so that the global market could be flooded with cheap oil and the Saudi-dominated cartel smashed.[106] The main consequences of the neocon plan would be the erosion of Saudi Arabia's financial muscle and ability to finance extreme Islamic groups, and the undermining of the whole oil-based economy of the Middle East, both the enormous profits of the oil-producing countries and the livelihoods of the guest workers from neighbouring Arab states whose families depended on their remittances. We shall return to the significance of this White House dispute in Chapter 4, but it is worth noting here that the biggest beneficiary of the neocons' plan to topple the Iraqi regime and at the same time destroy the Middle East's oil cartel was Israel, which would not only lose a potential military challenger in Iraq but also a significant rival in the shape of Saudi Arabia for influence in Washington and with the US oil lobby. These two Arab countries were also the Palestinians' most important patrons: Iraq in terms of its vocal ideological backing of the Palestinian cause, and Saudi Arabia for the financial help it provided. Under the neocons' arrangement, Israel's interests, already preferred by US administrations, would face no countervailing pressures whatsoever. That may have explained why one of the neocons' favourite slogans in the lead up to the attack on Iraq was: 'The road to Jerusalem runs through Baghdad.'

ISRAEL'S ROLE BEHIND THE SCENES

In pursuing their policies against Iraq, the neocons were in lock-step with the Israeli government, then headed by a former general, Ariel Sharon, known for his brutal military adventures and belief in pre-emptive wars. This was no surprise. As we shall see in later chapters, the partition of Iraq into three statelets – based on the Sunni, Shia and Kurdish populations – had been a Zionist ambition dating back decades. One neocon lobbyist, Thomas

Neumann, executive director of the Jewish Institute for National Security Affairs, described the Bush White House 'as the best administration for Israel since Harry Truman', referring to the president who recognised the newly established Israeli state in 1948. Shortly before the attack on Iraq a senior US official told the *Washington Post*: 'The Likudniks [Sharon supporters] are really in charge now.' And a former leading official in the Bush Snr's Administration observed that from the moment of 9/11 Sharon had been working on Bush Jnr to persuade him that they were facing the same threat: international terrorism. 'Sharon played the president like a violin: "I'm fighting your war, terrorism is terrorism," and so on. Sharon did a masterful job.'[107]

In February 2002, weeks after he had publicly defied the US by beginning a military rampage through Gaza, Sharon was a guest in the White House advising President Bush on plans for a strike against Iraq.[108] Two months later, according to reports by a British journalist who was leaked secret Downing Street memos, the White House made a pact with the British government to hit Iraq, and began seeking ways to 'wrong-foot' Saddam Hussein to provide the legal justification to wage war.[109] By the summer, more than six months before the US invasion, Sharon told the Israeli parliament: 'Iraq is a great danger. It could be said it is the greatest danger ... Strategic coordination between Israel and the US has reached unprecedented dimensions.'[110] That view was confirmed by a US Republican Senator, Chuck Hagel, after a fact-finding mission to Israel in December 2002. Following a private meeting, Hagel revealed to a confidant that Sharon was leaving 'no doubt that the greatest US assistance to Israel would be to overthrow Saddam Hussein's Iraqi regime'.[111]

The Israeli government was also happy to ratchet up the pressure on the wider international community to support American action. In August 2002, one of Sharon's closest aides, Rana'an Gissin, argued: 'Any postponement of an attack on Iraq at this stage will serve no purpose. It will only give him [Saddam Hussein] more of an opportunity to accelerate his program of weapons of mass destruction.' The Defence Minister, Binyamin Ben Eliezer, drove the point home: 'We will be one of the main targets [of

Iraq]. What I told the Americans, and I repeat it: "Don't expect us to continue to live with the process of restraint. If they hit us, we reserve the right of response."'[112] It was not only the Israeli right talking up war. Labor party veteran Shimon Peres, who was Foreign Minister in Sharon's cabinet, warned an audience in Washington in October 2002 that postponing a strike on Iraq would be 'taking maybe the same risk that was taken by Europe in 1939 in the face of the emergency of Hitler'.[113]

Claims widely publicised in the West that Saddam Hussein had secret stockpiles of biological and chemical weapons were exploited to good effect by Sharon, with the Prime Minister playing up the supposed anti-Semitism of the regime and Israel's uncomfortable proximity to Iraq. All of this flew in the face of assessments by Israel's military intelligence, which advised the government that, after more than a decade of sanctions, Iraq was in no position to inflict reprisals on Israel. Despite Israel supposedly being the prime target of Iraqi retaliation, the chance of an attack from Iraq, the cabinet was told, was just '1 per cent'.[114] Nonetheless, arguing that Saddam Hussein was planning to use his WMD against Israel, Sharon whipped up a national consensus in favour of prompt US action. By February 2003, 77 per cent of Israeli Jews were behind an attack. 'There is a majority of supporters of a war among all the parties and in all sectors of the Jewish public', reported the daily *Ha'aretz* newspaper.[115]

In fact, so solid was the support of the Israeli public and leadership for an invasion of Iraq – in stark contrast to the mass protests in Europe and America – that later, as US public opinion turned against continuing the occupation, Israeli officials hastily began rewriting history, claiming that Sharon had been at best agnostic about the wisdom of an attack, if not downright hostile. Danny Ayalon, who was Israel's ambassador to the US at the time, claimed that the Israeli Prime Minister had warned Bush that Iraq was not ready for a 'democratic culture'. Ayalon added that, though Israeli officials had been closely involved in advising the White House, they had 'never cross[ed] the red line of recommending policy' for fear that this could provoke accusations later that Israel led the US into the war. By that stage Sharon was in a coma and in no position to be challenged on Ayalon's improbable account of the meetings.[116]

In Chapter 3, we shall examine how Israel 'sold' the neocons a vision of a remade Middle East, and how the neocons then sold that same vision to the rest of the Bush Administration. But in the meantime, it is worth sketching out Israel's own motives in promoting a deeper US involvement in the Middle East. The Bush Administration had decided even before the 9/11 attacks that it wanted to 'remake' the region so that its control of oil would be secured. Israel too needed the Middle East remade, in its case so that it would have no significant regional challengers, its usefulness to the US would be unrivalled by any other Middle Eastern state, and it would continue being rewarded with billions of dollars each year to ethnically cleanse the occupied territories of their Palestinian inhabitants. A senior Israeli commentator, Aluf Benn, explained days before the attack on Baghdad:

> Senior IDF [Israeli army] officers and those close to Prime Minister Ariel Sharon, such as National Security Advisor Ephraim Halevy, paint a rosy picture of the wonderful future Israel can expect after the war. They envision a domino effect, with the fall of Saddam Hussein followed by that of Israel's other enemies: [Yasser] Arafat, Hassan Nasrallah [of Hizbullah], [Syria's President] Bashar Assad, the ayatollah in Iran and maybe even Muhammar Gadaffi [of Libya]. Along with these leaders, will disappear terror and weapons of mass destruction.[117]

Israel's rationale for promoting a US attack on its regional rivals neatly chimed with the war on terror: that the Arab world was engulfed by a genocidal anti-Semitism that wanted Israel destroyed as a nation just as the Jews had nearly been destroyed as a people by the Nazis. This coincidence of interests and pretexts produced a unifying theme much exploited by the neocons: the 'clash of civilisations'.

2

THE LONG CAMPAIGN AGAINST IRAN

In late January 2007, Israel and America's political and security establishments descended on an exclusive seaside town just north of Tel Aviv. Named after the father of Zionism, Theodor Herzl, and today home to foreign diplomats and wealthy Israelis, Herzliya has been hosting an annual conference – under the banner 'The Balance of Israel's National Security' – since the outbreak of the second Palestinian intifada in late 2000.[1] The Herzliya conference quickly established itself as the premier event in Israel's political calendar. Hundreds of politicians, including most of the cabinet, generals, diplomats, academics, journalists and policy makers meet to discuss the most pressing issues they believe to be facing the country. There is rarely much dissent; the point of Herzliya is to set out the coming year's national agenda for Israel's Jewish majority.

Until the 2007 conference, the delegates' main concern had been clear: Israel's struggle against the Palestinians and, in particular, the 'existential threat' posed to the Jewish state by the rapid growth of the Palestinian populations inside Israel and the occupied territories.[2] These demographic discussions foreshadowed Ariel Sharon's scheme to withdraw from Gaza in August 2005 and to end, in his own mind at least, Israel's responsibility for the 1.4 million Palestinians crowded into the Strip. Indeed, it was at one of the Herzliya conferences, in December 2003, that Sharon announced the Disengagement Plan.[3]

The 2007 conference, however, was different from its predecessors in at least two respects. First, on this occasion a host of non-Israelis – US policy makers, past and present – had been invited. Forty-two Americans, among them the Deputy

Defense Secretary, Gordon England; the Under-Secretary of State for Political Affairs, Nicholas Burns; and Democratic presidential candidate John Edwards, took part alongside half the Israeli cabinet and the Prime Minister, Ehud Olmert. For the first time, Herzliya looked like a joint Israeli and American production. And second, the conference turned its attention away from the Palestinian question, an issue seen by Israelis as essentially a domestic matter, to the regional arena and, in particular, the threat from the Shia 'arc of extremism'. The words 'Iran' and 'Hizbullah' featured prominently in the titles of many of the debates.

One reluctant participant, Yonatan Mendel, a leftwing Israeli journalist, later wrote of his surprise at the line-up of speakers for a talk he was assigned to cover for his news agency:

> The panel was entitled 'The Changing Paradigm of Israeli-Palestinian Relations in the Shadow of Iran and the War against the Hizbullah'. The session was to be chaired by a former Israeli ambassador to the UN, Dore Gold, who is currently president of the Jerusalem Centre for Public Affairs. I vaguely remembered coming across one of his books as an undergraduate at Tel Aviv University: *Hatred's Kingdom: How Saudi Arabia Supports the New Global Terrorism*. The second speaker was Professor Bernard Lewis of Princeton University. I knew his work well – who didn't? The title of one of his books encapsulates his views: *What Went Wrong? The Clash between Islam and Modernity in the Middle East*. Clash of Civilisations: here we come. The third speaker was Moshe Yaalon, the former Israeli chief of staff. After his retirement in 2005 he told *Haaretz* that the Palestinians were still looking for ways to exterminate Israel; therefore Israeli withdrawal to the 1967 borders would never solve the conflict ... He now works at the Shalem Centre, an education and research institution that is identified with the Israeli right and American neo-conservatives. I assumed that the panel would include at least one speaker who thought differently from his colleagues and started to feel bad for the fourth speaker. Poor fellow, I thought, facing those three. I read on. The poor fellow was revealed to be James Woolsey, a former director of the CIA.[4] I knew nothing about him. I googled his name and found out that in July [2006] Woolsey had called on the US to bomb Syria.[5]

Mendel went on to describe the shared message of the four panellists: that Iran was on the verge of gaining nuclear weapons, and would then fulfil a long-standing dream to destroy Israel. The speakers were echoing Washington's widely accepted claim that Tehran was secretly trying to develop a nuclear warhead. The fact that Iran's clerical leaders, including the late Ayatollah Khomeini, had repeatedly issued fatwas – binding religious edicts – banning the country from developing nuclear weapons was considered of no interest in Western media coverage.[6] The basis for Western fears was Iran's work on enriching uranium, a component in the development both of a civilian nuclear energy programme and of nuclear weapons. Iran, as a signatory of the Nuclear Non-Proliferation Treaty, had the right to enrich uranium as part of its civilian programme but had failed to inform the United Nations watchdog body, the International Atomic Energy Agency, about efforts it had made to do so. Although Iran quickly agreed to abide by the code and inspections when this breach was discovered in 2002, the White House had the pretext it needed to begin a campaign to stop Tehran's work on its civilian programme, forcing an inevitable confrontation between the two. The rhetoric in Washington soon included not only the unsubstantiated claim that Iran was secretly working on nuclear warheads, despite the UN inspections, but that its sole reason for wanting to develop such weapons was to destroy Israel and possibly the rest of the world.

Stripped of their bluster, American and Israeli concerns were neatly summed up in an approving editorial from the conservative *Economist* magazine.

> Even if Iran never used its bomb, mere possession of it might encourage it to adopt a more aggressive foreign policy than the one it is already pursuing in Iraq, Lebanon and the Palestinian territories. And once Iran went nuclear other countries in the region – such as Saudi Arabia, Egypt and perhaps Turkey – would probably feel compelled to follow suit, thereby entangling the Middle East in a cat's cradle of nuclear tripwires.[7]

In other words, the US and Israel were worried that they might no longer be able to dictate policy in the Middle East. Interestingly, *The Economist* did not question the premise supporting its main conclusion: why, if Iran's supposed efforts at acquiring a nuclear bomb had to be prevented so that its neighbours were not encouraged to play a game of catch-up, did Israel's own nuclear arsenal not need to be destroyed or regulated to remove the incentive from Iran to play its own version of catch-up? Instead, America's pre-emptive overthrow of the neighbouring Iraqi regime and its chorus of threats against Iran only added to the pressure on Tehran to head down the path of developing nuclear weapons. By summer 2007 the White House even justified a controversial plan to site US anti-ballistic missiles in former Eastern bloc countries (in reality, designed to be a show of force against Russia)[8] on the grounds that they could be used to protect the West from Iran's imminent nuclear arsenal.[9] Analyst Dilip Hiro explained the thinking in Tehran:

> With Saddam's regime destroyed and North Korea armed and dangerous, Iran was the member of that 'axis' left exposed to the prospect of regime change ... From the Iranian leaders' viewpoint, surrendering their right to enrich uranium, as demanded by the Bush administration and its allies, means giving up the path to a nuclear weapon in the future. Yet, the history of the past half century indicates that the only effective way to deter Washington from overthrowing their regime is by developing – or, at least, threatening to develop – nuclear weaponry. Little wonder that they consider giving up the right to enrich uranium tantamount to giving up the right to protect their regime.[10]

Hiro's analysis was supported by Israel's leading military historian, Martin van Creveld:

> Even if the Iranians are working on a bomb, Israel may not be their real concern. Iran is now surrounded by American forces on all sides – in the Central Asian republics to the north, Afghanistan to the east, the Gulf to the south and Iraq to the west ... Wherever U.S. forces go, nuclear weapons go with them or can be made to follow in short order. The world has witnessed how the United States attacked Iraq for, as it turned out, no reason at all. Had the Iranians not tried to build nuclear weapons, they would be crazy.[11]

Despite the profound implausibility of much of the debate about Iran and nuclear weapons, and a manufactured climate (as we shall see) in which Tehran was assumed to want to destroy Israel, the Herzliya panel's warnings received an enthusiastic reception from the distinguished audience, as Yonatan Mendel recounted:

> 'Destroying Israel and the US is the essence of the Iranian state,' Woolsey said, 'and trying to convince Iran to stop it is like trying to convince Hitler not to be anti-semitic.' The crowd was now his. Woolsey didn't lose his momentum. 'I agree with Dr Gold,' he said, as he looked over at the panellists. 'Wahhabi Islam [the ultra-conservative Sunni Islam of the Saudi regime], al-Qaida and Vilayat e-Faqih [Iran's Shia clerical leadership] cannot be treated individually. Those who say that they will not co-operate with one another are as wrong as those who claimed that the Nazis and Communists would not co-operate.' The audience couldn't contain its excitement and started clapping riotously. Woolsey kept his grip. 'We should listen to what they say,' he said, silencing the crowd, 'just like we needed to listen to Hitler.' An attentive silence spread through the room. 'We must not accept totalitarian regimes,' he said, 'and we should not tolerate a nuclear weapon capability for Iran ... If we use force, we should use it decisively, not execute some surgical strike on a single or two or three facilities. We need to destroy the power of the Vilayat e-Faqih if we are called upon and forced to use force against Iran.' Next Woolsey took his audience to Syria. 'It is a shame,' he said, that Israel and the US failed to 'participate in a move against Syria last summer'. He paused. 'Finally,' he said, looking into his audience's eyes, 'we must not forget who we are. We, as Jews, Christians and others, are heirs of the tradition deriving from Judaism.'[12]

THE PROPAGANDA WAR

Although the Bush Administration and the neocons had focused their early attention on the supposed threat posed by Iraq, there are strong grounds for suspecting that, though Israel was pleased to see the Iraqi regime overthrown, Iran was regarded as the more pressing danger. Israel's obsession with Iran had developed at least a decade earlier as Tehran grew stronger in the wake of the 1991 Gulf War and the effective emasculation of Iraq from the combined effect of Operation Desert Storm, the crippling sanctions regime and the imposition of no-fly zones. Tehran, in contrast, had begun a slow process of economic and military recovery after the exhausting war with Baghdad; was nurturing Israel's main foe in Lebanon, the Hizbullah; had an enduring alliance with Syria, Israel's relatively strong and recalcitrant neighbour; and was suspected of assisting Hamas in the occupied Palestinian territories. Israel started a prolonged propaganda campaign against Iran from the early 1990s which had strong echoes of the climate being manufactured in the US more than a decade later. Then, as now, Iran was said to be only years or months away from developing nuclear weapons, and determined to destroy not only Israel but the whole world. In reality, Iran was quite open in the early 1990s about trying to find a European partner to help it develop a civilian nuclear energy programme, as it was entitled to do under the Nuclear Non-Proliferation Treaty. However, under US pressure, European states refused to cooperate.

These US concerns about a nuclear Iran were shared by Israel, as a review of the media of the time reveals. In early 1993, for example, Yo'av Kaspi, the political correspondent of the newspaper *al-Hamishmar*, referring to the crushing sanctions imposed by the West on Baghdad, reiterated the Israeli government's view that 'Iran needs to be treated just as Iraq [has] been'. Kaspi interviewed a retired senior officer in military intelligence, Daniel Leshem, who suggested that Tehran should be lured into a trap – possibly encouraged to make a mistake similar to Saddam's of invading Kuwait – thereby justifying massive retaliation. 'If they [Iran] nevertheless refrain from starting a war', he added, it might still be possible to find a pretext. 'We should take advantage of their involvement in Islamic terrorism which already hurts the entire world.'[13] In summer 1994 *Ha'aretz* analyst Aluf Benn explained why dealing with Iran was considered the Israeli army's top priority: 'Iran could aspire to regional hegemony and ruin the peace process by virtue of having nuclear weapons and long-range missiles, of building a modern air force and navy, of exporting terrorism and revolution and of subverting Arab secular regimes.'[14] What this appeared to mean, once the prism of Israel's security obsessions had been lifted, was that Iran might soon become a genuine military rival and, as a result, Israel's dictates would not be the only ones shaping the Middle East.

By October 1994, *Ha'aretz* reported that Prime Minister Yitzhak Rabin and his deputy, Shimon Peres, were organising the campaign against Tehran through a new government office under the Orwellian name of the 'Peace in the Middle East Department'. Its job was to suggest that Iran was 'a major threat to stability in the Middle East'. This was ascribed not only to 'its support for terror and sabotage and its attempts to become nuclearized' but also to its 'being an exemplar not only for Islamic fundamentalists but for other resistance movements in Arab countries'. Rabin and Peres were already reported to be thinking in terms of presenting this as a clash of civilisations. *Ha'aretz* noted that 'Israeli *hasbara* [propaganda] was ordered to depict the rulers of Iran as "a danger to peace in the entire world and a threat to equilibrium between Western civilization and Islam"'.[15] The then Chief of Staff, Ehud Barak, adopted a similar tone, stating that Tehran 'posed a danger to the very foundations of world order'. Barak reached his conclusion, wrote Aluf Benn, because Iran 'opposes the flow of oil to the developed world and because it wants to upset the cultural equilibrium between the West and Islam'.[16]

In addition, there were long-standing fears in the Israeli military that a nuclear Iran would pass on its knowledge to Syria, making the two countries a very effective regional counterweight to Israel. In April 1992 General Uri Saguy, head of Israel's military intelligence, replied to a question about whether Iran would assist Syria with developing a bomb:

> When Iran itself becomes nuclearized, I cannot see how it can avoid cooperating [in this matter] with Syria. Such a prospect should worry us ... In ten years' time Iran will certainly become a decisive factor in the entire region, and as such an ever-present threat to its peace. This can hardly be prevented, unless somebody intervenes directly.[17]

It was not surprising, therefore, that Sharon should have seen a double opportunity to be grasped in Washington's new aggressive engagement with the Middle East following 9/11. Saddam's removal was a boon: he had offered symbolic and vocal support to the Palestinians; and his regime, crippled by the Gulf War and the long sanctions regime, was the weak link in the oil cartel OPEC, apparently a prize wanted by the neocons in their designs to smash Saudi influence. But Sharon regarded Iran as the bigger threat to Israel's regional dominance, both because of its rapid advances in nuclear technology[18] and its links to the Shia militia Hizbullah, which had effectively evicted the occupying Israeli army from south Lebanon in 2000 and become an inspiring example of resistance for the Palestinians. Days before the US-led invasion of Iraq in 2003, *Ha'aretz* noted that the chief concern of Israeli policy makers was that 'Iran might take advantage of the war [against Iraq] to strengthen its status in the region and accelerate development of nuclear weapons ... Israel regards the Iranian atom bomb as the gravest threat to its security, and has been trying to muster international pressure to halt the project, with the United States' help'.[19] In other words, for Israel the destruction of Iraq and Iran had to come as a package; weakening only one would simply make the other stronger.

Sharon had hoped that a US invasion of Iraq would serve as a model for attacking Iran, just as the neocons had used the US war in Afghanistan as a model for their 'pre-emptive' strike on Iraq. Speaking of Iran, Syria and Libya in early 2003, shortly after the invasion of Iraq, Sharon noted: 'These are irresponsible states, which must be disarmed of weapons of mass destruction, and a successful American move in Iraq as a model will make that easier to achieve.'[20] (Although Libya was included in the list at this stage, within months its dictator, Colonel Muammar Gaddafi, had signed up on the US side in the war on terror and abandoned his own, unconvincing attempts at developing nuclear weapons.) During Sharon's visit to the White House more than a year before the invasion of Iraq, and only months after 9/11, Ben Eliezer took time out to explain to the international media that the Israeli Prime Minister was warning President Bush that Tehran posed as much of a threat to peace in the Middle East as Baghdad. 'I know that today the name of the game is Iraq, which is very relevant, but I would say they are twins, Iran and Iraq.'[21]

In November 2002, Sharon told the London *Times* about his conversation with the US President:

> One of the things I mentioned [to Bush] is that the free world should take all the necessary steps to prevent irresponsible countries from having weapons of mass destruction: Iran, Iraq of course, and Libya is working on a nuclear weapon ... Iran is a centre of world terror and Iran makes every effort to possess weapons of mass destruction on the one hand and ballistic missiles. That is a danger to the Middle East, to Israel and a danger to Europe.[22]

Sharon told the newspaper that Iran should come under pressure 'the day after' Baghdad was hit.

In February 2003, only a month before the attack on Iraq, Sharon used his meeting with a leading neocon in the Bush Administration, John Bolton, then an Under-Secretary of State, to press the case for targeting Iran next. Bolton was reported to have responded that 'he had no doubt America would attack Iraq, and that it would be necessary thereafter to deal with threats from Syria, Iran and North Korea'.[23] Bolton was already referring to the White House's new 'axis of evil' – Syria was to replace Iraq following the latter's occupation by US forces. Over the coming months, Israel would increasingly focus on a similar axis of evil: Iran, Syria and Hizbullah in Lebanon (with Hamas officially joining later, in early 2006, after its election to lead the Palestinian Authority). Iran was portrayed as the centre of world terrorism, using as a proxy the Hizbullah militia of its co-religionists, the Shia in Lebanon. Syria, wedged between Lebanon on one side and Iraq and Iran on the other, was accused of assisting Iran in supplying Hizbullah, as well as stoking the Sunni insurgency in post-invasion Iraq. The latter allegation could reasonably be doubted: the secular Syrian regime, dominated by the small Shia sect of the Alawis, had been ruthlessly suppressing Sunni militants inside its own borders and had no interest in helping a similar insurgency in neighbouring Iraq.

Sharon's keen interest in Iran was well known to the Israeli media. In early 2002 the country's most celebrated columnist, Nahum Barnea of *Yed'iot Aharonot*, noted that Israel's top priority was persuading the US Administration that Iran was 'the real strategic threat' and that they would have to 'deal with it diplomatically or militarily, or both. If they don't, Israel will have to do it alone.'[24] And hours before the attack on Iraq, Uzi Benziman, one of *Ha'aretz*'s most informed commentators, amplified the point:

> The war on terror and on weapons of mass destruction is the banner under which President Bush is going to war in Iraq. Then why is he passing over Iran when the smoking gun is there for all to see? After the war in Iraq, Israel will try to convince the US to direct its war on terror at Iran, Damascus and Beirut. Senior defense establishment officials say that initial contacts in this direction have already been made in recent months, and that there is a good chance that America will be swayed by the Israeli argument.[25]

Even as the US was preparing to declare victory in Iraq after its rapid push to Baghdad, Sharon's 'point man' in Washington, the lawyer Dov Weisglass, was pressing the Iran line yet again. 'Israel will suggest that the United States also take care of Iran and Syria because of their support for terror and pursuit of weapons of mass destruction', reported the Israeli media.[26]

ISRAEL'S FEAR OF A NUCLEAR RIVAL

One veteran Middle East analyst, David Hirst, explained Israel's view of Iran:

> Israel classifies Iran as one of those 'far' threats – Iraq being another – that distinguish it from the 'near' ones: the Palestinians and neighbouring Arab states [Egypt, Jordan, Syria, Lebanon] ... The closer their [Iraq and Iran's] weapons of mass destruction programmes come to completion, the more compelling the need for Israel – determined to preserve its nuclear monopoly in the region – to eliminate them.[27]

The core concern for Israel was that should either of these 'far threats' manage to rival Israel's power in the Middle East, they would be able to influence the peace process in ways that might benefit the Palestinians and possibly bring an end to decades of occupation.[28] Israel, therefore, had every reason to exaggerate both the advanced stage Tehran had reached in its nuclear programme and its malicious intentions towards Israel and the world. The

US echoed these claims as it blocked dialogue with Tehran at almost every turn. Zbigniew Brzezinski, the hawkish National Security Adviser during Jimmy Carter's presidency, called the US approach 'clumsy' and 'stupid', effectively forcing the Iranians out of the negotiating process that would have ensured a closer cooperation with the international community. The US had insisted that the Iranians 'give something up [their right to enrich uranium] as a precondition for a serious dialogue on the subject', observed Brzezinski. 'I frankly don't understand how anyone in his right mind would make that condition if he were serious about negotiations, unless the objective is to prevent negotiations.'[29]

As the US further isolated Tehran over its nuclear energy programme, Iran's populist president, Mahmoud Ahmadinejad, dug in his heels. In 2007 he boasted that his country was making rapid progress on nuclear technology. Tehran was in fact a long way from its stated goal of achieving civilian nuclear energy, let alone nuclear weapons. Exactly 15 years after Israel's lobbying against Iran had begun, the head of the International Atomic Energy Agency, Muhammad el-Baradei, reported that Iran had only a few hundred centrifuges up and running.[30] Even assuming Ahmadinejad was not exaggerating in claiming that his scientists at the Natanz plant had begun operating 3,000 centrifuges to make enriched uranium, the *Guardian* newspaper observed that experts 'doubt whether continuous operation has been achieved – another key part of the calculation. Three thousand centrifuges operating smoothly in tandem would produce enough enriched uranium to produce one bomb in a year.' In assessing the value of an attack on Iran, the *Guardian* observed:

> If, as the Oxford Research Group has claimed, it is the case that bombing Natanz could hasten an Iranian bomb (because you can't bomb the knowledge that Iranian scientists have gained, and getting a nuclear bomb after an attack would become a national imperative), that leaves only one option: changing Iranian behaviour through cooperation and negotiation.

Furthermore, intimidation was likely only to encourage Tehran to opt out of the Non-Proliferation Treaty and thereby end the inspections it was allowing the International Atomic Energy

Agency to make. The *Guardian* suggested another way of dealing with Iran's nuclear ambitions: 'One suggestion is an enrichment process [for a civilian programme of nuclear power] that takes place physically on Iranian soil but under multilateral ownership and supervision. There may be other ways of satisfying both Iran's claim for a nuclear cycle and our desire to stop it getting the bomb.'[31]

The neocons and Israel appeared to have other ideas.

Behind the scenes, the Israel lobby in Washington began its own covert efforts to help Tel Aviv influence Washington policy makers against Tehran. Most controversially, Larry Franklin, a Pentagon staffer working for Douglas Feith, began passing classified information about US defence policy on Iran to two senior staff at Israel's chief Washington lobby group, AIPAC, and an Israeli diplomat. Franklin was tried and jailed in early 2006.[32] In the subsequent trial of the AIPAC officials, Steve Rosen and Keith Weissman, their lawyer argued that neither had reason to believe he had done anything wrong in receiving classified information from Franklin because senior Bush Administration officials, including Secretary of State Condoleezza Rice, had passed on documents at least as sensitive. Also named as assisting AIPAC were: Stephen Hadley, National Security Adviser to the White House; Elliott Abrams, Hadley's deputy at the National Security Council; Anthony Zinni and William Burns, two former US envoys to the Middle East; and David Satterfield, Burns' former deputy and the deputy ambassador to Iraq.[33]

By May 2003, according to an article in the American Jewish weekly newspaper the *Forward*: 'Neoconservatives advocating regime change in Tehran through diplomatic pressure – and even covert action – appear to be winning the debate within the administration.' With American Jewish groups pressing for action against Iran, the *Forward* observed: 'The emerging coalition is reminiscent of the buildup to the invasion of Iraq.'[34]

A month later, as US forces were facing the early stages of an insurgency in Baghdad, Michael Ledeen, a scholar at the American Enterprise Institute and an adviser to President Bush's Deputy Chief of Staff, Karl Rove, wrote in the *Washington Post*:

> We are now engaged in a regional struggle in the Middle East, and the Iranian tyrants are the keystone of the terror network. Far more than the overthrow of Saddam Hussein, the defeat of the mullahcracy and the triumph of freedom in Tehran would be a truly historic event and an enormous blow to the terrorists.[35]

To realise his vision, Ledeen promoted in the US media the unfounded story that Iranian agents had smuggled enriched uranium out of Iraq shortly before the US invasion, thereby neatly both explaining the West's failure to find evidence of a nuclear programme in Iraq and proving a new level of nuclear threat posed by Iran.[36] Ledeen had already established an organisation called the Coalition for Democracy in Iran along with Morris Amitay, a former executive director of AIPAC.

US READIES FOR A MILITARY STRIKE

There was no debate in Israel about which country should be targeted after Iraq; it was taken for granted that Iran should be next. The question was simply one of how to isolate Tehran and neutralise its threat to Israel's regional hegemony, particularly its presumed quest for a nuclear arsenal to rival Israel's own. Would Europe shrink from the task and insist on negotiations with Tehran, especially as the latter appeared increasingly open to compromise? Would the US find a way to impose effective sanctions on Iran and force it to back down? Or would Israel or the US mount an attack? Iran, despite the terrifying scenarios created by Israel and the neocons, was no 'military behemoth', in the words of analyst Dilip Hiro. Its military industry was smaller than Belgium's and during its savage eight-year war with Iraq it had purchased only a tenth of the arms bought by its neighbour. Nonetheless, no one in the Israeli or American governments appeared to want a repeat of the invasion and occupation of Iraq. As *The Economist* observed, the military operation being considered was 'an attack from the air, aimed at disabling or destroying Iran's nuclear sites'.[37]

In the US, the drumbeat of war grew weaker in late 2003 and early 2004, as the Bush Administration became absorbed with the growing insurgency in Iraq, and as Tehran agreed to tougher inspections from the International Atomic Energy Agency. As a consequence, Israel began leaking reports through 2004 that it might go it alone in attacking Iran's nuclear sites, similar to the strike it launched against Iraq's Osiraq nuclear reactor in 1981. Israeli defence officials were quoted saying: 'Israel will on no account permit Iranian reactors – especially the one being built in Bushehr with Russian help – to go critical ... If the worst comes to the worst and international efforts fail, we are very confident we'll be able to demolish the ayatollah's nuclear aspirations in one go.' The *Sunday Times* quoted from a classified official Israeli document entitled *The Strategic Future of Israel*. Drafted by four senior defence officials and presented to Sharon, it concluded: 'All enemy targets should be selected with the view that their destruction would promptly force the enemy to cease all nuclear/biological/chemical exchanges with Israel.' Describing Iran as a 'suicide nation', the report called on Israel to develop a multi-layered ballistic missile defence system. An Israeli strike on Iranian nuclear facilities, it was noted, could provoke 'a ferocious response' that might involve rocket attacks on northern Israel from Iran's ally in Lebanon, Hizbullah.[38]

By early 2005, with Bush re-elected president, the US quickly shifted its attention back to Iran – in line with Israel's position. In January, Vice-President Cheney declared: 'Given the fact that Iran has a stated policy that their objective is the destruction of Israel, the Israelis might well decide to act first, and let the rest of the world worry about cleaning up the diplomatic mess afterwards.'[39] Cheney's suggestion that Israel was facing a tight deadline – supported by endless Israeli statements that Iran was only months away from developing nuclear weapons[40] – contradicted that year's National Intelligence Estimate, the first updated US intelligence report on Iran since 2001. It found that Iran was at least ten years away from having the technology to make a nuclear bomb and that, although Tehran was doing clandestine civilian research, there was no evidence it was directly working on developing nuclear weapons. 'What is clear is that Iran, mostly through its [civilian nuclear] energy program, is acquiring and mastering technologies that could be diverted to bombmaking', reported the *Washington Post*.[41]

Nonetheless, the Bush Administration set about creating a legal framework – as it had done previously with Iraq – that might later justify an attack. Paradoxically, in summer 2005, shortly after the inspectors of the International Atomic Energy Agency gave Iran a relatively clean bill of health, the strong US lobbying finally paid off: the Agency's board of governors, a more politicised body, issued a statement finding Tehran in 'non-compliance' and threatening to refer Iran to the UN Security Council if it did not improve its cooperation. Even then the report was carried by the bloc vote of the NATO countries, with, unusually, many voting nations, including Russia and China, abstaining.[42] Asli U Bali, of Yale Law School, noted that the timing of the board's statement suggested that behind the vote lay 'the political objective of persuading Iran to halt enrichment [of uranium], rather than enforcement of treaty obligations'.[43] A subsequent UN resolution, passed in July 2006, demanded that Iran suspend uranium enrichment-related and reprocessing activities by 31 August 2006 or face sanctions.[44] In December 2006 a harsher resolution, 1737, was adopted, condemning Iran's nuclear research programme and imposing limited sanctions.[45] Another UN resolution passed in March 2007, applying further sanctions.

In parallel to these legal manoeuvres, the White House was also reported to be preparing for a covert military strike. Scott Ritter, the former UN chief weapons inspector in Iraq who had angered Washington by arguing before the US invasion that Saddam Hussein's stockpiles of WMD no longer existed, claimed that the Pentagon had been ordered to be ready for an attack on Tehran from summer 2005 onwards. 'In October 2004,' Ritter said, 'the President of the United States ordered the Pentagon to be prepared to launch military strikes against Iran as of June 2005. That means, have all the resources in place so that, if the President orders it, the bombing can begin.'[46] The timing may not have been arbitrary: two months later Israel was due to withdraw its few thousand settlers from the Gaza Strip in what it called a 'disengagement'. Israel had publicised fears that 'Iran, or more likely its Hizbullah allies on the northern border in Lebanon, and Syria might take advantage of Israel's vulnerability while its forces were tied up in the country's south. Israel and the US may have believed that they could use any such move as a pretext to hit Iran.

Ritter's account was in part corroborated by a series of reports from Seymour Hersh in the *New Yorker*. Drawing on an array of sources in the Pentagon and intelligence community, Hersh charted the strategies of the White House – and, to a lesser extent, Israel – in undermining Iran during the key period of 2005 and early 2006. He also revealed that the Administration was facing opposition from senior military staff in the Pentagon and from European states, which wished to pursue a diplomatic policy. In early 2005, Hersh reported that Defense Department officials under Douglas Feith had been working with Israeli military planners and consultants to pinpoint nuclear and chemical weapons sites and missile targets inside Iran. In addition, US Central Command had been asked to revise its war plans, providing for a ground and air invasion of Iran.[47] By spring 2006, the White House had, according to Hersh,

> increased clandestine activities inside Iran and intensified planning for a possible major air attack. Current and former American military and intelligence officials said that Air Force planning groups are drawing up lists of targets, and teams of American combat troops have been ordered into Iran, under cover, to collect targeting data and to establish contact with anti-government ethnic-minority groups.

Among the military options being considered was using tactical nuclear warheads to hit underground bunkers, such as Natanz, where, officials believed, nuclear weapons research was being conducted.[48] Much of the spying on Iran's nuclear programme was being carried out by Israeli secret agents, according to Hersh's informants.[49] It was possible that, in a practice used before by Israel in Arab states, former Iranian Jews now living in Israel were spying for their country while claiming to be visiting relatives in Iran. (Some 30,000 Jews live in Iran, the Middle East's largest Jewish population outside Israel. Their relative success in Iran and their repeated refusal to leave, despite financial incentives offered by Israel and American Jewish groups for them to emigrate, have proved an enduring embarrassment to those claiming that the Iranian regime is driven by genocidal anti-Semitism.)[50]

By early summer, Hersh reported, Bush was facing stiff opposition from his generals.

> Inside the Pentagon, senior commanders have increasingly challenged the President's plans, according to active-duty and retired officers and officials. The generals and admirals have told the Administration that the bombing campaign will probably not succeed in destroying Iran's nuclear program. They have also warned that an attack could lead to serious economic, political, and military consequences for the United States. A crucial issue in the military's dissent, the officers said, is the fact that American and European intelligence agencies have not found specific evidence of clandestine activities or hidden facilities [in Iran]; the war planners are not sure what to hit.

Hersh quoted a Pentagon consultant: 'There is a war about the war going on inside the building.' Many military commanders reportedly feared the effect of bombing Iran on the insurgency in neighbouring Iraq – and the consequent loss of US personnel.

By that stage, according to Hersh, tactical nuclear warheads had been taken off the table because of concerns that their use would be politically unacceptable, though there were still debates about whether bunker-busting bombs could be used to similar effect. Bush's new strategy, argued Patrick Clawson, a fan of the president's policy and the deputy director for research at the Washington Institute for Near East Policy, was to assuage Europe, as well as Russia and China, for a time when their votes, or abstentions, at the United Nations would be needed if talks broke down and the US decided to seek Security Council sanctions or a UN resolution that allowed the use of military force against Iran. Hersh concluded: 'Several current and former officials I spoke to expressed doubt that President Bush would settle for a negotiated resolution of the nuclear crisis.' A former senior Pentagon official claimed that Bush remained 'confident in his military decisions'.[51]

TURNING THE CLOCK BACK 20 YEARS IN LEBANON

On 24 May 2006, Israel's prime minister, Ehud Olmert, was invited to address a joint session of Congress. In his widely publicised speech, he claimed that Iran stood 'on the verge of acquiring nuclear weapons', a development that would pose 'an existential threat' to Israel. He added: 'It is not Israel's threat alone. It is a threat to all those committed to stability in the Middle East and to the well-being of the world at large.'[52] Less than two months later, on 12 July 2006, Israel launched a war against the Lebanese Shia militia Hizbullah, publicly – if simplistically – identified by Israel and the US as a proxy for Iran.[53] After a month's futile fighting, 119 soldiers and 43 civilians had been killed in Israel, and at least 1,000 civilians and a small but unknown number of Hizbullah fighters had died in Lebanon.

There were obvious reasons why Israel and the US might have regarded the destruction of Hizbullah as the necessary gambit before an attack on Iran. Were Tehran to be targeted first, Israel would be vulnerable to retaliation not only from long-range Iranian missiles but also, as Israel's defence officials had suggested two years earlier, from Hizbullah's short-range Katyusha rockets across the northern border. And if Israel launched a combined attack on Iran and Hizbullah, almost inevitably drawing in Syria too, Israel would face military reprisals on three fronts at once. Instead, dealing with Hizbullah's rockets first – and at the very least intimidating the Syrian army – would isolate Tehran militarily and free Israel and the US to attack Iran at a time of their choosing. That was the assessment of the White House, according to Seymour Hersh's conversations with officials.[54]

The July 2006 hostilities began with a relatively minor incident by regional standards: Hizbullah launched a raid on an Israeli military post on the border with Lebanon, during which three Israeli soldiers were killed and two captured. A brief Hizbullah rocket strike on sites close to the northern border left no one seriously hurt and was described at the time by the Israeli army as a 'diversionary attack'.[55] Five more soldiers died shortly afterwards when their tank crossed over into Lebanon in hot pursuit of the captured Israelis and hit a landmine. This was the latest in a long-running round of tit-for-tat strikes by Israel and Hizbullah since Israel's withdrawal from its military occupation of south Lebanon in May 2000. A few weeks before Hizbullah captured the two soldiers, for example, Mossad had been strongly suspected in the assassination of two Islamic Jihad militants in a car bombing in the port city of Sidon in south Lebanon.[56]

Israel was well aware of the reasons for the Hizbullah attack. The Shia militia had several outstanding points of friction with Israel since the latter had withdrawn from its two-decade occupation of south Lebanon in May 2000. First, as recorded by United Nations peacekeepers stationed in south Lebanon, Israeli war planes had been flying almost daily over Lebanon to carry out spying operations in violation of the country's sovereignty, and to wage intermittent psychological warfare by creating sonic booms to terrify the local civilian population.[57] Second, since Israel's withdrawal, its army had continued occupying a small corridor of land known as the Shebaa Farms. Israel, backed by the United Nations after Tel Aviv had exerted much pressure on the international body,[58] claimed that the Farms area was Syrian – part of the Golan – and that it could only be returned in negotiations with Damascus; Lebanon and Syria, meanwhile, argued that the land was Lebanese and should have been handed back when Israel withdrew.[59]

But third and most important in explaining the July 2006 border raid was a bitter dispute between Hizbullah and Israel over prisoners. Israel had refused after its withdrawal in 2000 to hand over a handful of Lebanese prisoners of war (the exact figure was difficult to establish as Israel had opened a secret prison, called Facility 1391, into which many Lebanese captives disappeared during the occupation of south Lebanon).[60] Regarding this issue as a point of honour, Hizbullah had vowed to capture Israeli soldiers so that they could be exchanged for the remaining Lebanese prisoners. It had seized three soldiers in October 2000, six months after the Israeli withdrawal, without incurring major reprisals.[61] Although on that occasion the soldiers had died during their capture, Israel later agreed an exchange of 23 Lebanese, 12 other Arab nationals and 400 Palestinians it was holding for the return of the soldiers' bodies and a captured Israeli businessman.[62] According to reports in the Israeli media, there had subsequently been three unsuccessful attempts by Hizbullah to capture soldiers to ensure the return of the last two or three remaining Lebanese prisoners, and especially Samir Kuntar, who had been held by Israel since 1979.[63] The day after the eruption of the July 2006 hostilities, a *Ha'aretz* editorial noted:

> The major blow Israel suffered yesterday, the circumstances of which will certainly demand explanations, is particularly harsh primarily because this did not come as a surprise. Hezbollah leader Hassan Nasrallah warned in April that he planned to get back Samir Kuntar, even by force ... Freeing Kuntar along with the other Lebanese prisoners and captives may have prevented yesterday's kidnapping.[64]

As expected, following the border raid, Hizbullah's leader, Hassan Nasrallah, offered a prisoner swap for the two soldiers.[65]

Israel, however, was in no mood to compromise or negotiate.[66] Calling the seizure of the soldiers an 'act of war', Israel began bombing Lebanon from the air the same day and launched a limited ground invasion. (Notably, a senior Israeli army commander later admitted that the point of destroying Lebanon was not the return of the two Israeli soldiers but to weaken Hizbullah.[67]) The next day Israeli war planes destroyed airports, roads and bridges, factories, power stations and oil refineries – part of Israel's campaign to 'turn back the clock in Lebanon 20 years', as the Chief of Staff, Dan Halutz, phrased it.[68] Was Halutz referring, even if unconsciously, to better times for Israel, before Hizbullah's establishment in the early 1980s? The civilian death toll in Lebanon rose rapidly. Hizbullah responded, cautiously at first, by firing its primitive rockets at areas near the northern border, including the towns of Kiryat Shmona and Nahariya, that were well prepared for such strikes. The Shia militia waited four days before extending its reach and hitting Haifa with a volley of rockets that killed eight railway workers. By then more than 100 Lebanese civilians were dead from the Israeli bombing.[69]

When Israel failed over the course of four weeks to significantly dent Hizbullah's military capabilities – the rocket attacks continued and expanded, and the army's attempts at invading south Lebanon were repeatedly repulsed – Israel and the US were forced to go down diplomatic channels, seeking a United Nations resolution, 1701, that they hoped would limit Hizbullah's ability in the future to resist Israel. The two demanded disarmament of the militia by the Lebanese army and enforcement by UN peacekeepers. However, given the weakness of Lebanon's army and the reluctance of the international community to commit troops, the chances of defanging Hizbullah looked remote. Israel, therefore, spent the last three days before the ceasefire was due to come into effect dropping some 1.2 million US-made cluster bombs over south Lebanon.[70] The use of these old stocks of US munitions, which were reported to have a failure rate as high as 50 per cent,[71] meant that hundreds of thousands of bomblets – effectively small land mines – were left littering south Lebanon after the fighting finished. The intention seemed clear: to make the country's south as uninhabitable as possible, at least in the short term, and the job of isolating Hizbullah fighters that much easier should Israel try another attack.

There were three early indications that Israel might be seeking to widen the war to Iran and Syria. First, within hours of the attack, the deputy director-general of Israel's Foreign Ministry, Gideon Meir, was trying to implicate Iran in Hizbullah's capture of the two soldiers, and by extension Syria too: 'We have concrete evidence that Hezbollah plans to transfer the kidnapped soldiers to Iran. As a result, Israel views Hamas, Hezbollah, Syria and Iran as the main players in the axis of terror and hate that endangers not only Israel, but the entire world.'[72] The 'concrete evidence' never emerged from the dark corridors of the Mossad.

Second, Israel claimed that Hizbullah's arsenal of some 12,000 rockets hidden across south Lebanon – from which it managed to fire as many as 200 a day into northern Israel – had been supplied by Iran and Syria.[73] This may have been true but applied a double standard typical of Israel's relations with its neighbours: Israel was supplied by the US with the latest weaponry, including cluster bombs. Arriving at the Haifa railway depot where the workers had been killed, Shaul Mofaz, Israel's Transport Minister and a former Chief of Staff, said the fatal rocket contained Syrian ammunition.[74] At the same time, Israeli military commanders held a press conference at which they claimed that they had destroyed a Syrian convoy trying to re-supply Hizbullah. 'These are rockets that belong to the Syrian army. You can't find them in the Damascus market, and the Syrian government is responsible for this smuggling', said the army's head of operations, Gadi Eisenkott.[75] Both Iran and Syria had good reasons to want Hizbullah strong: Israel's difficulties invading Lebanon might deter it from attacking them; and Israel's problems with Hizbullah on the northern border were one of the few leverage points Syria and Iran possessed in international negotiations.

And third, Israel's leaders took advantage of the Western media's instant and convenient amnesia about the chronology of Hizbullah's rocket strikes. Israel argued that its army's massive bombardment of Lebanon, far from being an act of barely concealed aggression, was a necessary defensive response to Hizbullah's rockets.[76] The attacks were popularly referred to by Israeli officials and commentators as Hizbullah's attempt to 'wipe Israel off the map' – a clear echo of a phrase closely (though wrongly, as we shall see later) associated with Iran's leader, Mahmoud Ahmadinejad. In fact, the Hizbullah rockets had been fired in retaliation for the Israeli aerial onslaught, and Nasrallah had repeatedly used his TV appearances to call for a ceasefire.[77] When at one point the US Secretary of State, Condoleezza Rice, won Israel's agreement to a 48-hour suspension of air strikes on south Lebanon, Israel broke its promise within hours while Hizbullah largely honoured the pause in hostilities, even though it was not party to it.[78] Nasrallah appeared keen to show that his militia was disciplined and that it had a specific aim: namely, a prisoner swap.[79] The Western media, however, concentrated on Israeli arguments that Hizbullah was seeking the Jewish state's destruction – with the implication that Iran was really behind the plan.[80]

There was one sense, however, in which Hizbullah's rockets may have been fired for Tehran's benefit – though few seemed to understand the significance. Most critics, including international human rights organisations, regarded the rocket fire from south Lebanon either as 'indiscriminate' or as targeted at Israeli civilians. But while Hizbullah's projectiles were not precise enough to hit specific or small targets, they were often accurate enough to suggest the intended target. Though not reported by the local and international media, some observers on the ground, including myself, saw that a significant proportion of the rockets landed close by – and in some cases hit – military sites in northern Israel, including weapons factories, army bases, airfields, communication towers and power stations.[81] Israel was able to conceal this fact through its military censorship laws, which ensured that reporters were unable to explain what had been hit, or what military targets might exist, at the site of Hizbullah strikes. Nazareth, for example, was repeatedly mentioned as a target of rocket attacks, with the implication that the Shia militia was trying to hit a 'Christian' city (most observers appeared not to appreciate that the city has a Muslim majority),[82] without journalists noting that military facilities were located close by Nazareth. I can reveal this information now only because a subsequent *Ha'aretz* article noted in another context the existence of an armaments factory in Nazareth.[83]

The same conclusion – that Hizbullah had been trying, at least on some occasions, to target military sites in Israel – was subsequently reached by the Arab Association for Human Rights, based in Nazareth. Its researchers found a close correlation between the existence of a military base or bases close by Arab communities in the north and the high number of Hizbullah strikes officially recorded against the same communities.[84] After the war, the Israeli media admitted a few successful strikes on military sites, including a hit on an oil refinery in Haifa.[85] Hizbullah's ability to direct its fire towards such targets, if less often hit them, was possible because on several earlier occasions pilotless Hizbullah drones, supplied by Iran, photographed much of northern Israel, mimicking on a small scale Israel's own spying operations.[86]

Another direct hit was reported by Robert Fisk, a British journalist based in Beirut who was not subject to the censor.

Fisk revealed that the army's most important military planning centre in the Lebanon war, an underground bunker in the hillside of Mount Miron close to the border, had been repeatedly struck by rockets – a fact later confirmed by Israel's leading military correspondent Ze'ev Schiff. Fisk wrote:

> Codenamed 'Apollo', Israeli military scientists work deep inside mountain caves and bunkers at Miron, guarded by watchtowers, guard-dogs and barbed wire, watching all air traffic moving in and out of Beirut, Damascus, Amman and other Arab cities. The mountain is surmounted by clusters of antennae which Hizbollah quickly identified as a military tracking centre. Before they fired rockets at Haifa, they therefore sent a cluster of missiles towards Miron. The caves are untouchable but the targeting of such a secret location by Hizbollah deeply shocked Israel's military planners. The 'centre of world terror' – or whatever they imagine Lebanon to be – could not only breach their frontier and capture their soldiers but attack the nerve-centre of the Israeli northern military command.[87]

Hizbullah's futile targeting of these well-protected military sites with their Katyusha rockets served a purpose, however. It suggested to Israel not only that Hizbullah knew where Israel's military infrastructure was located but that Iran knew too. Why reveal this to Israel? Because, we can surmise, Tehran may have hoped that, by showing just how exposed Israel was militarily to Iran's more powerful, long-range missiles, Israel's leaders might think twice before attacking Iran after Hizbullah.

EVIDENCE THE WAR WAS PLANNED

Iran and Hizbullah had good reason to fear that the assault on Lebanon – and whatever was supposed to follow it – had been planned well in advance. Nasrallah's deputy, Sheikh Naim Qassem, certainly thought so. He told the *an-Nahar* daily that two days into the fighting Hizbullah learnt that Israel and the United States had been planning an attack on Lebanon in September or October. 'Israel was not ready. In fact it wanted to prepare for two or three months more, but American pressure on one side and the Israeli desire to achieve a success on the other ... were factors which made them rush into battle.'[88] Are there any grounds for Qassem's belief that Israel was working to a prepared, if secret, script with the Americans rather than, as the official version suggests, improvising after the two soldiers' capture? There are several strong indications that it was.

First, in an interview and separate article published shortly after the ceasefire between Israel and Hizbullah was agreed, respected American investigative journalist Seymour Hersh revealed that Vice-President Dick Cheney and his officials, led by neocon advisers Elliott Abrams and David Wurmser, had been closely involved in the war. US government sources told him that earlier the same summer several Israeli officials had visited Washington 'to get a green light for the bombing operation and to find out how much the United States would bear. Israel began with Cheney. It wanted to be sure that it had his support and the support of his office and the Middle East desk of the National Security Council.' After that, 'persuading Bush was never a problem, and Condi Rice was on board'.[89] With these agreements in place between Washington and Tel Aviv, a war of reprisal could be launched the moment a Hizbullah violation of the border took place. A hawkish former head of intelligence at Mossad, Uzi Arad, expressed it this way: 'For the life of me, I've never seen a decision to go to war taken so speedily. We usually go through long analyses.'[90]

The main concern in Tel Aviv and Washington, Hersh pointed out, was with Hizbullah's rockets. 'You cannot attack Iran without taking them [the rockets] out, because obviously that's the deterrent. You hit Iran, Hezbollah then bombs Tel Aviv and Haifa. So that's something you have to clean out first.'[91] But the neocons had other reasons for supporting an Israeli attack on Hizbullah, according to Hersh. First, they wanted the Lebanese government of Fuad Siniora, seen as loyal to Washington, to be able to challenge a weakened Hizbullah and assert the Lebanese army's control over south Lebanon.[92] And second, the US air force was hoping that their Israeli counterparts would be able to field-test US bunker-busting bombs against Hizbullah before they were turned on Iranian sites. From the spring, he added, the US and Israeli military worked closely together. 'It was clear this summer, the next time Hezbollah made a move ... the Israeli Air Force was going to bomb, the plan was going to go in effect ... I think the best guess people had is it could have been as late as fall, September or October, that they would go. They went quickly.'[93] Hersh noted that a US government consultant had confided in him: 'The Israelis told us it would be a cheap war with many benefits.'[94]

Second, a report by Matthew Kalman in the *San Francisco Chronicle*, published a week into the war, supported Hersh's account:

> More than a year ago, a senior Israeli army officer began giving PowerPoint presentations, on an off-the-record basis, to US and other diplomats, journalists and think tanks, setting out the plan for the current operation in revealing detail. Under the ground rules of the briefings, the officer could not be identified. In his talks, the officer described a three-week campaign: The first week concentrated on destroying Hezbollah's heavier long-range missiles, bombing its command-and-control centers, and disrupting transportation and communication arteries. In the second week, the focus shifted to attacks on individual sites of rocket launchers or weapons stores. In the third week, ground forces in large numbers would be introduced, but only in order to knock out targets discovered during reconnaissance missions as the campaign unfolded.[95]

And third, there is the self-serving, though nonetheless revealing, evidence about the build-up to war from Israel's Prime Minister, Ehud Olmert, to the Winograd Committee, a panel he set up to investigate the army's dismal performance against Hizbullah. Olmert told the Committee that he spoke to the Israeli General Staff in January 2006, as he became acting prime minister after Ariel Sharon was felled by a brain haemorrhage, about preparing a contingency plan for attacking Lebanon should a soldier be captured by Hizbullah, an event Israel was expecting but seems to have done little to prevent. Olmert said he then held further talks with the military in March about drawing up more definite plans. He claimed that he was the one directing the army to ready itself for war.[96] There is good reason to believe that Olmert's testimony is right in respect of there existing by July 2006 a military plan for attacking Lebanon, but wrong about when the plan was drawn up and about his role in its preparation.

In fact, after Olmert's testimony was leaked to the media, members of the General Staff criticised him for having kept them out of the loop: if Olmert was planning a war against Lebanon, they argued, he should not have left them so unprepared.[97] That claim can quickly be discounted as a red herring. Apart from the improbability of Olmert being able to organise a war without the senior command's knowledge, references can be found in the Israeli media from the time of the war acknowledging the fact that the army was readying for a confrontation with Lebanon, just as Olmert claimed. On the first day of fighting, for example, the *Jerusalem Post* reported of the planned ground invasion: 'Only weeks ago, an entire reserve division was drafted in order to train for an operation such as the one the IDF is planning in response to Wednesday morning's Hizbullah attacks on IDF forces along the northern border.'[98]

But even more importantly, there is every reason to doubt that in Israel's highly militarised system of government – where prime ministers are almost always generals too – Olmert, a military novice, would have been allowed to take a significant role in the army's plans for how to deal with a regional enemy. The General Staff would have had their own plans for such an eventuality, regularly revised according to changing circumstances and coordinated in part with Washington. Olmert would at best have been able to choose from the plans on offer. That was certainly the view of General Amos Malka, a former head of military intelligence, when he testified to the Winograd Committee. He told the panel that politicians came to the army to discuss a military operation 'as if coming for a visit', adding that the politician

does not come with anything of his own, he has no [military] staff, no one prepared papers for him, he has not held a preliminary discussion, he comes to a talk more or less run by the army. The army tells him what its assessment is, what the intelligence assessment is, what the possibilities are, option A, option B and option C.

Malka also dismissed Chief of Staff Dan Halutz's claim that he was following the orders of politicians in prosecuting the war against Lebanon. Such a relationship, he said, 'does not exist in Israeli decision making. The army is part of the political echelon.' Giving the Committee members a brief history lesson, Malka concluded: 'David Ben-Gurion [Israel's first Prime Minister] was both defense minister and prime minister, and the army was his executive branch, for education and establishing settlements as well. Since then, we've placed strategy in the hands of the army, but we forgot to take it back when the reasons for doing so ceased to exist.'[99] Malka's view was supported by Binyamin Ben Eliezer, the Infrastructures Minister and a member of the war cabinet, who told the Winograd Committee that Olmert had been 'misled, to put it mildly' by the army. 'Olmert said to me: "I am not a company, platoon or brigade commander, nor am I a general, as opposed to my predecessor [Ariel] Sharon. All of the generals I met with did not present any plans".'[100]

Experienced military analysts also inferred the same conclusions from the Winograd Committee's heavily censored interim report, published in May 2007. While endlessly castigating the Israeli leadership over its 'failures' in prosecuting the war against Lebanon, the report revealed almost nothing on the most important questions: what had happened at the start of the war and why had Israel's leaders taken the decisions they did? The reporter Ze'ev Schiff of *Ha'aretz* observed:

> The main conclusion emerging from the testimony given to the Winograd Committee by the three most important players – Prime Minister Ehud Olmert, Defense Minister Amir Peretz and former chief of staff Dan Halutz – is that the army dominates in its relationship with the government ... The conclusion is that the Israel Defense Forces has too big an impact on decision making.[101]

That may in part explain the Committee members' failure to understand the process by which Olmert reached his decision to go to war.

Our impression is that the prime minister came to the fateful discussions in those days with his decision already substantially shaped and formulated. We have no documented basis from which it is possible to obtain hints as to his process of deliberation, as to what alternatives he considered, nor as to the timeline of the decisions that he made and their context.[102]

This passage echoed the conclusions of Aluf Benn of *Ha'aretz* two days into the war: 'The brief time that passed between the abduction [of the two soldiers] and Olmert's announcement of a painful response indicates that his decision to undertake a broad military operation in Lebanon was made with record speed. That he had no doubts or hesitations.'[103] Unusually, the Committee could find no evidence of the conversations between Olmert and Halutz that preceded the war, and therefore concluded that this was because the Prime Minister made the decision 'in haste' and 'informally' – in other words, that Olmert did not consult with anyone. A more convincing explanation is that Olmert and the Israeli military concealed the true circumstances surrounding the launching of the war because the decision had been taken in advance.

Both the General Staff and Olmert probably had additional reasons for wanting to muddy the waters on the issue of responsibility for the war. After the army's dismal performance in Lebanon, commanders were keen to restore a little of their dignity and the army's deterrence power by claiming that the politicians had interfered in ways that damaged their ability to defeat Hizbullah. Olmert, on the other hand, was facing some of the lowest popularity ratings ever for a serving prime minister, almost universally regarded as a leader without the military experience needed to cope with the new climate of confrontation in the Middle East. Admitting that he had simply rubber-stamped the General Staff's plans would have damaged him even further, underlining to Israelis that he was not a warrior like Ariel Sharon they could trust in difficult times. It would also have set him on course for a clash with the army, a fight he would have inevitably lost against one of the institutions most respected by Israeli society.

A far more probable scenario was that from the moment Olmert took up the reins of power, he was slowly brought into the army's confidence, first tentatively in January and then more fully after his election in March. He was allowed to know of the senior command's secret plans for war – plans, we can assume, his predecessor, Ariel Sharon, a former general, had been deeply involved in advancing and that had been approved by Washington. Olmert was brought into the picture relatively late. If the observations of Hersh and the Hizbullah leadership are to be believed, the hasty and chaotic nature of Israel's prosecution of the war – and the resulting dismal military failures – reflected, at least in part, the fact that the Israeli army was pushed into war too early, before it had fully prepared, by Hizbullah's capture of the soldiers. Comments from an anonymous senior officer to *Ha'aretz* suggested that the army had intended an extensive ground invasion of Lebanon in addition to the aerial campaign, but that Olmert and possibly the Chief of Staff, Dan Halutz, shied away from putting it into effect after the unexpected failure of the aerial bombardment in defeating Hizbullah. 'I don't know if he [Olmert] was familiar with the details of the plan, but everyone knew that the IDF had a ground operation ready for implementation.'[104]

SYRIA WAS SUPPOSED TO BE NEXT

Had Hizbullah been beaten, what would this plan have required next? The answer, it seems, is an attack on Syria, with Israeli air strikes forcing Damascus into submission.[105] According to reports in the Arab media during the early stages of the war against Lebanon, that was the fear in Syria and Iran. The newspaper *al-Watan* reported a phone conversation in which President Bashar Assad of Syria was supposedly told by the Iranian leader Ahmadinejad: 'The Zionist-American threat on Damascus has reached a dangerous level, and there is no choice but to respond with a strong message so the aggressors will reconsider whether to launch a preventive attack against Syria.'[106]

The evidence for a planned attack on Damascus comes from an impeccable source. After the summer's war, Meyrav Wurmser, the Israeli wife of David Wurmser, Dick Cheney's adviser on the Middle East, gave an interview to the website of Israel's most popular newspaper, *Yed'iot Aharonot*. Meyrav Wurmser is a leading neocon in her own right, a director of an American rightwing think-tank, and one of the authors of the document *A Clean Break*. She revealed that the neocons in the Bush Administration, including presumably her husband, had delayed the imposition of a ceasefire for as long as possible so that Israel would have more time to expand its attack to Syria. Only Hizbullah's unrelenting rocket strikes on northern Israel, she implied, had prevented the plan from being put into effect.

> The anger [in the White House] is over the fact that Israel did not fight against the Syrians. The neocons are responsible for the fact that Israel got a lot of time and space. They believed that Israel should be allowed to win. A great part of it was the thought that Israel should fight against the real enemy, the one backing Hizbullah. It was obvious that it is impossible to fight directly against Iran, but the thought was that its [Iran's] strategic and important ally [Syria] should be hit ... It is difficult for Iran to export its Shiite revolution without joining Syria, which is the last nationalistic Arab country. If Israel had hit Syria, it would have been such a harsh blow for Iran that it would have weakened it and [changed] the strategic map in the Middle East.[107]

These were doubtless the expected 'birth pangs' that Condoleezza Rice referred to a week into the fighting with Hizbullah.[108] Wurmser's view certainly makes sense of reports in the Israeli media that Washington wanted Syria targeted next. On 30 July, the *Jerusalem Post* reported: '[Israeli] Defense officials told the *Post* last week that they were receiving indications from the US that America would be interested in seeing Israel attack Syria.'[109] That followed an unguarded moment during the G8 summit in Russia on 17 July when President Bush was caught on a live microphone telling British prime minister Tony Blair: 'What they need to do is get Syria to get Hezbollah to stop doing this shit.'[110] A few days later, on 21 July, the White House issued a press release claiming that Bush's foreign policy was succeeding. Strangely, it ended with a link to an article by a leading neocon military historian and newspaper columnist, Max Boot, entitled 'It's time to let the Israelis take off the gloves'. In his piece, Boot argued: 'Syria is weak and next door. To secure its borders, Israel needs to hit the Assad regime. Hard. If it does, it will be doing Washington's dirty work.'[111]

Wurmser's account is partly confirmed by another leading neocon, John Bolton, at the time of the attack on Hizbullah the US ambassador to the United Nations and the key American official responsible for negotiating the ceasefire between Israel and Lebanon. He told the BBC in an interview several months after the fighting that the Bush Administration had resisted calls for a ceasefire to give Israel more time to defeat Hizbullah. Stating that he was 'damned proud' of the US role in blocking a ceasefire, he added that the US had also been 'deeply disappointed' at Israel's failure to remove the threat of Hizbullah and the subsequent lack of any attempt to disarm its forces.[112] Wurmser's account is also corroborated by the evidence of an Israeli government minister, Ophir Pines Paz, to the Winograd Committee. He told the panel that many members of the cabinet had been led to expect that the international community would stop the war within a few days. 'The leading diplomatic sources ... gave us [a] working premise that we didn't have much time to work with, and that we needed to act until we would be stopped – but then no one stopped us. This is what happened. Not only did no one stop us, they encouraged us, and we let this go to our heads.'[113]

The disappointment of Wurmser and Bolton could be explained, at least to a degree, by the neocons' conviction that the Shia coalition of Hizbullah and Iran needed to be split asunder by force, and that this could not achieved without transforming Syria from an ally of this Shia confederation into an obstacle. Iran could not easily supply and support Hizbullah if Damascus refused to turn a blind eye to such activities.

Following the August 2006 ceasefire, all signs were that another round of fighting against Lebanon and Syria would be launched again soon – this time, Israel presumably hoped, more successfully.

That has certainly been the widely held view of the Israeli public, government officials and the army.[114] It also explained the army's obsession with protecting an Achilles' heel exposed in the war against Lebanon: the home front.[115] For the first time in one of its conflicts, Israel faced a military threat – in the form of rockets – on its own soil that quickly sapped the public's morale. Since the Lebanon war, Israel has concentrated on finding a solution to its domestic vulnerability, from installing Arrow and Patriot anti-ballistic missiles and a home-grown defence system known as Iron Dome to developing a laser-based system known as Skyguard and what the Israeli media termed a 'missile-trapping' steel net designed to shield buildings from attack.[116]

Typifying this manufactured consensus for 'more war' were the views of Martin van Creveld, a professor at Hebrew University in Jersualem and one of the country's most respected military historians with intimate knowledge of the army's inner workings and its collective ethos. He wrote a commentary in the American Jewish weekly the *Forward* in March 2007 arguing that Syria was planning an attack against Israel, possibly using chemical weapons, no later than October 2008. He predicted that Syria would create a pretext for a military confrontation: 'Some incident will be generated and used as an excuse for opening rocket fire on the Golan Heights and the Galilee [in Israel].' In the professor's view, Syria hoped to 'inflict casualties' and ensure Jerusalem 'throws in the towel'. The evidence, said Van Creveld, was that the Syrian military had been on an armaments shopping spree in Russia and studying the lessons of the Lebanon war.[117] He did not interpret this as evidence that Damascus feared, given the hostile rhetoric from Israel and the US, that an attack was imminent and that therefore it should be ready to defend itself.[118] The implication of Van Creveld's article was that Israel was entitled to launch a pre-emptive strike to foil Damascus' plans.

Strangely, Van Creveld's gloomy forecast contradicted another article he had written just a few weeks earlier for the same publication, in which he argued that Israel should negotiate with Syria as a way to weaken Israel's Shia enemies, notably Iran and Hizbullah. 'Syria forms the critical link between Hezbollah and

Iran. The airport in Damascus is the gateway through which Iranian weapons and Iranian military advisers have been reaching Lebanon for some two decades. Close the gateway, and the flow of aid will be much diminished, if not eliminated.' As the leader of a relatively poor and small country, argued Van Creveld, 'Syrian President Bashar al-Assad finds himself more dependent on his Iranian counterpart, Mahmoud Ahmadinejad, than perhaps he would like.'[119] Exploiting this vulnerability, Israel and the US could wrestle Syria away from the 'Shia arc of extremism', concluded the professor.

The basis for his optimism was a growing number of credible reports in the Israeli media that Assad had been seeking for two years to negotiate with Israel a deal on the Golan Heights. Not only that, but he had used a back channel, mediated by the Swiss, to offer Israel the best terms it could possibly expect for the Golan's return: its demilitarisation and transformation into a peace park open to Israelis. In addition, Assad had gone a long way to meeting Israel's concerns about its continuing access to the area's water supplies.[120] The Israeli government appeared convinced of Assad's sincerity: assessments by the National Security Council and the Foreign Ministry concluded that the offer of talks on the Golan was genuine.[121] Other reports, however, indicated that both the Israeli Prime Minister and US Vice-President Dick Cheney, although aware of the talks, had decided not to pursue the offer from Damascus.[122] In fact, if Meyrav Wurmser was right, they had not only rebuffed Syria but had also planned to attack it at a time when Assad was desperately trying to make peace.

The Israeli and American leaderships stuck to their position of no talks with Damascus through early 2007, even as a group of Israeli intellectuals and former officials pushed for the talks to be renewed,[123] and as senior US politicians, including Nancy Pelosi, the new Democratic Speaker of the House of Representatives, visited Syria.[124] President Bush accused Pelosi of sending 'mixed signals' to Damascus. She, on the other hand, saw Syria as the key to ameliorating the disastrous situation of American forces in Iraq. The Israeli dissidents, meanwhile, believed a deal with Syria on the Golan would ensure that the Shebaa Farms were returned to Lebanon and that a major justification for Hizbullah's continuing hostilities with Israel would be removed. As summer 2007 approached, there were at least hints that the US and Israel might begin engaging Damascus, possibly in an attempt to isolate Iran further, though no substantive progress was made on this front. Their good faith was at least put in question by comments from Elliott Abrams, one of the most resilient of the State Department's senior neocon officials, in May 2007. Referring to the mooted possibility of a renewal of the peace process between Israel and the Palestinians, but implicitly also alluding to Israel's wider relations with its neighbours, Abrams reassured a group of powerful American Jews that such talk was designed to dissipate criticism of the US from the Arab world and the European Union for its failure to initiate a peace process. Talks, he said, were sometimes nothing more than 'process for the sake of process'.[125]

Given this context, what did Van Creveld's rapid change of tune about talking to Syria signify? After his initial guarded optimism, why did he claim in his later article that peace talks with Damascus were futile and that a military confrontation was all but inevitable. His reasoning was to be found in the following argument:

> Obviously, much will depend on what happens in Iraq and Iran. A short, successful American offensive in Iran may persuade Assad that the Israelis, much of whose hardware is either American or American-derived, cannot be countered, especially in the air. Conversely, an American withdrawal from Iraq, combined with an American-Iranian stalemate in the Persian Gulf, will go a long way toward untying Assad's hands.[126]

In other words, Van Creveld was now arguing, against all the evidence but presumably in line with Israeli official policy, that the waverers in Washington and Tel Aviv were wrong to contemplate withdrawal from Iraq or risk 'appeasement' with Iran or Syria, that Israel faced a dire threat from this axis of evil, and that a US attack on Iran was the key to Israel's regional survival. It looked suspiciously as if the professor, after writing his original conciliatory piece, had been persuaded to return to the fold.

A POWER STRUGGLE IN WASHINGTON

Israel's failure in Lebanon, and the dismal performance of Bush's Republican party in the mid-term Congressional elections in November 2006, put in doubt the ascendancy of the neocons for the first time. With the Democrats taking decisive control of the House of Representatives, tensions in the Bush Administration started to surface and a change of direction in the Middle East seemed possible – if far from certain. One of the major points of friction was over the recommendations of a report by a Congressional panel called the Iraq Study Group published in late 2006. Led by James Baker, a former Republican Secretary of State and a close ally of the oil industry, and Democratic Congressman Lee Hamilton, the panel argued that US forces should be gradually withdrawn from Iraq and that Washington should engage its main neighbours, Iran and Syria, to help in the task of stabilising what was clearly now a failed state.[127]

The Iraq Study Group's proposals were a direct reversal of neocon policy. Bush's key advisers continued to argue that the US 'stay the course' in Iraq – or as one leading neocon ideologue, Daniel Pipes, suggested:

> My solution splits the difference, 'Stay the course – but change the course.' I suggest pulling coalition forces out of the inhabited areas of Iraq and redeploying them to the desert. This way, the troops remain indefinitely in Iraq, but remote from the urban carnage. It permits the American-led troops to carry out essential tasks (protecting borders, keeping the oil and gas flowing, ensuring that no Saddam-like monster takes power).[128]

The neocons therefore focused on a different claim, one that required deeper US involvement in the region rather than an exit. They argued that Tehran was trying to undermine American determination to stay in Iraq by interfering in its neighbour's internal politics. Iran was widely blamed both for stirring up Iraq's majority Shia community against US forces and for helping arm the Sunni-led insurrection.[129] Although Tehran undoubtedly had an interest in American forces becoming bogged down in Iraq, not least because it might prevent the White House from trying to

extend its Middle East wars to Iran, there was an improbability
to claims that Iraq's mainly Sunni insurgents were cooperating
closely with Shia Iran – in fact, these claims echoed earlier fanciful
US accusations that Iraq was giving sanctuary to al-Qaeda. In
line with the White House's position, a US commander in Iraq,
General George Casey, accused Iran of 'using surrogates to
conduct terrorist operations in Iraq, both against us and against
the Iraqi people'.[130] However, other Pentagon generals broke
ranks to present Iran's involvement in a different light. Chairman
of the Joint Chiefs of Staff, Peter Pace, observed that, although
individual Iranians were assisting the insurgency, Tehran was not
obviously implicated. 'It is clear that Iranians are involved and
it is clear that materials from Iran are involved, but I would not
say, based on what I know, that the Iranian government clearly
knows or is complicit.'[131]

Later, in April 2007, as the White House sought to widen the case
against Iran, it claimed the Shia regime was supplying weapons to
the Sunni fundamentalists of the Taliban in Afghanistan, the other
Middle East quagmire in which US forces were sinking.[132] By late
May 2007, an anonymous Washington official was quoted in the
Guardian newspaper stating that Tehran was behind many of the
attacks on US soldiers in Iraq and was secretly forging ties with
al-Qaeda and Sunni militias in Iraq to launch an offensive against
the occupation forces to oust them from the country. Implying
that responsibility for these developments lay directly with the
Iranian leadership, the official claimed: 'The attacks are directed
by the Revolutionary Guard who are connected right to the top [of
Iran's government].' He added that Syria was a 'co-conspirator'
that was allowing jihadis to infiltrate across the border.[133]

Despite much speculation following the publication of the
Baker-Hamilton report on Iraq that the neocons' influence was
waning, Bush ignored the Iraq Study Group's recommendations
for a gradual withdrawal and announced a 'surge' of 30,000
additional troops to Iraq.[134] Most analysts assumed that these
forces were being sent to try to restore order, even if it was widely
recognised that their presence would be little more than a drop in
the ocean. However, another possibility was suggested by dissident

intellectual Noam Chomsky, who argued that the surge troops might move into Khuzestan, an Arab area of Iran and the location of its main oilfields, during an attack on Tehran. The attack could then concentrate on destroying Iran's nuclear installations without interrupting the flow of oil. 'If you could carry that off, you could just bomb the rest of the country to dust', Chomsky observed.[135] Shortly afterwards, in April 2007, during a standoff with the West over the capture of 15 British sailors found in or near Iranian waters, reporter Robert Fisk noted: 'The Iranian security services are convinced that the British security services are trying to provoke the Arabs of Iran's Khuzestan province to rise up against the Islamic Republic. Bombs have exploded there, one of them killing a truck-load of Revolutionary Guards, and Tehran blamed MI5.'[136]

By late 2006, it was difficult to decipher whether the diplomatic or military option was preferred. The White House had put concerted pressure on other nations to isolate Tehran in the United Nations through a regime of economic, travel and arms sanctions,[137] and it had also sent an armada of US aircraft carriers to the Gulf.[138] Claims from the Bush Administration that Iran was meddling in Iraq and helping the insurgency against US forces were growing louder by the day. The question was: were the signals from Washington reflecting high-level disagreements or were they designed to provide cover for America's real intentions? Was this a war of words and brinkmanship, or was Washington manoeuvring the international community to justify an attack on Iran, just as it had previously done in the case of Iraq?

AHMADINEJAD: THE NEW HITLER

With Washington apparently wavering, Olmert took the chance in his closing speech to the Herzliya delegates in late January 2007 to focus on the threat from Iran. He ramped up the rhetoric.

> The Jewish people, on whom the scars of the Holocaust are deeply etched, cannot allow itself to again face a threat against its very existence. In the past, the world remained silent and the results are known. Our role is to

prevent the world from repeating this mistake. This is a moral question of the highest degree ... When the leader of a country announces, officially and publicly, his country's intention to wipe off the map another country, and creates those tools which will allow them to realize their stated threat, no nation has the right to weigh its position on the matter. This is an obligation of the highest order, to act with all force against this plot.

Olmert also accused Iran of being the hidden hand behind all of Israel's enemies in the region:

Iranian support of Palestinian terror – through financial support, provision of weapons and knowledge, both directly and through Syria – Iranian assistance of terror in Iraq, the exposure of the capabilities which reached the Hizbullah from Iran during the fighting in Lebanon [in 2006] and the assistance which they offered just recently to Hamas, have demonstrated to many the seriousness of the Iranian threat.[139]

There were still a few voices inside the Israeli security establishment prepared quietly to point out that, even assuming Tehran had the desire to destroy Israel, it did not have the capability, especially given Israel's own formidable nuclear arsenal. In late 2006, for example, Ephraim Halevy, a former head of the Mossad, told a convention in Budapest that Iran's development of a nuclear programme posed no threat to Israel.[140] Yiftah Shapir, an expert on missile warfare at Tel Aviv University's Institute for Strategic Affairs, believed Iran wanted Israel's destruction but assessed the chances of it ever launching a first strike of nuclear weapons – if it possessed them – as 'low'. He argued that Tehran would want a 'dialogue' with its enemies. 'Strategic logic is stronger than any ideology', he observed.[141] And Yitzhak Ravid, once the head of military studies at Israel's Rafael Armaments Development Authority, pointed out that Iran was not only far off developing a nuclear warhead but had not even mastered the technology of the missiles that would be needed to deliver them. Quoting Uzi Rubin, head of ballistic missile research for the Ministry of Defense, he said: 'The Iranians are almost frantic in volunteering information about their weapons capabilities, sometimes to the point of incredulity ... they [their missiles] are meant to impress before they are meant to be used in anger.'[142]

Hans Blix, the former chief UN weapons inspector who had overseen the inspection programme in Iraq before the American invasion and was also a former head of the International Atomic Energy Agency, highlighted the West's double standards. He noted that, unlike North Korea, which the West was engaging in negotiations over its known nuclear arsenal, Tehran was instead being isolated and threatened with 'humiliating' punishments over mere suspicions that it planned to manufacture weapons. Faced with what he called a 'neocolonial attitude', Blix observed: 'The Iranians have resisted all the time saying, no, we are willing to talk, we are willing to talk about the suspension of enrichment, but we are not for suspension before the talks. I would be surprised if a poker player would toss away his trump card before he sits down at the table. Who does that?'[143]

But the messages of Halevy, Ravid and Blix were being drowned out, both in Israel and the United States. After months of bellicose talk from Israeli leaders, there was a wide consensus among the country's Jewish public – just as there had been before for an attack on Iraq. According to *Ha'aretz* in March 2007, as the world waited in trepidation to see what would unfold next in the Middle East, Israelis were in no mood for compromise: 'The Israeli Jewish public sees eye to eye with the government's position', reported *Ha'aretz*. 'Eighty-two percent of people believe [Iran's] nuclear armament constitutes an existential danger to Israel. And a majority – albeit smaller at 48.5 percent – say Israel should attack Iran's nuclear facilities and destroy them even if it has to do so on its own.'[144]

At Herzliya in January 2007, Olmert, head of the centrist Kadima party founded by Sharon, used his speech to neatly merge two themes that were the stock-in-trade of his chief political rival, Binyamin Netanyahu, leader of the Likud party, and his coalition ally, Shimon Peres, a veteran of the Labor party.[145] For many months Netanyahu, in particular, had been accusing Iran's leader, Mahmoud Ahmadinejad, both of being a 'new Hitler', who like his predecessor was consumed with a visceral hatred of Jews, and of planning to carry out a new Holocaust by exterminating the Jews with a nuclear attack. Where once the Nazis herded Jews into concentration camps before sending them to the gas chambers, argued Netanyahu, now Iran was treating Israel as a readymade death camp which could be 'wiped out' with a nuclear bomb. In late 2006, Netanyahu told American Jewish leaders: 'It's 1938 and Iran is Germany. And Iran is racing to arm itself with atomic bombs. Believe him [Ahmadinejad] and stop him ... He is preparing another Holocaust for the Jewish state.'[146] On another occasion, Netanyahu told Israel's Army Radio that, after an Iranian attack on Israel, an apocalypse would engulf the rest of the world:

> Israel would certainly be the first stop on Iran's tour of destruction, but at the planned production rate of 25 nuclear bombs a year ... [the arsenal] will be directed against 'the big Satan', the US, and the 'moderate Satan', Europe ... Iran is developing ballistic missiles that would reach America, and now they prepare missiles with an adequate range to cover the whole of Europe.[147]

Netanyahu's campaign reached its climax in London at about the same time as the Herzliya conference, when he told members of the British parliament that Ahmadinejad should be brought before the World Court for his 'messianic apocalyptic view of the world' and for inciting genocide against the Jewish people.[148]

It should be pointed out that none of these genocidal positions could be convincingly attributed to Ahmadinejad, let alone the country's supreme leader, Ayatollah Ali Khameini, who, it was rarely mentioned in Western coverage, is in charge of foreign policy.[149] The quote endlessly attributed to Ahmadinejad that he wanted to 'wipe Israel off the map' – a reimagining of a familiar Zionist fear that the Arabs want to 'drive the Jews into the sea' – was a straightforward mistranslation of one of his speeches, an error that quickly gained a life of its own after the mistake was originally made by the overworked translators of an Iranian news agency. Accurate translations were quickly offered by Farsi experts, including Juan Cole, a professor of the Modern Middle East at the University of Michigan and former editor of *The*

International Journal of Middle East Studies. On his website, he noted that Ahmadinejad was actually quoting from the late Iranian spiritual leader Ayatollah Khomeini, who was himself comparing Israel's survival as an ethnic state with the illegitimate regime of the former Western-backed Shah of Iran.

> The phrase [Ahmadinejad] then used as I read it is 'The Imam [Khomeini] said that this regime occupying Jerusalem (*een rezhim-e ishghalgar-e qods*) must [vanish from] from the page of time (*bayad az safheh-ye ruzgar mahv shavad*).' Ahmadinejad was not making a threat, he was quoting a saying of Khomeini and urging that pro-Palestinian activists in Iran not give up hope – that the occupation of Jerusalem was no more a continued inevitability than had been the hegemony of the Shah's government.[150]

Arash Narouzi, an Iranian intellectual who was no friend of the regime in Tehran, made much the same point:

> What exactly did he [Ahmadinejad] want 'wiped from the map'? The answer is: nothing. That's because the word 'map' was never used. The Persian word for map, 'nagsheh' is not contained anywhere in his original Farsi quote, or, for that matter, anywhere in his entire speech. Nor was the western phrase 'wipe out' ever said. Yet we are led to believe that Iran's president threatened to 'wipe Israel off the map' despite never having uttered the words 'map', 'wipe out' or even 'Israel.'[151]

Nonetheless, world leaders cited and condemned this unuttered 'quote' almost daily as proof of Iran's malevolent intentions towards Israel. Much mileage was also made by the US and Israel of Ahmadinejad's decision to call what was widely referred to as a 'Holocaust denial' conference in Tehran in December 2006. In fact, the aim of the conference was not to deny that the Holocaust had happened; rather it was officially billed as questioning the Western historical record of the Nazi death camps and the number of Jews killed in them. Offensive as Ahmadinejad's stunt undoubtedly was (and was designed to be) to Western sensitivities, it was also clear from what Iranian officials and Ahmadinejad himself had to say about the event that two transparent goals lay behind it.

First, the conference was supposed to illustrate Western hypocrisy in denying Muslims the legitimacy of their sensitivities in the recent

'Danish cartoons' affair, in which a Danish newspaper, followed by several other European publications, printed denigrating representations of the Prophet Mohammed, including one of him as a suicide bomber. By staging the conference, Ahmadinejad was questioning how Muslims' sensitivities on this subject were different from the West's own sensitivities about the Holocaust. If Islam's most precious beliefs were public property, ripe for exploitation and abuse, reasoned Ahmadinejad, why not also the West's most taboo issue, the Holocaust?[152]

And second, the conference was meant to expose Israel's exploitation of the Holocaust to justify its decades-long occupation of the Palestinians and the violation of their right to statehood and justice. Why did a crime committed by Europe against the Jews subsequently indemnify Israel against all criticism of its own crimes against the Palestinians? Or as Manouchehr Mohammadi, a research and education officer at the Iranian foreign ministry, observed: 'Our policy doesn't mean we want to defend the crimes of Hitler ... This issue [of the Holocaust] has a crucial role regarding the west's policies towards the countries of the Middle East, especially the Palestinians.'[153] As preparations for the conference were announced in January 2006, Ahmadinejad made a similar argument: 'If you [the West] started this killing of the Jews, you have to make amends yourself. This is very clear. It's based on laws and legal considerations. If you committed a mistake or a crime, why should others pay for it?'[154]

It was a question Israel desperately did not want anyone, let alone its chief rival in the Middle East, asking. The issue now was whether the US would help Israel silence Ahmadinejad and the Iranian regime for good.

3

END OF THE STRONGMEN

By the end of 2006 President Bush was reportedly facing stiff opposition to an attack on Iran from, on one side, members of his own White House team, including Condoleezza Rice and his new Defense Secretary, Robert Gates, as well as the Pentagon's senior command, and, on the other, Dick Cheney and the neocons.[1] Israel's failure to destroy Hizbullah a few months earlier had, according to one Middle East expert, proved 'a massive setback for those in the White House who want to use force in Iran. And those who argue that the bombing will create internal dissent and revolt in Iran are also set back.'[2] With these obstacles keenly on his mind, as well as his falling popularity, Bush attended a meeting of the United Nations. There he held a private discussion with France's President Jacques Chirac about a possible attack on Tehran. Asked by Chirac whether Israel should be allowed to strike Iran in place of the US, Bush is said to have responded: 'We cannot rule this out. And if it were to happen, I would understand.'[3] The message seemed clear: even if the political climate in the US would not indulge the launching of such an operation, the US president nonetheless willed it.

What was the view in Israel? If the participants at the Herzliya conference in January 2007 had not made the general feeling of Israel's security and political establishments self-evident, here was what Uzi Arad, a former head of intelligence at Mossad and the organiser of the conference, had to say two months later about hitting Iran: 'A military strike may be easier than you think. It wouldn't just be aimed at the nuclear sites. It would hit military and security targets, industrial and oil-related targets such as Kharg island [Iran's main oil export terminal in the Gulf], and regime targets ... Iran is much more vulnerable than people realise.'[4] These were not idle words: Israel had been practising test bombing runs on mock-ups of the Natanz reactor, simulating the use of 'low-yield' nuclear bunker-busting bombs, as well as running long-distance test flights to Gibraltar.[5] The idea that Israel was considering taking unilateral action if the US failed to act was not as improbable as it sounded, according to Israeli analysts. Writing in the *Jerusalem Post*, Ya'acov Katz argued that Israel, aware that the use of tactical nuclear weapons against Iran could lead to a bloody war across the region, would take the decision with great reluctance. 'If, however, Iran is Israel's greatest existential threat ever, as Prime Minister Ehud Olmert claims it is, then even the hitherto unthinkable might be considered – even tactical nukes – when it comes to Israel's survival.'[6] In April 2007, a former head of the Mossad, Meir Amit, argued that, if Iran could not be stopped by severe sanctions, then the West 'must unite to do away with' Ahmadinejad, adding that a third world war was coming that would be different from all the others. 'This time it will be between cultures and not between peoples', he observed.[7]

The disaster steadily unfolding in Iraq, and the deepening crisis in Lebanon and Syria provoked by Israel's ill-fated attack in the summer of 2006, raised an obvious question: why were Israel and the most senior figures in the US Administration, including Bush himself, cheerleading the extension of the 'war on terror' to Iran, the strongest state after Israel in the Middle East and the one that apparently held the key to alleviating the crisis in Iraq? And why were Israel and the US so conspicuously turning what was essentially a showdown between the US and a recalcitrant Middle Eastern nation into an epic religious struggle, a 'clash of civilisations' not only between the Judeo-Christian and Islamic worlds, but also, beyond that, between the two rival Islamic worlds of the Shia and the Sunni?

The potential consequences were apparent to veteran commentators like Anatol Lieven well before the threatened attack on Tehran. Writing in 2002 of the menacing build-up to the assault on Iraq, he pointed out:

The most surprising thing about the push for war is that it is so profoundly reckless. If I had to put money on it, I'd say that the odds on quick success in destroying the Iraqi regime may be as high as 5/1 or more, given US military superiority, the vile nature of Saddam Hussein's rule, the unreliability of Baghdad's missiles, and the deep divisions in the Arab world. But at first sight, the longer-term gains for the US look pretty limited, whereas the consequences of failure would be catastrophic. A general Middle Eastern conflagration and the collapse of more pro-Western Arab states would lose us the war against terrorism, doom untold thousands of Western civilians to death in coming decades, and plunge the world economy into depression.[8]

True to Lieven's predictions, it had become clear by late 2006 that several Middle Eastern states, particularly those seen as a threat to Israel's dominance of the region, were either sinking into civil war or were on the very precipice of such war. That tendency looked as if it was being exacerbated by parallel US attempts to create a coalition of loyal, Sunni regimes, led by Saudi Arabia, to oppose the supposed Shia 'arc of extremism'.[9] Given that many key Middle Eastern states were uncomfortable amalgams of Sunni and Shia populations – forced into unnatural nationhood early last century by Western colonial powers – this policy threatened to light a powder keg. Israeli and US policies, whether intentionally or not, seemed to be encouraging a descent into social disorder and communal fighting.

The most obvious case was Iraq, where the US-led invasion had unleashed not only a Sunni-dominated insurgency but also spiralling sectarian violence between the Sunni, Shia and Kurdish populations. In abolishing the Iraqi army, and making some 400,000 armed and embittered soldiers jobless, Washington not only gutted the ability of the country's security services to impose law and order but also acted as a recruiting sergeant for the insurgency. As the already bankrupt economy collapsed under US-imposed free market reforms designed to allow Western firms to rake off huge profits, unemployment rocketed to 70 per cent, oil production plummeted and the electricity and water services barely functioned. The scramble for limited resources only increased social disorder. In confronting and humiliating Iraq's two neighbours, Syria and Iran, the only countries that could help calm tensions there, rather than engage with them, the US simply poured more oil on the flames of the sectarian fighting, as well as on an insurgency claiming an increasing number of US soldiers' lives. As already noted, some four million Iraqis, out of a total population of 27 million, were reported either to have fled abroad or to have been displaced to other areas of Iraq, in what was becoming a de facto partition of the country. As far as the White House was concerned, all of this seemed preferable to its opposite: unity among the various communal groups that might lead to a resistance that could oust the US occupation forces.

Similarly, what point had the destruction of much of Lebanon's infrastructure by the Israeli air force in summer 2006 served? In Israel the widely held assumption at the start of the war was that Lebanon's Christians and Sunnis would rise up and turn on the Shia Hizbullah when their country was bombed back 20 years. The point of the war, it seemed, had been to provoke a civil war, a repetition of the sectarian fighting that raged in Lebanon for 15 years from 1975. In reality, however, the destruction had quite the opposite effect, galvanising support for the Shia militia. Nonetheless, after the war, Israel and the US were more successful in stoking sectarian tensions by siding openly but largely ineffectually with Fuad Siniora's government against the political aspirations of Hizbullah.[10] There was also much speculation about the arrival on the scene in Lebanon of small violent Sunni jihadi groups like Fatah al-Islam, whom observers rushed to link with the country's Palestinian refugees or with Syria, though most of their members appeared to have been recruited from countries like Saudi Arabia, Yemen and Morocco. A vicious battle erupted in one of the refugee camps, Nahr al-Bared, between Fatah al-Islam and the Lebanese security forces in late May 2007. Although it was early to draw firm conclusions, there were at least plausible suggestions that the CIA and Saudi Arabia might have had a hand in the development of these Sunni militias in an attempt to undermine the power of Hizbullah.[11]

In the occupied Palestinian territories of the Gaza Strip and the West Bank, the US refusal to recognise the Hamas government there, the imposition of a regime of economic sanctions by the international community on the Palestinian Authority, regular attacks on Gaza and its infrastructure, and the arming of Fatah factions loyal to President Mahmoud Abbas were all pushing the Palestinians into bitter feuding and a scramble for limited resources. Israel could barely conceal its irritation at the agreement of Fatah and Hamas to set up a national unity government in early 2007, thereby temporarily lifting the threat of civil war.[12] The economic siege continued, as did US and Israeli machinations. Forces loyal to Abbas and a Fatah strongman, Mohammed Dahlan, were further bolstered, prompting yet more internal Palestinian violence in May 2007.[13] A month later outright confrontation between Hamas and elements within Fatah broke out, with Hamas claiming that the Fatah militants were conspiring, with outside help, to overthrow it as the Palestinian government. The power struggle culminated in summer 2007 in Hamas taking over Gaza, and Fatah establishing a rival government, backed by Israel and the US, in the West Bank, cementing a geographic separation of the two occupied territories that had been a long-standing ambition of Israel.

The closed society of Syria was, as ever, more difficult to read, but the intention of US and Israeli policies was less hard to fathom. The passage of the Syria Accountability Act through Congress in late 2003 offered the Bush Administration easy justification for a military attack, either by the US or Israel, at any time in the future. A clause declaring Syria 'accountable for any harm to Coalition armed forces or to any United States citizen in Iraq if the government of Syria is found to be responsible' appeared to dispense even with the need for proof.[14] Damascus' growing international isolation and its humiliating eviction from Lebanon, the determination to pursue a UN investigation into its suspected role in assassinating a former Lebanese prime minister, Rafik Hariri, the constant hints that Israel was about to attack, plus the embarrassing revelations that Assad had been rebuffed in his secret attempts at making peace with Israel, were destabilising the regime, it could be assumed, and weakening a leader who gave every indication of being ready to cooperate with the West, including over Iraq. Even the CIA had been forced to admit that Damascus was helping the US in its fight against al-Qaeda and the Taliban, offering information that, according to a US official, 'exceeded the Agency's expectations'.[15] Nonetheless, Damascus seemed to be able to do little to end its pariah status.

Meanwhile, US and Israeli policies of naked aggression were reaching their height against Iran, one of the more socially cohesive societies in the Middle East. In October 2005, in an indication of the direction of Washington's thinking, a leading neocon forum, the American Enterprise Institute, hosted representatives from Iran's Kurdish, Azeri and Baluchi opposition groups in exile. 'For the US ... the temptation to use the ethnic lever against the Islamic Republic might prove irresistible', warned an independent Iranian analyst.[16] US forces seized five Iranian junior diplomats in Irbil in northern Iraq in early 2007, disappearing them into the local prison system.[17] Two months later a report by the American ABC News channel highlighted US backing since 2005 for a Pakistani militant group, led by a former Taliban fighter, that was launching guerrilla raids into Baluchi areas of Iran. The group was kidnapping and murdering Iranians, as well as exploding bombs, in what appeared to be attempts at destabilising the region.[18] In addition to these repeated humiliations, the concerted attempts by the US and Israel to denigrate Iran's leader, the constant drumbeat of war against Tehran and the UN-imposed sanctions regime were pushing in the same direction: the weakening of social ties holding Iran together. In a predictable response, Iran's government increased its repressive policies, reversing a liberalisation process begun under the previous President, Mohammed Khatami, that further strained social cohesion.[19]

The one light on the horizon, an initiative from Saudi Arabia – backed by the Arab League – for Arab states to make peace with Israel in return for Israel's withdrawal from the occupied territories, received lacklustre support from Washington and downright obstruction from Israel.[20] A similar offer of peace from the Arab world had first been put to Israel in spring 2002, when

Sharon was launching his destructive rampage through the West Bank early in the intifada. He studiedly ignored it then,[21] and his successor, Ehud Olmert, seemed almost as determined to do the same now. Conditions imposed by Olmert before agreeing to meet Arab leaders led one veteran Israeli commentator, Gideon Levy, to observe that Israel did not want peace:

> Until recently, it was still possible to accept the Israeli refrain that 'there is no partner' for peace and that 'the time isn't right' to deal with our enemies. Today, the new reality before our eyes leaves no room for doubt and the tired refrain that 'Israel supports peace' has been left shattered.[22]

By summer 2007 the normally close ties between the White House and Saudi Arabia had become noticeably cooler as Riyadh pressed on with its peace plan and was blamed by US officials for funding Hamas.

The official excuses for US belligerence towards Iran, Syria, Lebanon, the occupied Palestinian territories – and, earlier, Iraq – hardly stood up to scrutiny. None of these states appeared to pose a serious threat to the US mainland, and none had any obvious connection to al-Qaeda. None also posed a realistic physical threat to a nuclear-armed Israel. Repeated claims by the White House that it wanted to export 'democracy' to these states sounded more than hollow, not least in regard to the occupied territories, where the Palestinian electorate was being punished for making its democratic choice. The elections in Iraq in January 2005, much trumpeted by the White House, had in fact occurred, as the conservative *Financial Times* noted, only because of 'the insistence of the Grand Ayatollah Ali Sistani [Iraq's main Shia leader], who vetoed three schemes by the US-led occupation authorities to shelve or dilute them'.[23] Washington also showed no interest in responding to the will of the overwhelming majority of Iraqis, who polls consistently showed wanted the occupying soldiers out of their country. In any case, no nation in history had ever acted on such a vast and costly scale simply out of altruistic motives like 'encouraging democracy'.

An uncomfortable question suggested itself: if Washington's interests were to calm the sectarian pressures in Iraq that were making the country ungovernable, and if the key to achieving that goal was talking to Iran and Syria, as an increasing number of US Democratic and Republican politicians believed, why had no realistic efforts been made by the Bush Administration in that direction? What interests were shaping US policy in the region? Were the neocons simply pushing a US agenda for oil or, as a number of dissident voices suggested, an Israeli one for its own regional dominance? And if the latter, what idea of their own interests did Israel's leaders have: would civil war unleashed across the region not spell disaster too for a small non-Arab, non-Islamic state like Israel?

WHO CONTROLS AMERICAN FOREIGN POLICY?

Outside the mainstream debates that presented the confrontation with Iran in simple colours of black and white – the good, Judeo-Christian world against evil Islamic extremism – two more plausible but opposed answers were offered to these questions. In shorthand, they were referred to as 'the dog wagging the tail' and 'the tail wagging the dog' scenarios.[24]

The first, championed by Noam Chomsky, argued that the contradiction between US interests and its policies on the ground was only apparent rather than real. In truth, the US was pursuing its long-standing strategy of bullying non-compliant states in the Middle East to secure its control of oil resources. Certainly it had become increasingly clear that the Bush Administration was intending to cream off much of Iraq's oil wealth, giving Anglo-American corporations the right to plunder the riches from many of the country's oilfields for the foreseeable future. By late 2006, President Bush was even daring to link the occupation to oil, claiming that, if US forces pulled out, extremists would control Iraq and 'use energy as economic blackmail' and try to pressure the United States to abandon its alliance with Israel. The extremists, he said, would be 'able to pull millions of barrels of oil off the market, driving the price up to $300 or $400 a barrel'.[25]

'There are several issues in the case of Iran', Chomsky told an interviewer in early 2007 when asked about the reasons for a possible attack on Tehran.

> One is simply that it is independent and independence is not tolerated. Sometimes it's called successful defiance in the internal record. Take Cuba. A very large majority of the US population is in favor of establishing diplomatic relations with Cuba and has been for a long time with some fluctuations. And even part of the business world is in favor of it too. But the [US] government won't allow it. It's attributed to the Florida vote but I don't think that's much of an explanation. I think it has to do with a feature of world affairs that is insufficiently appreciated. International affairs is very much run like the mafia. The godfather does not accept disobedience, even from a small storekeeper who doesn't pay his protection money. You have to have obedience otherwise the idea can spread that you don't have to listen to the orders and it can spread to important places.

Chomsky added:

> It's not only that [Iran] has substantial resources and that it's part of the world's major energy system but it also defied the United States. The United States, as we know, overthrew the parliamentary government [in 1953], installed a brutal tyrant, was helping him develop nuclear power, in fact the very same programs that are now considered a threat were being sponsored by the US government, by Cheney, Wolfowitz, Kissinger, and others, in the 1970s, as long as the Shah was in power.[26]

Although Chomsky's argument offered a necessary part of the answer, it hardly seemed to provide sufficient justification for the US Administration's apparent desire to launch an attack on Iran – or, for that matter, its earlier decision to invade and occupy Iraq. Even for Washington hawks, it was hard to deny that the policy of containment of Iraq in the 1990s, for example, had been more successful than the chaos that followed invasion. Chomsky's view also suggested that Washington had a consistent, predictable and monolithic view of American interests abroad and how to secure them. But, as we have seen, in occupying Iraq, the Bush Administration pursued policies that contradicted the advice of many of its own advisers and the known goals of the powerful oil industry.

It undertook 'regime overthrow' rather than 'regime change', allowing violence and sectarianism to spiral out of control in Iraq instead of installing another strongman – as colonial experience dictated, and Big Oil wanted. Similarly, a strike against Iran to teach it that disobedience does not pay would inevitably come at a very high price for the US: greater lawlessness and killing in neighbouring US-occupied Iraq, the almost certain fall of a loyal regime in Lebanon, and chaos across the region, including in Saudi Arabia, Syria, Jordan and the occupied Palestinian territories, whose consequences it would be all but impossible to predict. The additional costs should such a strike involve nuclear warheads seemed incalculable.

Also, the analogy with Cuba was not entirely convincing. Cuba had been threatened shortly after its revolution with the US-funded invasion by Cuban exiles of the Bay of Pigs, while Iran had been attacked, with US backing, by its neighbour Iraq. In both cases, US action had failed to bring about regime change. So why not continue in the case of Tehran, as well as Baghdad, the US model for Cuba: containment and punishment? Was Chomsky suggesting that there were no other ways to secure the flow of oil, or Tehran's compliance in helping to stabilise Iraq, or to prevent Iran from developing a nuclear bomb?

Certainly, it was known that Tehran had been ready to enter a dialogue with Washington since at least early 2003, fearful that, after the US attack on Iraq, it was next in line. According to the *Washington Post*, Iran had sent a document to the State Department, offering 'to put a series of US aims on the agenda, including full cooperation on nuclear safeguards, "decisive action" against terrorists, coordination in Iraq, ending "material support" for Palestinian militias and accepting a two-state solution in the Israeli-Palestinian conflict'. Flynt Leverett, a State Department staffer, said he had placed the faxed document on the desk of Elliott Abrams, a prominent neocon in the department who was responsible for Middle East policy. In the summer of 2006, Condoleezza Rice admitted knowing about the document: 'What the Iranians wanted earlier was to be one-on-one with the United States so that this could be about the United States and Iran.'[27]

Rice was Bush's National Security Adviser at the time. Later, when the US media picked up on this embarrassing revelation, Rice changed her story and denied having ever seen the document. Instead she suggested that recognition of Israel would have been a precondition for entering into talks with Tehran. 'We had people who said, "The Iranians want to talk to you," lots of people who said, "The Iranians want to talk to you." But I think I would have noticed if the Iranians had said, "We're ready to recognize Israel" ... I just don't remember ever seeing any such thing.'[28]

An alternative to Chomsky's theory was proposed by two American professors, John Mearsheimer and Stephen Walt.[29] In an article published in the *London Review of Books*, after American publications refused it, the pair claimed that the pro-Israel lobby, uniquely among Washington lobby groups, had managed to push US foreign policy in a totally self-destructive direction. Although Israel was not a vital strategic asset, argued the professors, its policy goals were being pursued above Washington's. 'The Israeli government and pro-Israel groups in the United States have worked together to shape the administration's policy towards Iraq, Syria and Iran, as well as its grand scheme for reordering the Middle East.' This had been made possible because of the oppressive influence of the pro-Israel lobby in American politics:

> The thrust of US policy in the region derives almost entirely from domestic politics, and especially the activities of the 'Israel Lobby'. Other special-interest groups have managed to skew foreign policy, but no lobby has managed to divert it as far from what the national interest would suggest, while simultaneously convincing Americans that US interests and those of the other country – in this case, Israel – are essentially identical.[30]

Plausible as many of Mearsheimer and Walt's arguments were, their theory implied that much of the foreign policy making process in the US had been effectively hijacked by agents of a foreign power, and that it was Israel really pulling the levers in Washington through its neocon allies and groups like AIPAC. Though there seemed little doubt that AIPAC was seeking to promote Israeli interests over US interests, Mearsheimer and Walt's thesis went further in arguing that AIPAC was successfully determining US foreign policy – in contrast to Chomsky's view that the positions of AIPAC and the Israel lobby mainly reflected US interests in the Middle East. If the two professors were right, why had Washington been so supine in allowing a foreign power to bypass the well-established system of checks and balances? How had other powerful elites, including the oil industry, failed to find a way to expel these 'foreign bodies' and reassert US national interests?

There were a couple of major problems with the Mearsheimer-Walt position, at least in the hard-line versions expounded by some. First, although all recent US Administrations had been cravenly 'loyal' to Israel, the second Bush White House appeared to have taken that to an unprecedented level. If such commitment to Israeli interests was simply an effect of the pro-Israel lobby, and not the result of what were perceived, at least in part, also to be real US interests, why had the previous Bush Snr and Clinton presidencies not pursued similar policies in the Middle East to Bush Jnr? Why did Bush Snr, for example, not ensure Saddam Hussein was deposed during the 1991 Gulf War, at a time when the logic for such an action appeared far more compelling? According to the Mearsheimer-Walt thesis, there could be only two possible explanations: that Israel did not want to achieve Saddam's downfall in the early 1990s, or that the Israel lobby had accreted far more power in the meantime. Neither argument looked convincing.[31] And second, even if it could be persuasively argued that the Jewish neocons really were putting loyalty to Israel before loyalty to the US, how was it possible to explain the motivation of the non-Jewish neocons like John Bolton, James Woolsey, or their White House patrons like Dick Cheney and Donald Rumsfeld? Were they in the pay of the Israeli government, or being intimidated or blackmailed? And if not, how to explain their neoconservatism?

THE DOG AND TAIL WAG EACH OTHER

I propose a different model for understanding the US Administration's wilful pursuit of catastrophic goals in the Middle East, one that incorporates many of the assumptions of both the Chomsky and Walt-Mearsheimer positions. I argue that Israel persuaded the US neocons that their respective goals (Israeli regional dominance and US control of oil) were related and compatible ends. As we shall see, Israel's military establishment started developing an ambitious vision of Israel as a small empire in the Middle East more than two decades ago. It then sought a sponsor in Washington to help it realise its vision, and found one in the neocons. The Jewish neocons, many of them already with strong emotional ties to Israel, may have been the most ready to listen to the message coming from Tel Aviv, but that message was persuasive even to the non-Jewish neocons precisely because it placed US interests – especially global domination and control of oil – at the heart of its vision.

Israel's ideas about how to achieve these goals had a long heritage in Zionism, as will become clear. The Israeli security establishment argued that Israel's own regional dominance and US control of oil could be assured in the same way: through the provocation of a catastrophe in the Middle East in the form of social breakdown, a series of civil wars and the partition of Arab states. What many informed observers assumed to be a self-defeating US policy, the neocons and Israel regarded as a positive outcome. In other words, it was not that the dog was wagging the tail or the tail wagging the dog: the dog and tail were wagging each other. In a sense, this was the actual goal of the Israeli strategy. By tying the fates of Israel's occupation of the Palestinian territories to the US occupation of Iraq, by miring the American forces directly in the same, constant human rights abuses that Israeli forces committed daily in the West Bank and Gaza, the two projects stood or fell together. The futures of the Israeli and US occupations became inextricably entwined.

The neocons' vision of global American supremacy drew heavily for its inspiration on earlier Israeli plans for dominating the region that required recalcitrant Middle Eastern states such as Iran, Iraq and Syria, and states within their influence such as Lebanon, to be broken up into smaller units. Then, once more primal sectarian and tribal allegiances asserted themselves, they could be accentuated, exploited and managed. Israel's scheme may also have envisioned the weakening of Saudi Arabia, Israel's only Middle Eastern rival for influence in Washington, by fatally undermining its control of OPEC. This was a policy of 'divide and rule' in the Middle East promoted by a tiny state with imperial ambitions on an extravagant scale. What Israel planned for the region – and was finally in a position to implement with the rise of the neocons to prominent positions of power in the US – was what I have referred to elsewhere as 'organised chaos'.[32] One of the leading neocon ideologues, Michael Ledeen, a former Pentagon staffer, expressed this philosophy very clearly:

> Creative destruction is our middle name, both within our own society and abroad. We tear down the old order every day, from business to science, literature, art, architecture, and cinema to politics and the law. Our enemies have always hated this whirlwind of energy and creativity, which menaces their traditions (whatever they may be) and shames them for their inability to keep pace. Seeing America undo traditional societies, they fear us, for they do not wish to be undone. They cannot feel secure so long as we are there, for our very existence – our existence, not our politics – threatens their legitimacy. They must attack us in order to survive, just as we must destroy them to advance our historic mission.[33]

Vice-President Dick Cheney presented an outline of a similar vision of the future in a speech in January 2004 in which he described a West surrounded by enemies and permanently at war – the replication on a global scale of Israel's view of its own place in the Middle East. 'One of the legacies of this administration will be some of the most sweeping changes in our military, and our national security strategy as it relates to the military and force structure ... probably since World War II.' In an ambitious reimagining of the Carter Doctrine, Cheney said the Bush Admin-istration was planning to expand its military forces into more overseas bases so that the US could wage war quickly around the world.

> Scattered in more than 50 nations, the al Qaeda network and other terrorist groups constitute an enemy unlike any other that we have ever faced. And

as our intelligence shows, the terrorists continue plotting to kill on an ever-larger scale, including here in the United States. Instead of losing thousands of lives, we might lose tens or even hundreds of thousands of lives as the result of a single attack, or a set of coordinated attacks.[34]

There are two additional points to remember about the model I am proposing. The first is that relations between the neocons and Israel have always been dynamic; Israel did not simply sell a vision to the neocons and then seek its implementation. The neocons were persuaded of the basic Israeli strategy for dominating the Middle East (and that it was in both parties' interests), and then set about devising their own policies to realise these goals. It is quite possible, on this reading, that at times Israel found itself being dictated to by the neocons, or pushed to deliver on promises it struggled in practice to attain. That was certainly how it looked during the assault on Lebanon, when the Israeli leadership quickly realised it could not defeat Hizbullah with an air campaign and that it could not afford the losses of a ground invasion. The war seemed to drag on mostly at the instigation of the neocons, committed absolutely to the strategy of removing the threat of Hizbullah as a precondition for launching an assault on Tehran but not faced, like Israel's politicians, with the costs to their domestic popularity posed by a greater loss of soldiers' lives.[35]

The second is that Washington's apparent hesitation in implementing the next stage of the vision – attacking Iran – appeared to reflect the US and Israel's inability to manage the civil wars and insurrections, as well as opinion back home, as successfully as they had imagined. Israel's fantastically lavish vision of the Middle East under joint Israeli and US rule was just that: fantastic. It made simplistic assumptions typical of the Israeli security establishment that Arabs and Muslims were pawns who could be easily manipulated by superior Israeli and Western intrigues. It posited a view of a primitive 'Arab mentality' familiar from Israeli academia and the security establishment.[36] It was hardly surprising that one of the most influential books on the Middle East among the neocons and the US army was a notoriously racist tract called *The Arab Mind* (1976) written by Raphael Patai, a Hungarian Jew who had spent many years teaching at Israeli universities before moving to the US. Patai developed a theory of the Arab personality suggesting that it understood only force and that its biggest weaknesses were shame and sexual humiliation. Such principles apparently drove the torture regime set up by the US army at the Abu Ghraib prison in Iraq.[37]

ISRAEL'S RELATIONS WITH ITS PATRONS

Before considering the Israeli-US plan for destabilising the Middle East, we should briefly examine Israel's traditionally complex relations with its patrons. After its creation in 1948, Israel continued to seek the protection of a superpower – just as the Jewish community in Palestine had done in the pre-state era – while at the same time pursuing its own discrete aims. The most important was the development of nuclear weapons, a goal that was seen as the key to Israel not only securing its place within a hostile Middle East but also rethinking its role as an agent of change in the region. An example of how Israel exploited this strategy was its close involvement with two fading European powers, Britain and France, who initiated the Suez War of 1956 as a way to punish Egypt's leader, Gamal Abdel Nasser, who had nationalised the Suez canal. Israel agreed to invade the neighbouring Egyptian peninsula of Sinai, offering the Europeans the pretext they were seeking, under cover of 'intervening' between the two warring parties, to occupy the canal zone. All three – Israel, Britain and France – had their own interests in curbing the Arab nationalism of Nasser.[38] Their plan failed when the US and Soviet Union jointly applied pressure, including undermining the strength of the pound, to bring about a ceasefire and a withdrawal by Israel.

Both Britain and France were the substantial losers in this last-gasp colonial venture; Israel, on the other hand, turned the episode strongly to its advantage. For its participation in the Suez War, it won help from France with its nuclear research. Recently released documents show that two years later, in 1958, for reasons that have yet to be explained, Britain supplied Israel with the heavy water it needed.[39] During this period Israel's nuclear programme, closely supervised by Shimon Peres, was successfully concealed from the US, which was led to believe that the reactor at Dimona was, at first, a textile factory, then a water-pumping station and finally a desalination plant. A US spy plane managed to photograph the reactor in 1960, though subsequent inspections failed to reveal its true purpose. Israeli officials constructed false walls at the site to prevent inspectors from accessing sensitive areas.[40] According to recent revelations from the historian Tom Segev, Israel was producing its first nuclear warheads by the mid-1960s, shortly before the outbreak of the Six-Day War of 1967.[41] Today Israel is believed to have an arsenal of at least 200 warheads.

It is often argued that Washington only appreciated the value of Israel as a strategic ally after the 1967 war, in which Israel defeated the combined armies of its neighbours in six days. Certainly, the initial assessments of the State Department and CIA were that a close US alliance with a Jewish state in the Middle East would prove a strategic liability. In 1947, as President Harry Truman was seeking Jewish votes by backing the Zionist cause of statehood, CIA officials warned that the Jewish leadership in Palestine was 'pursuing objectives without regard for the consequences' and was thereby damaging Western strategic interests 'since the Arabs now identify the United States and the United Kingdom with Zionism'.[42] However, the argument that the US-Israeli alliance was simply a consequence of the Six-Day War oversimplifies matters:[43] Israel and Washington already had unusually close ties, as was revealed in early 2007 with the release, after a 40-year delay, of transcripts of private meetings of the Senate's Foreign Relations Committee shortly before and during the 1967 war. They reveal the powerful grip that Israel and its lobbyists already had on the hearts, minds and pocketbooks of the US representatives. In a debate on 9 June about the unusual financial relationship between Israel and American Jewish groups, there was the following exchange between the Senators on Jewish power in the US:

Senator Bourke Hickenlooper: Do we not give tax forgiveness for monies contributed to Israel, which is rather unusual? We could stop that.

Secretary of State Dean Rusk: I believe contributions to the UJA [United Jewish Appeal] are tax exempt, yes.

Committee chairman J. William Fulbright: That is right. The only country. Do you think you have the votes in the Senate to revoke that?

Senator Clifford Case: Are you in favor yourself?

Hickenlooper: I think we ought to treat all nations alike.

Case: That is correct. But are you in favor of it?

Hickenlooper: As long as we do not give it to other nations, I do not –

Fulbright: The trouble is they think they have control of the Senate and they can do as they please.

Senator Stuart Symington: What was that?

Fulbright: I said they know they have control of the Senate politically, and therefore whatever the Secretary [of State] tells them, they can laugh at him. They say, 'Yes, but you don't control the Senate.'

Symington: They were very anxious to get every Senator they could to come out and say we ought to act unilaterally, and they got two, three.

Fulbright: They know when the chips are down you can no more reverse this tax exemption than you can fly. You could not pass a bill through the Senate.

Hickenlooper: I do not think you could.[44]

In addition to the Senators' concern about the financial intimidation the pro-Israel lobby was already able to exercise in Congress, there were signs that some Senators were convinced that Israel was a vital ally in the region. Days before the outbreak of the war, Senator George Aiken asked of Secretary of State Dean Rusk: 'If Israel should fall, her [America's] entire interests in the Middle East would be jeopardized, wouldn't they, sir?'[45]

But if there were already warm ties between the two states, those relations only solidified in the wake of the war. The growing closeness can in part be explained by the Israeli army's success in humiliating Soviet-allied Egypt and Syria, which convinced President Lyndon Johnson that Israel was a useful Cold War asset. At the end of the war, a State Department official told the media:

Israel has probably done more for the United States in the Middle East in relation to money and effort than any of our so-called allies elsewhere around the globe since the end of the Second World War. In the Far East we can get almost no one to help us in Vietnam. Here the Israelis won the war singlehandedly, have taken us off the hook and have served our interests as well as theirs.[46]

The special relationship was also mutually beneficial: the US believed Israel had proved itself a formidable, even inspirational,[47] military ally in the Middle East; and for Israel, an exclusive alliance with the US, as European influence waned in the region, offered access to the world's biggest arms developer. The logic of the Cold War, in which leading Arab states were being courted by the Soviet Union, only reinforced Washington and Tel Aviv's sense that their futures lay together. But possibly more significant than these reasons was the perception in Washington that a nuclear-armed Israel had to be either cultivated or confronted at a dangerous cost. That was the view of Francis Perrin, High Commissioner of the French Atomic Energy Agency: 'We thought the Israeli bomb was aimed against the Americans, not to launch against America, but to say "if you don't want to help us in a critical situation we will require you to help us, otherwise we will use our nuclear bomb".'[48] In other words, the US had little choice but to ensure that Israel was always armed sufficiently that it need not resort to the 'bomb in the basement'. That would become a particularly pressing concern for the US a few years later, in 1973, when Israel found itself facing defeat in the Yom Kippur War.

Whatever the motives for the alliance, what followed, according to George Ball, a senior official in the Kennedy and Johnson Administrations, was the emergence in Washington of a deepening 'passionate attachment' to Israeli interests. The ever more confident pro-Israel lobby offered the American political class a simple and persuasive message, says Ball: 'A prosperous and well-armed Israel could, [the lobbyists] contended, serve America as a staunch ally, blocking the spread of Soviet and radical influences, safeguarding the Gulf and the oilfields on the Gulf's littoral, and providing irrefutable intelligence on the whole Middle East.'[49] The basis of the lobby's success in Washington, in both its Jewish and Christian Zionist forms,[50] as Ball admits, was its power to raise huge sums of money that could work for or against candidates standing for election to public office. Few members of Congress dared to be outspoken on matters that Israel believed related to its security for fear that their opponent would be riding a wave of lobby financing come election time.[51] This unbalanced degree of support for a foreign power was reinforced by a public climate in the US that readily encouraged the labelling of criticism of Israel as anti-Semitism.[52] As a result, few dared challenge America's ever-growing financial support for Israel, which by 2002 had cost American taxpayers more than $370 billion. If the cost over the years of protecting Israel from threats was factored in, the price rose to $1.6 trillion, according to one economist.[53]

The sense of mutual advantage continued into the 1970s. At the turn of the decade, shortly after the Nixon Doctrine had been adopted, Israel proved its value again, helping Jordan's King Hussein, an ally of Washington, in suppressing a rebellion by the Palestinians, then seen as a Soviet proxy. When Israel briefly looked in danger of defeat during the 1973 Arab-Israeli war, Nixon and his National Security Adviser, Henry Kissinger, hurriedly agreed an airlift of weapons to Israel, risking the wrath of the Arab world, which imposed a costly oil embargo on the West as a result. But contrary to the Walt-Mearsheimer thesis of the pro-Israel lobby's power, there were notable instances of the US disregarding Israeli wishes and even punishing Israel. Two Middle East analysts noted some of the most obvious:

> From Reagan's sale of AWACS planes to Saudi Arabia to the first Bush administration's threat to withhold loan guarantees from Israel, there are scattered examples of Israel and the pro-Israel lobby proving unable to veto executive branch decisions. Ongoing disputes over Israeli arms sales to China (and previously to India), the current Bush administration's quiet non-response to Israeli requests for financial compensation for its Gaza 'withdrawal' and its message to the Olmert government that it should not ask for funding for its 'convergence plan' are additional examples.[54]

Conversely, there were other incidents that suggested the relationship was not one in which Israel simply did the bidding of its superpower ally. Just as Israel had successfully extracted nuclear privileges from France and Britain, it now made regular demands that its interests be given special treatment by the US. One of the earliest and starkest examples was the agreement of the Johnson Administration to hush up an almost certainly intentional attack by the Israeli air force and navy on a US spy ship, the *Liberty*, during the 1967 war, killing 34 American sailors and wounding at least 100 more.[55] Ball argues that Johnson's failure to punish Israel in any way was an important lesson: 'Israel's leaders concluded that nothing they might do would offend the Americans to the point of reprisal. If America's leaders did not have the courage to punish Israel for the blatant murder of American citizens, it seemed clear that their American friends would let them get away with almost anything.'[56] Ball's account of Menachem Begin's relations with the Carter Administration shows the Americans regularly frustrated by their Israeli allies and forced into humiliating climbdowns, including during Israel's invasion and occupation of south Lebanon in 1978.[57]

But, though there are repeated examples of Israel defying US Administrations even on important foreign policy matters, it may still be the case that on strategic issues Israeli policy was seen in Washington as according with larger US interests. Possibly small sins were being forgiven because overall the right objectives were being pursued. One possibility is that Israel was the key to the success of US military industries in fuelling an arms race in the region. Stephen Zunes, a Middle East policy analyst, has argued that the US-subsidised arming of Israel to the tune of billions of dollars each year forced a desperate game of catch-up from its neighbours: 'The benefit to American defense contractors is multiplied by the fact that every major arms transfer to Israel creates a new demand by Arab states – most of which can pay in hard currency from oil exports – for additional American weapons to respond to Israel.'[58] In summer 2007, the Bush Administration was accused of fuelling just such an arms race in the Middle East when it announced plans to sell $20 billion of advanced weaponry to Saudi Arabia and other Gulf states, as well as $13 billion to Egypt, in what was widely seen as an attempt to bolster Washington-friendly regimes in the region against Iran and to offer a carrot to Saudi Arabia to entice it to attend a regional peace conference called by President

Bush for late 2007. The White House also promised to maintain Israel's military edge with a $30 billion increase in defence aid over ten years. 'Other than the increase in aid, we received an explicit and detailed commitment to guarantee Israel's qualitative advantage over other Arab states', Israeli Prime Minister Ehud Olmert told journalists, adding: 'We understand the US's desire to help moderate states which stand at a united front with the US and Israel in the struggle against Iran.'[59]

In addition, Israel doubtless also had an integral role to play in the US strategy of controlling the Middle East through a traditional policy of divide and rule. Israel's intermittent wars with uncooperative or hostile neighbours, and its peace agreements with others, meant that the danger of the kind of Arab nationalism once invoked by Egypt's Nasser – that even led to a brief experiment in political union between Egypt and Syria in the late 1950s – was over. With Israeli help, the main Middle Eastern states had been split into different and irreconcilable camps: the weak Gulf states became dependent on the US for military protection and for legitimation of their oil cartel, OPEC; the reliable strongmen of states like Egypt, Jordan and Iran (under the Shah) were bolstered with US support; and 'rogue' states like Syria, Libya, Iraq and Iran (after the 1979 revolution) were isolated and contained. In practice, the US barometer for determining the extent of Middle Eastern states' legitimacy was their willingness to make peace with, or at least feign acceptance of, Israel.[60]

It is in this context that the decision by Israel's Defence Minister, Ariel Sharon, to launch an ambitious invasion of Lebanon in 1982 can be understood. By installing Bashir Gemayel, a strongman from the minority Christian Maronites, Israel hoped to gain several significant benefits: a peace treaty signed on Israeli terms; the chance to effectively annex the area of south Lebanon up to the Litani River, with its important water resources; the eviction of the Palestinian leadership and fighters from their bases in the refugee camps; the reduction of Syrian influence in Lebanon; and the creation of another non-Muslim ethnic state alongside Israel. These aims had a long pedigree of support from Israel's leaders, including the country's first prime minister, David Ben Gurion, who repeatedly urged that Israel push into Lebanon to proclaim a 'Christian state'.[61] In 1954 the country's Chief of Staff, Moshe Dayan, backed the same Machiavellian intrigue: 'The Israeli army will enter Lebanon, will occupy the necessary territory, and will create a Christian regime which will ally itself with Israel.'[62] But although Israeli interests were primarily being pursued, they did not conflict, and probably accorded, with US interests: a compliant strongman would diminish Syrian and Soviet influence in the region, help in the process of isolating recalcitrant Arab states, and further strengthen Israel.

SHARON'S DOCTRINE OF EMPIRE

It is noteworthy that shortly before he instigated the invasion of Lebanon, Sharon had written a speech in which he set out a new vision of Israel's role in the Middle East. It was a radical departure from the traditional understanding of Israel's need simply to protect itself from hostile neighbours, and it shocked some domestic commentators. Sharon's vision could not be realised without either Israel's sole possession of nuclear weapons in the Middle East or its intimate alliance with the US.

The lecture was never given to its intended audience, at the Institute for Strategic Affairs at Tel Aviv University, because the event was cancelled in the wake of the controversy surrounding Israel's decision in December 1981 to annex Syrian territory it was occupying, the Golan Heights, in violation of international law. But it was published shortly afterwards in the daily *Ma'ariv* newspaper. In his undelivered speech, Sharon developed a new security philosophy for Israel in which it no longer thought in terms of peace with its neighbours or of combating the danger of direct confrontation with Arab states on its borders. Instead it sought to widen its sphere of influence to the whole region.

Beyond the Arab countries in the Middle East and on the shores of the Mediterranean and the Red Sea, we must expand the field of Israel's strategic and security concerns in the eighties to include countries like

Turkey, Iran, Pakistan, and areas like the Persian Gulf and Africa, and in particular the countries of North and Central Africa.[63]

Israel's success depended on 'a clear qualitative and technological superiority' in military weapons, particularly 'our decision to prevent the confrontation countries or potential confrontation countries obtaining the nuclear weapon'.[64]

This view of Israel as a regional superpower quickly became known as the Sharon Doctrine, and invited severe criticism. Zvi Timur, a correspondent with the leftwing *al-Hamishmar* daily, observed that Sharon was proposing the establishment of an 'Israeli empire'. 'This doctrine can be dismissed with such expressions as "mania", "megalomania" or "lack of realism". But we must remember that while Ariel Sharon holds the post of Minister of Defence, Israel may be involved in a series of world or local conflicts with which, in fact, Israel has no direct concern.'[65]

By Israeli standards, Sharon was far from the eccentric or hard-line warrior he was often painted in the West. Although he enjoyed greater visibility than any Israeli general with the possible exceptions of Moshe Dayan and Yitzhak Rabin, he also undoubtedly represented many of the core values of Israel's military establishment. It is often forgotten that many leading generals of Sharon's generation – including Rehavam Ze'evi, Rafael Eitan and Yehoshafat Harkabi – held views at least as extreme, if not more so, than Sharon's for all or much of their lives. Sharon's worldview was also acknowledged to have deeply influenced many younger officers, including some nominally on the left such as Ehud Barak.[66] Israel's recent Chiefs of Staff, including Shaul Mofaz and Moshe Ya'alon, were well known for hard-line views that matched and on occasion exceeded Sharon's. Where Sharon did excel was in his ability to persuade others to adopt his plans and to turn his visions into reality.

In fact, there is more than circumstantial evidence that the Sharon Doctrine quickly became integrated into the Israeli security establishment's view of its potential role in the Middle East. In his book *Open Secrets*, Israel Shahak collected and translated many of the comments made in the Hebrew media by senior army officers in the early 1990s supporting a regional role for Israel's military. An example is an op-ed penned by Shlomo Gazit,[67] a former head of Israeli military intelligence, for the *Yed'iot Aharonot* newspaper in 1992, in which he sets out Israel's strategic role:

> The geographical location of Israel at the centre of the Arab-Muslim Middle East predestines Israel to be a devoted guardian of stability in all the countries surrounding it. Its [role] is to protect the existing regimes: to prevent or halt the processes of radicalization and to block the expansion of fundamentalist religious zealotry. Israel has its 'red lines', which have a powerful deterrent effect by virtue of causing uncertainty beyond its borders, precisely because they are not clearly marked nor explicitly defined. The purpose of these red lines is to determine which strategic developments or other changes occurring beyond Israel's borders can be defined as threats which Israel itself will regard as intolerable to the point of being compelled to use all its military power for the sake of their prevention or eradication.[68]

In other words, Israel's role was to impose dictates and terrify other states in the region with threats of punishment so that they dare not step out of line. Gazit's 'red lines' included revolts, whether military or popular, that might bring 'fanatical and extremist elements to power in the states concerned'.[69] As a result, wrote Gazit, Israel's influence extended beyond its immediate neighbours and 'radiates on to all the other states of our region'. By protecting reliable Middle Eastern regimes, Israel performed a vital service for 'the industrially advanced states, all of which are keenly concerned with guaranteeing the stability in the Middle East'.[70]

The Sharon Doctrine also underpinned comments made in December 2001, shortly after the 9/11 attacks on the US, by Israel's National Security Adviser, General Uzi Dayan, and the head of the Mossad, Ephraim Halevy. The pair reportedly told that year's Herzliya conference that the 9/11 attacks were a 'Hannukkah miracle', offering Israel the chance to sideline and punish its enemies. Halevy spoke of the imminent arrival of 'a world war different from all its predecessors' and the emergence after 9/11 of a common perception combining 'all the elements of Islamic terror into one clear and identifiable format', creating 'a genuine dilemma for every ruler and every state in our region.

Each one must reach a moment of truth and decide how he will position himself in the campaign.' Dayan, meanwhile, identified the targets, after Afghanistan, for the next stage of the regional campaign: 'The Iran, Iraq and Syria triangle, all veteran supporters of terror which are developing weapons of mass destruction.' He argued: 'They must be confronted as soon as possible, and that is also understood in the US. Hezbollah and Syria have good reason to worry about the developments in this campaign, and that's also true for the organizations and other states.'[71]

In spring 2007, Meron Benvenisti, a former deputy mayor of Jerusalem and long-time commentator on Israeli affairs, offered an insight into what he called the 'fiery belligerence of arrogant generals'. Explaining their aversion to peace initiatives such as the Saudi plan that offered Israel recognition by the whole Arab world, he wrote:

> The governing ideology maintains that Arab hostility is a permanent situation, that the Arabs lack a basic willingness to relate to the Jewish state as a legitimate entity, and that the violent nature of the region does not allow for real peace but, in the best case scenario, a cease-fire that will be violated the very moment its enemies sense Israel's weakness.[72]

It sounded very much like Cheney's view of permanent war. Like Cheney, Israel's General Staff favoured 'pre-emptive' wars to diminish the threat posed by the more powerful among the Middle East's Arab and Muslim states.

This would not have been of critical importance were it not for the fact that Israeli policy towards its Arab neighbours had been largely determined by the army, not the government, for decades. As we have already seen, General Malka, a former head of military intelligence, told the Winograd Committee as much in early 2007. In 2001, an anonymous Congressional source made a similar assessment to a news agency. All Israeli governments, he said, had given 'a tremendous amount of attention' to the army's suggestions because they represented 'the permanent government'.[73] Israeli military commentator Amir Oren made the same point in Ha'aretz: 'In the last six years, since October 1995, there were five prime ministers and six defence ministers, but only two chiefs of staff.'[74] Guy Bechor, a columnist for the popular *Yed'iot Aharonot* newspaper, was even more plain-spoken: 'The government and the decision-makers, the Knesset, the press, the State Attorney's Office and the other civil and economic institutions follow the military piper from Hamlyn. Not that there are no exceptions, but that is what they are – exceptions.'[75]

Reminiscences by the doyen of military correspondents, Ze'ev Schiff of *Ha'aretz*, also offered an insight into how the army could bypass the country's political leadership when it chose to. In 2007 he recalled a conversation with Ariel Sharon in the days following Israel's success in the 1967 war. Sharon had asked Schiff to stop criticising the weak Prime Minister of the time, Levy Eshkol. Schiff asked why. 'Understand,' said Sharon,

> at a time like this in particular, after the victory, it's desirable that Israel should have a weak prime minister. This will make it possible to quickly transfer the Israel Defense Forces' training camps and military exercises to the West Bank. That will be my job ... A weak prime minister will be wary of interfering in a move of this kind. But he must not be made too weak; otherwise he could be toppled.

Sharon also joked to Schiff that shortly before the war, when the Israeli army had faced hesitation from Eshkol over its plans to launch a pre-emptive strike against the neighbouring Arab states, Sharon and the other young generals had considered a 'military revolt'. 'We would not have had to do much. We could have locked the ministers in the room and gone off with the key. We would have taken the appropriate decisions and no one would have known that the events taking place were the result of decisions by major generals.'[76]

Shlomo Gazit, however, noted that the value of Israel's military role to the US had dwindled in the 1990s following the fall of the Soviet empire. This was apparent, he added, during the 1991 Gulf War when Israel was excluded from participating because no Arab state 'can be a party to any military or security-aimed alliance, if Israel is also a party to it'. In these circumstances, what kind of strategic asset was Israel, asked Gazit rhetorically? He concluded that Israel still served a vital purpose because it filled the vacuum created by the disappearance of the Soviet Union, when 'a number of Middle Eastern states lost a patron guaranteeing their political, military and economic viability'. This had increased the region's instability, meaning that Israel's role as the guarantor of regional order had been 'elevated to the first order of magnitude'.[77]

When a decade earlier Sharon had proposed his doctrine of Israel as an empire – if one dependent on the US – he had been thinking of its role in a bipolar world in which the US faced off with the Soviet Union. 'I believe that strategic cooperation between Israel, the US and other pro-Western countries in this area headed by Egypt, with which Israel is now developing a new system of relations, endorsed by a peace treaty [the 1978 Camp David agreement], is the only realistic way of preventing further Soviet conspiracies.'[78] Israel's role was to maintain order in the Middle East, an order that would benefit its patron, the US, against excessive Soviet influence in the region.

But following the collapse of the Soviet empire, a new set of 'conspiracies' was needed to justify this philosophy. Israel's left and right quickly grasped the need for a shift in their approach. As we saw in the previous chapter, in 1994, months after Samuel Huntington had popularised the term 'the clash of civilizations' first in an article in the *Foreign Affairs* journal and then in a best-selling book,[79] Rabin, Peres and Barak started using the same terminology, claiming that the West and Islam were doomed to be in a permanent state of confrontation. And after 9/11, as Halevy and Dayan had predicted at the 2001 Herzliya conference, the US public and political establishment would be ready to accept the need for a war against Islamic extremism. Israel's conception of its place in the Middle East, as an outpost of Judeo-Christian civilisation surrounded by a sea of Muslim barbarians, could now – in the post 9/11 world – be presented as one of the central pillars of the US war on terror.

MAKING THE MIDDLE EAST COLLAPSE

But there was, I believe, a more significant, though less well understood, effect of the fall of the Soviet empire on the evolution of the Israeli army's thinking. Sharon's vision of Israel as a Middle Eastern empire was not the only one circulating in the Israeli security establishment of the early 1980s. An even more far-reaching scheme for the region was proposed in an essay published in Hebrew in February 1982 by the World Zionist Organisation, and written by an Israeli journalist, Oded Yinon. He had previously been a senior official in the Foreign Affairs Ministry, meaning he almost certainly enjoyed close ties to the Mossad. In an essay entitled *A Strategy for Israel in the Eighties*, Yinon advocated transforming Israel into an imperial regional power, much in line with the Sharon Doctrine, but added a further goal: making the Arab world disintegrate into a mosaic of ethnic and confessional groupings that could be more easily manipulated in Israel's interests. What little attention the article aroused outside Israel derived from two separate translations into English offered shortly afterwards by the *Journal of Palestine Studies* and the dissident Israeli scholar Israel Shahak.[80]

The timing of the essay's publication was probably significant too. As Hassan Nafaa, a professor of political science at Cairo University, has observed, Yinon published his article a few months after the assassination of Egyptian President Anwar Sadat, and a few weeks before Israel was due to return the Sinai to Egypt. Yinon spends part of the essay arguing that withdrawal from Sinai would be folly, especially given the peninsula's oil and gas reserves, which could be used to strengthen an Egyptian regime that was, in his view, close to collapse. Instead Israel should work to expose Egypt as a 'paper tiger', depriving it of economic resources and destabilising the state by sowing discord between its Muslim and Coptic citizens. Yinon believed a Muslim mini-state in the north and Christian mini-state in the south would be, in Nafaa's words, 'the best way to weaken the central state in Egypt and deprive the Arab world of the one country that could hold it together'. With Egypt marginalised, the rest of the Middle East could be dissolved with relative ease by Israel. A few months after Yinon's essay appeared, Sharon would launch his ambitious invasion of Lebanon, a barely concealed attempt to weaken Israel's northern neighbour and establish a Christian state there.[81]

Much like Huntington's fashionable thesis of a 'clash of civilisations', published more than a decade later, Yinon proposed that we were witnessing cataclysmic times and the 'collapse of the world order'. The success of totalitarian Communist regimes, ruling over 'three-quarters' of the world's population, argued Yinon, had emptied ideas like liberty of meaning.[82] 'The dominant process is the collapse of the rational humanistic view which has been the major theme of the life and prosperity of Western Civilization since the Renaissance.'[83] The central threat to Israel and the Western world was clear: 'The strength, dimension, accuracy and quality of nuclear and non-nuclear weapons will overturn most of the world in a few years.' We were entering an era of terror, and Israel in particular would be faced with growing militancy from its Arab neighbours.

In his diagnosis of the crisis and his prescription of a remedy, Yinon pointed out, and overstated, facts well known to the colonial European powers when they established nation states in the Middle East, largely for their own benefit. One strategy for ensuring that the government of each country would remain dependent on its colonial master, even after nominal independence, was to install a leader of a minority population to run the regime. This was achieved in Lebanon, where the electoral system ensured the Christian Maronites effectively ruled over the Islamic – Sunni and Shia – majority; the small Shia sect of the Alawis had long been in charge of Syria, despite being little more than a tenth of the population; until the US invasion, Iraq had had a series of Sunni rulers, even though its majority population was Shia; and Jordan was ruled by Hashemite monarchs, claiming ancestry from Saudi Arabia and the Prophet Mohammed, even though a majority of Jordanians had been Palestinian since Israel's demographic transformations of the area through its 1948 and 1967 wars. As a result,

> The Arab-Islamic world is built like a 'temporary tower of cards', which was constructed by foreigners (French and British in the 1920s) without taking into consideration the will and desires of the inhabitants. It is divided into 19 countries which are composed of combinations of minorities and which

are hostile to each other, such that the ethnic-social framework of every Arab-Muslim country can potentially crumble up to the point of civil war that exists in some of them.[84]

This pattern was observable throughout the region, wrote Yinon:

> In Kuwait, the Kuwaitis compose a quarter of the entire population; in Bahrain, the Shiites are the majority, while the Sunnis rule. Similarly, in Oman, in North Yemen, and even in Marxist South Yemen, there is a large Shiite majority. In Saudi Arabia, one half of the population is composed of foreigners, Egyptians, Yemenites, and others, while a Saudi minority is in power ... One half of Iran is Persian speaking, and the other is of Turkish ethnic origin, language and nature. Turkey is divided between Sunni Muslim Turks and two large minorities, 12 million Shiite Alawis and 6 million Sunni Kurds. In Afghanistan, 5 million Shiites compose almost one third of the total population; and in Sunni Pakistan there are 15 million Shiites; in both cases, they endanger the existence of the state.[85]

Yinon argued that most of these states were in dire financial trouble. Even in the oil-rich states, the 'beneficiaries of this resource are a small minority of elites of the total population, who have a narrow base, and lack both self-confidence and an army that can secure their survival'.[86] They could be dissolved with great ease.

> The total disintegration of Lebanon into five regional localized governments is the precedent for the entire Arab world including Egypt, Syria, Iraq and the Arab peninsula, in a similar fashion. The dissolution of Egypt and later Iraq into districts of ethnic and religious minorities following the example of Lebanon is the main long-range objective of Israel on the Eastern Front. The present military weakening of these states is the short-term objective. Syria will disintegrate into several states along the lines of its ethnic and sectarian structure, as is happening in Lebanon today. As a result there will be a Shiite Alawi state, the district of Aleppo will be a Sunni state, and the district of Damascus another state which is hostile to the northern one ... [Iraq's] sub-division is more important than that of Syria. Iraq is stronger than Syria, and in the long run the strength of Iraq is the biggest danger to Israel ... Iraq can be divided on regional and sectarian lines just like Syria in

the Ottoman era. There will be three states around the three major cities, Basra, Baghdad, and Mosul, while Shiite areas in the south will be separate from the Sunni north which is mostly Kurdish.[87]

In fact, Yinon's approach had long antecedents. European colonialists from the nineteenth century onwards had seen the Middle East as a mosaic of ethnic, tribal and religious affiliations. And, following in that tradition, the early Zionists had believed that to secure the Jewish state's place in the region it was in their interests to weaken, and ideally eliminate, their chief enemy: Arab nationalism. In his official biography of David Ben Gurion, Michael Bar-Zohar reports the Israeli prime minister's comments in 1956, in the immediate build-up to the Suez War. As Ben Gurion met with French officials to discuss Israel's invasion of the Sinai peninsula that was being proposed by the British, he spelt out an ambitious plan that he hoped might win backing from his French hosts. 'Before all else, naturally, the elimination of [Egyptian leader] Nasser.' After that, reported Bar-Zohar, Ben Gurion argued for 'the partition of Jordan, with the West Bank going to Israel and the East Bank to Iraq. Lebanon's boundaries would also be moved, with part going to Syria, and another part, up to the Litani River, to Israel; the remaining territory would become a Christian state.'[88] One witness to Ben Gurion's outburst, Abba Eban, Israel's ambassador to the United Nations, called the plan 'grotesquely eccentric',[89] while the Prime Minister himself admitted it was 'fantastic'. Nonetheless, according to Israeli historian Avi Shlaim, a series of entries on the subject in Ben Gurion's diaries suggest he was in 'deadly earnest'. In Shlaim's words, his thinking

was that a Christian Lebanon would of its own accord make peace with Israel; that Iraq would be allowed to take over the East Bank of the Jordan on condition that it made peace with Israel; and that a defeated, humiliated and occupied Egypt would be compelled to make peace on Israel's terms.[90]

Saleh Abdel Jawwad, a professor of politics at Bir Zeit University in the West Bank and one of the few Palestinian scholars of Zionism, noted that Ben Gurion had developed two complementary theories about how to undermine Arab nationalism: the 'Theory of Allying with the Periphery' required that the Jewish state make alliances with other states opposed to Arab nationalism, both in the West and East, in order to create a bloody struggle of 'us versus them', familiar later as the clash of civilisations; while the 'Theory of Encirclement' required that the Jewish state establish a ring of adversaries around the Arab nations by building strategic relationships with Turkey, African nations such as Ethiopia, Iran (before the 1979 revolution) and India. 'It is against this backdrop that Israel has supported secessionist movements in Sudan, Iraq, Egypt and Lebanon and any secessionist movements in the Arab world which Israel considers an enemy',[91] wrote Abdel Jawwad.

Michael Bar-Zohar recounted Ben Gurion's determined attempts to persuade the US of the benefits of establishing a clandestine 'Periphery Alliance' between Israel, Iran, Turkey and Ethiopia in the late 1950s, finally winning backing from President Dwight Eisenhower in 1958 as independence movements threatened or overthrew the Western-backed monarchies in Iraq and Jordan.

> In the most profound secrecy, a specter-like organization was born, and extended until it formed a ring around the Arab Middle East. The terms 'clandestine' and 'specter' are no exaggeration. In the course of several years, Israel conducted intensive activity throughout the Middle East under the mantle of almost total secrecy. Using different disguises, traveling under false names, by indirect routes, Ben-Gurion's emissaries repeatedly flew off into the night for the capitals of Israel's new allies.[92]

Ben Gurion, observed Bar-Zohar, realised that this alliance could put Israel at the heart of American plans for the Middle East. Israel 'was no longer a small, isolated country, but the leader and connecting link of a group of states ... whose population exceeded that of all the Arab states together'.[93]

Regarding both Iraq and Iran, Abdel Jawwad pointed out a long history of shadowy involvement by the Mossad, dating back decades. The pre-state Jewish authorities in Palestine, for example, began developing links with the Kurds in Iraq from the 1920s.

> By the end of the 1950s and the early 1960s, Israel became the primary source of arms and military training for the Kurds in their fight against

the Iraqi central government. While full details have yet to be revealed, thousands of Mossad agents and Israeli military personnel were located throughout northern Iraq under different covers (military advisors, agricultural experts, trainers, and doctors).

This practice was observed again after the US-led invasion of Iraq when reports by Seymour Hersh and others pointed out the presence of Israeli agents in Kurdish areas.[94]

Similarly, Mossad's deep involvement in Iran could be traced back to the 1950s:[95]

The beginning of Israel's relationship with the Shah was formed when the Mossad, acting in accord with British (MI6) and American (CIA) intelligence, worked to bring about the collapse of the democratically elected Iranian leader [Mohammed] Mossadeq in 1953 ... The relationship forged with the Shah enabled Iran to be the primary importer of Israeli products until the rise of [Ayatollah] Khomeni. Israel also played a role in training the SAVAK, the infamous and brutal intelligence service which protected the Shah.

In fact, the relationship continued even after the Islamic Revolution, according to an interview in the *Boston Globe* in 1982 with Moshe Arens, at the time when he was Israeli ambassador to the US but would soon be promoted to Israeli Defence Minister. Arens said Israel had been selling arms to the new Iranian regime, with US approval, 'to see if we could not find some areas of contact with the Iranian military, to bring down the Khomeini regime'.[96]

'War as an end in and of itself, is an ever-present Israeli objective', concluded Abdel Jawwad. 'Sequential wars with the Arab world have given Israel opportunities to exhaust the Arab world, as well as tipping the demographic and political situation against Palestinians. Even regional wars which Israel has not participated in have benefited Israel and weakened the Palestinian national movement.' Israel's 1948 and 1967 wars, for example, led to hundreds of thousands of Palestinians being displaced from their homeland, while the 1982 invasion of Lebanon expelled a further 200,000 Palestinians from close by Israel's northern border. The war between Iraq and Iran through the 1980s 'disempowered the Palestinian cause: the Arab world was split into two camps,

Arab resources were squandered, oil income was depleted, and Arab attention was taken away from the Palestinian question'. And the 1991 Gulf War left the Palestinians friendless after their leaders sided with Saddam Hussein and 'resulted in the expulsion of the Palestinian community from Kuwait, which formed one of the primary arteries of Palestinian income and power in the occupied territories'.

Strangely, given his later view that Israel was simply carrying out the will of Washington in the Middle East, Noam Chomsky had expressed similar suspicions about Israeli goals in the early 1980s. He argued then that Israel was desperately 'trying to stir up U.S. confrontation with Iran' after the 1979 revolution, recognising Tehran to be 'the most serious military threat that [Israel] faces'. Chomsky thought it 'unlikely' that the US would bow to Israeli demands because it was 'playing a somewhat different game in its relations to Iran'; it preferred 'seeking a long-term accommodation with "moderate" (that is, pro-U.S.) elements in Iran and a return to something like the arrangements that prevailed under the Shah'.[97] Chomsky appeared to agree with an Israeli analyst, Yoram Peri, a former adviser to Yitzhak Rabin, who feared that the US and Israel were potentially on a collision course over their preferred policies in the Middle East. In Chomsky's words:

> The reason is that the U.S. is basically a status quo power itself, opposed to destabilization of the sort to which Israel is increasingly committed. The new strategic conception is based on an illusion of power, and may lead to a willingness, already apparent in some of the rhetoric heard in Israel, to undertake military adventures even without U.S. support.[98]

According to Chomsky, the divergence of interests between the US and Israel in the early 1980s could be attributed to the fact that the Israeli military favoured policies to 'Ottomanize' the Middle East: that is, recreate the state of affairs that existed before the arrival of the European colonialists, with Israel replacing Turkey as the powerful centre of an empire in which 'much of the region [is] fragmented into ethnic-religious communities, preferably mutually hostile'. Given this worldview, Chomsky observed: 'It is only natural to expect that Israel will seek to destabilize the surrounding states.'[99] Chomsky cited several analysts in Israel, including Oded Yinon, who were thinking along these lines in the 1980s, and noted that Yinon's position was 'quite close to mainstream thinking'. The Israeli scholar Boaz Evron believed that underpinning all these conceptions of Israel as an empire, even Sharon's, was a fervour for the 'Ottomanization' of the Middle East. Under the Ottoman empire, noted Evron, a system known as the *millet* allowed each ethnic-religious group its own internal administration overseen by the Turkish rulers. 'Sharon is now offering to set up a "millet" of the same religious-ethnic kind, but one that is armed and tyrannising its own oppressed population.' The point of resurrecting the *millet* system was to empower weaker ethnic-religious groups, like the Christian Maronites in Lebanon, the Kurds and the Druze, and encourage them to enter into an alliance with the Jews of Israel 'against the supremacy of Sunni Muslim Arabism'.[100]

Yinon's plan, like Sharon's, was dated, its concerns specific to the time. He too was concerned with the threat posed by the Soviet Union, though those Cold War fears could easily be translated in the 1990s – as they were by the neocons – to the Islamic world. But more importantly, Yinon regarded the dissolution of Middle Eastern states as the key to Israel expelling the Palestinians both from inside Israel and from the occupied territories so that the remaining parts of historic Palestine could be annexed to Israel. His interest in taking back Sinai from Egypt can be explained, according to Hassan Nafaa, in terms of creating a space outside the borders of Greater Israel for the Palestinians. Yinon never makes this point explicitly, but as Nafaa points out: 'Sinai is an area that could be used to absorb the population growth among the Palestinians of Gaza, or even to offer a lasting solution to the [Palestinian] refugees' problem.'[101] Yinon, however, is more open about wanting the destruction of the Jordanian regime to create new possibilities for the relocation of Palestinians from the West Bank.

> Israel's policy in war or in peace should be to bring about the elimination of Jordan and its present regime and transfer it to the Palestinian majority.

Replacing the regime to the east of the Jordan River [Jordan] will also eliminate the problem of the Jordan River territories [the West Bank], which are densely populated by Arabs [Palestinians]; emigration from the territories and a demographic and economic freeze in these areas are the guarantees of the change already taking place on both sides of the river. We must be active to stimulate this change rapidly.[102]

Remaking the Middle East by dissolving its main Arab and Muslim states would ensure not only Israel's domination of the region but Israel's unchallenged right to continue the creeping process of ethnic cleansing of the occupied Palestinian territories.

4

REMAKING THE MIDDLE EAST

There seems little doubt that by the early 1990s, after the fall of the Soviet empire, Israel's military was conceiving of its role in regional terms and was actively persuading Washington of its usefulness in securing US interests in the Middle East. But which of these two regional conceptions was dominant inside the army: Sharon's of Israel as a bully enforcing order; or Yinon's of Israel as the guarantor of US and Israeli dominance by sowing disorder and instability? There are, of course, no public documents revealing which vision the Israeli army preferred. But we can reach some persuasive conclusions by examining recent trends in Israel's foreign policy and the military's assessment of its strategic place in the new world order after 9/11.

Before the collapse of the Soviet empire, Israel had been sitting on one of the key fault lines in the bipolar world of US-Soviet hostilities. Faced with what was seen as a monolithic enemy in the shape of the Soviet empire, the US and Israel had easily discernible interests: cajoling, intimidating and, if necessary, attacking the region's Arab and Muslim leaders to keep as many of them as possible out of the sphere of Soviet influence and thereby ensure the West's continuing control of oil. The terms of this 'Great Game' were clear to all. But in the post-Soviet world, nation states and their leaders became far less significant guarantors of stability. The US and Israel confronted two new kinds of Middle Eastern political and paramilitary actors (the distinction was blurred). The first were the Sunni jihadis, popularly referred to as al-Qaeda, who belonged to loose networks of militants that moved within and between states. These groups had little or no loyalty to the colonial constructs that were the Middle East's nations, and their mobility and fluidity made them almost impossible to fight or intimidate in traditional ways.[1] The second were groups such as the Taliban in Afghanistan and Hizbullah in Lebanon that, while participating in the political rituals of their own states, were not dependent on its institutions or infrastructure for their existence. They made serious challenges for political power while at the same time creating parallel organisations, including militias, that could not be easily intimidated or bullied either by the state itself or by outside forces. The US invasion of Afghanistan in 2001, for example, destroyed the Taliban's grip on the government but did little to destroy its ability to resist the US occupation or undermine the US puppet government. Similarly Israel's attack on Lebanon in summer 2006 crushed the country's infrastructure but left Hizbullah relatively unscathed.

In this new, unpredictable world, Sharon's vision of Israel as a guarantor of stability made little sense. What was the point of the US and Israel bullying or defeating states and their armies when the real enemy existed at the sub-state level? In contrast, Yinon's argument that Israel should encourage discord and feuding within states – destabilising them and encouraging them to break up into smaller units – was more compelling. Tribal and sectarian groups could be turned once again into rivals, competing for limited resources and too busy fighting each other to mount effective challenges to Israeli or US power. Also, Israeli alliances with non-Arab and non-Muslim groups such as Christians, Kurds and the Druze could be cultivated without the limitations imposed on joint activity by existing state structures. In this scenario, the US and Israel could manipulate groups by awarding favours – arms, training, oil remittances – to those who were prepared to cooperate while conversely weakening those who resisted. Yinon's argument was an early version of Cheney's case for 'permanent war'.[2]

There was a single threat to this vision of the region: the development of nuclear weapons by a Middle Eastern state other than Israel. Such a state would have the deterrence necessary to prevent an attack by the US or Israel designed to break it up. And furthermore, it would also have the ability to compete with Israel in influencing and manipulating sub-state actors such as Hizbullah and the Taliban by awarding its own favours. It could even, in the worst-case scenario, provide such groups with nuclear weapons that might be used to threaten Israel or the US. Given this context, it becomes possible to understand how, following the collapse of the Soviet empire, an Israeli military plan to spread 'organised chaos' across the Middle East, to secure its own regional dominance and US control of oil, may have been so persuasive to the neocons in Washington.

NEOCON MOTIVES IN BACKING ISRAEL'S VISION

As we saw in Chapter 1, the neocons effectively hijacked the State Department's plan to remove Saddam Hussein in Iraq and replace him with a more reliable strongman. Why did they do it? According to the American journalist Greg Palast, one of the key reasons for remaking Iraq, in the neocons' view, had been offered by Ariel Cohen, of the Heritage Foundation in Washington DC. He suggested dividing up Iraq's oilfields and selling them off to dozens of private operators, each of whom would try to maximise production against rivals. With millions of additional barrels produced a day, the Saudi-dominated oil cartel OPEC would be smashed and, as a consequence, Saudi Arabia brought to its knees. A weakened Saudi regime would no longer be able to finance radical Islamic groups, including resistance movements like Hamas in the occupied Palestinian territories. Cohen's plan was also likely to result in the dissolution more generally of the Middle East's oil-producing states, including Iraq and Iran, as the cartel and its financial power crumbled. Michael Ledeen, a former Pentagon official and an ideologue of the American Enterprise Institute, had given voice to this longer-term neocon ambition in 2002, before the invasion of Iraq:

First and foremost, we must bring down the terror regimes, beginning with the Big Three: Iran, Iraq, and Syria. And then we have to come to grips with Saudi Arabia ... Stability is an unworthy American mission, and a misleading concept to boot. We do not want stability in Iran, Iraq, Syria, Lebanon, and even Saudi Arabia; we want things to change. The real issue is not whether, but how to destabilize.[3]

A former Israeli Knesset member and long-time peace activist, Uri Avnery, a long way from Washington, was aware many months before the invasion of Iraq of similar goals being discussed in Israel. He wrote that once the US was occupying Iraq it would be in a position to manipulate oil prices to 'bring the kingdom [Saudi Arabia] to the brink of bankruptcy ... The new situation would finally break OPEC. Washington will decide the price of oil and how it is distributed.'[4] Certainly, the antipathy of the Israeli right to a strong Saudi Arabia, and the stability it craves as the basis for ensuring the profitable flow of oil westwards, was regularly on display in the Israeli media. In 2007 Caroline Glick, the deputy managing editor of the *Jerusalem Post*, a favourite destination for neocon commentaries, wrote disparagingly in her regular column of the Washington establishment's misconceptions about the region. She identified as at particular fault James Baker, like President Bush a close friend of the oil industry and the Saudi royals, as well as one of the heads of the Iraq Study Group that had urged an American withdrawal from Iraq. In addition, Glick noted Israel's vehement objections to the planned US sale of satellite-guided 'smart bombs' to Saudi Arabia because of fears that the regime might fall and such weapons end up in the hands of Islamic extremists. This criticism of the Saudis did not go far enough, according to Glick. 'The Saudis aren't simply vulnerable. They are culpable. In addition to being the creators of al-Qaida and Hamas's largest financial backers, the Saudis themselves directly threaten Israel.' How exactly? Because their allies in Washington like Baker had been promoting a 'foreign policy paradigm' based 'on the belief that it is possible and desirable to reach a stable balance of power in the Middle East'.[5]

Today, the notion that stability is a realistic aim is even more far-fetched. Specifically, the willingness of Muslim secularists to form strategic relations with jihadists and the willingness of Shi'ites to form strategic partnerships with Sunnis was unimaginable 20 years ago. Aside from that, the specter of a nuclear-armed Iran throws a monkey wrench into any thought of regional stability. A look around the region shows just how absurd Baker's notions truly are.

For the neocons, permanent war between the opposed Judeo-Christian and Muslim worlds was an inevitable state of affairs. Baker and the Saudis' attempts to halt the neocon plan to crush the forces of evil was simple appeasement, a betrayal that would ultimately lead to the triumph of the wrong side in the clash of civilisations. Glick, in an indication of the fears gripping the wider neocon community in summer 2007 that their moment may have passed, castigated the 'appeasers' in the White House.

> Sooner or later the US will pay a price for the Bush administration's decision to embrace the delusion of stability as its strategic goal. With jihadist forces growing stronger around the globe, if the Americans leave Iraq without victory, there is no doubt that Iraq (and Iran and Syria) will come to them. But whatever the consequences of America's behavior for America, the price that Israel will pay for embracing Baker's myths of stability will be unspeakable.[6]

As Glick sensed, the neocon plan for spreading chaos through the Middle East was facing concerted opposition from parts of the Washington establishment. As Greg Palast observes, the US oil industry is deeply opposed to the break-up of OPEC because of the agreements it has signed with OPEC countries that guarantee it a slice of the profits from rises in the price of crude. Like Saudi Arabia, it also believes that stability, rather than chaos, is best for business in the Middle East. Scenting belatedly the thrust of the neocon plan, the oil industry moved rapidly to block Cohen's hard-line version of privatisation, while ensuring that it would still win the largest slice of the profits from the new arrangement in Iraq.

Nonetheless, Big Oil has every reason to fear that Iran may benefit from the chaos already unfolding in Iraq and seek to increase its influence there through the Iraqi Shia majority. Shia control of oil in both Iran and Iraq would produce an oil titan that could wrench OPEC from Saudi dominance – inadvertently realising the neocon vision – but only at the cost of replacing Sunni control of oil with Shia control. The power struggle in Washington that emerged in late 2006 reflected not only a partial loss of influence among the neocons but also an uncertainty about how to deal with the fallout from the long-term US occupation of Iraq. The Democrats, in refusing to oppose outright the mess created by the Bush Administration in Iraq and the disaster looming over Iran, appeared to be waiting to reassert more traditional policies: to install a loyal strongman and possibly to withdraw to permanent military bases in the desert from which the flow of Iraq's oil could be controlled. With the growing strength of the insurgency and the accelerating sectarian war, however, it was uncertain whether the US still had the power to place its own man in charge in Baghdad, one who could secure oil for the US and counter Iranian influence.

But while it is still unclear whether the Bush Administration will pursue the neocon vision of the Middle East to its logical conclusion, the neocons had succeeded in setting in motion a process of destabilisation that was providing a taste of what they intended and what Israel wants for the region.

The Mearsheimer-Walt thesis suggests that, as long as Israel was the prime beneficiary of the attacks on Middle Eastern states, that was enough reason for the pro-Israel lobby – including, by implication at least, the neocons – to give their blessing. On this view, either the lobby was pressing for Israel's interests over US interests, or it believed that whatever was good for Israel was by definition good for the US too. That view, I believe, is too simplistic. Although AIPAC and the pro-Israel lobby have been primarily promoting Israel's interests, the neocons are far from in thrall to them, even if they are influenced by their lobbying and deeply sympathetic to their causes. Undoubtedly AIPAC worked strenuously to influence the neocons, and it is possible that individual neocons may have been working to advance Israel's interests, even if they conflicted with US interests, but that was not true for the movement as a whole. Rather, there were good reasons, as we have seen, why the neocons might have been persuaded that not only attacking Middle Eastern states but also bringing about their collapse would ultimately benefit the US as well as Israel. These motives are worth briefly listing.[7]

The first, as mentioned, was that, with the US taking control of key oil states like Iraq and Iran, production could be increased and the global markets flooded with cheap oil. For Israel, the policy had obvious benefits: rival Arab states would be economically and militarily crippled, as would the Palestinians in the occupied territories, who have traditionally relied on donations from the Gulf countries and remittances from Palestinians working in the oil states. The neocons may have concluded that US interests would be served in a similar fashion. Maxim Ghilan, a veteran Israeli peace activist, argued in April 2002, a year before the attack on Iraq, that the Israeli-neocon plan for remaking the Middle East was about undermining the oil states. He observed that the neocons had been persuaded that the Gulf nations, particularly Saudi Arabia and Kuwait, had become potential threats to the US. The fear was that their accumulating wealth in American banks and various financial institutions could be used as a tool to influence American politics,[8] an influence that might counter Israel's own lobbyists. Destroying Iraq and Iran, and taking direct control of their oil, was one way to weaken the Gulf states. Ghilan's view was that the real clash of civilisations, between the Judeo-Christian and Islamic worlds, was being waged in the world of international finance.

·From his vantage point in Washington in the months leading up to the attack on Iraq, Anatol Lieven suggested a possible related neocon goal.

> The planned war against Iraq is not after all intended only to remove Saddam Hussein, but to destroy the structure of the Sunni-dominated Arab nationalist Iraqi state as it has existed since that country's inception. The 'democracy' which replaces it will presumably resemble that of Afghanistan – a ramshackle coalition of ethnic groups and warlords, utterly dependent on US military power and utterly subservient to US (and Israeli) wishes ... Similarly, if after Saddam's regime is destroyed, Saudi Arabia fails to bow to US wishes and is attacked in its turn, then – to judge by the thoughts circulating in Washington think-tanks – the goal would be not just to remove

the Saudi regime and eliminate Wahabism as a state ideology: it would be to destroy and partition the Saudi state. The Gulf oilfields would be put under US military occupation, and the region run by some client emir; Mecca and the Hejaz might well be returned to the Hashemite dynasty of Jordan, its rulers before the conquest by Ibn Saud in 1924; or, to put it differently, the British imperial programme of 1919 would be resurrected.

In addition, according to Lieven, the neocons may have had a yet grander goal. 'It's worth bearing in mind that the dominant groups in this Administration have now openly abandoned the underlying strategy and philosophy of the Clinton Administration, which was to integrate the other major states of the world in a rule-based liberal capitalist order, thereby reducing the threat of rivalry between them.' Instead, argued Lieven, the true target of these Middle East adventures was China:

What radical US nationalists have in mind is either to 'contain' China by overwhelming military force and the creation of a ring of American allies; or, in the case of the real radicals, to destroy the Chinese Communist state as the Soviet Union was destroyed. As with the Soviet Union, this would presumably involve breaking up China by 'liberating' Tibet and other areas, and under the guise of 'democracy', crippling the central Chinese Administration and its capacity to develop either its economy or its Army.

Lieven concluded pessimistically: 'Given America's overwhelming superiority, it might well work for decades until a mixture of terrorism and the unbearable social, political and environmental costs of US economic domination put paid to the present order of the world.'[9]

In fact, Lieven's implication that the Bush Administration had finished with the business of crushing Russia may have been misplaced. Certainly Vladimir Putin, the president of Russia, did not think so. In a speech ignored by the Western media in June 2007, he noted the rapidly deteriorating state of US–Russian relations since 9/11. The Bush Administration had implemented an aggressive strategy of surrounding Russia with military bases, it had recruited former Soviet states to Nato and then installed missiles on Russia's borders, it had toppled allied regimes in Central

Asia and built permanent military bases there, and it had incited political upheaval in Moscow through US-backed 'pro-democracy' groups in Serbia, Ukraine and Georgia. One observer pointed out: 'These openly hostile actions have convinced many Russian hard-liners that the administration is going forward with the neocon plan for "regime change" in Moscow and fragmentation of the Russian Federation. Putin's testimony suggests that the hard-liners are probably right.'[10]

Although Lieven did not mention it, China has a strong stake in the security of the Middle East, taking almost half its oil imports from the region.[11] Direct American control of the Middle East's oilfields would remove any threat of China gaining an edge over the US in its relations with the region's oil producers. By occupying the Middle East's oilfields, the US would have an effective stranglehold on the main artery to the Chinese economy. The alternative for the US was set out by Noam Chomsky. Were Iraq to be allowed to set up an independent government, controlled by the Shia, it would forge alliances with the Shia leadership in Iran and with the Shia minority in neighbouring Saudi Arabia, who live in the country's main oil-producing areas.

> The outcome could be a loose Shia alliance comprising Iraq, Iran and the major oil regions of Saudi Arabia, independent of Washington and controlling large portions of the world's oil reserves. It's not unlikely that an independent bloc of this kind might follow Iran's lead in developing major energy projects jointly with China and India. Iran may give up on Western Europe, assuming that it will be unwilling to act independently of the United States. China, however, can't be intimidated. That's why the United States is so frightened by China. China is already establishing relations with Iran – and even with Saudi Arabia, both military and economic. There is an Asian energy security grid, based on China and Russia, but probably bringing in India, Korea and others. If Iran moves in that direction, it can become the lynchpin of that power grid.[12]

THE OCCUPIED TERRITORIES AS A LABORATORY

Yinon's argument, rather than being a radical departure from Israeli military thinking, built on two well-established principles.

First, since the 1967 war the idea of expelling the Palestinians to Jordan – the 'Jordan is Palestine' option – had been advocated at various times by much of the Israeli leadership, including Ariel Sharon. The debate had been about how best to achieve such an outcome, not whether it was desirable. Second, for some time there had been widely held discussions in the military command about breaking up the Arab countries into feuding mini-states. In the early 1980s Ze'ev Schiff, the military correspondent for *Ha'aretz* and the best informed commentator on the army's thinking, wrote that Israel's 'best' interests would be served by 'the dissolution of Iraq into a Shi'ite state, a Sunni state and the separation of the Kurdish part'.[13]

Israel had the chance to put into practice this theory of internal dissolution of states – and sell it to influential sympathisers, including the neocons, in the United States – by testing the principles on a small scale inside the occupied territories. The West Bank and Gaza were the perfect laboratories for these ideas, just as they also proved a useful place to test urban warfare tactics, new weapons technology and crowd control techniques,[14] the lessons of which would later be used by US forces in fighting Iraq's insurgents. In fact, as investigative journalist Naomi Klein has pointed out, Israeli business was booming on the back of the chaos unfolding across the Middle East, with Israel exporting to America the military technology it developed in, and the expertise it acquired from, controlling Palestinians in the occupied territories.

> Many of the country's most successful entrepreneurs are using Israel's status as a fortressed state, surrounded by furious enemies, as a kind of 24-hour-a-day showroom, a living example of how to enjoy relative safety amid constant war. And the reason Israel is now enjoying supergrowth is that those companies are busily exporting that model to the world.[15]

In a period of seven years Israel had more than quadrupled its sales of 'security products' to the US, and by 2006 its defence exports had reached $3.4 billion, making Israel the fourth biggest arms dealer in the world, overtaking Britain. The US Department of Homeland Security was one of Israel's most reliable markets, buying hi-tech fences, unmanned drones, biometric IDs, video and audio surveillance gear, air passenger profiling and prisoner interrogation systems.[16]

From the lessons learnt in the laboratories of Gaza and the West Bank, Israel believed it could break with the policies developed by the European colonial powers in the Middle East. They had installed or propped up a loyal strongman, while keeping him weak enough to rely on the support of his Western patron. This could be done by ensuring ethnic or sectarian rivalries beset his area of authority. On these grounds, Britain and France favoured the introduction of the 'nation state' in the region as a model of sovereignty because it created territorial units in which these dramas could be constructed and encouraged. Establishing states in which hostile ethnic and sectarian groups were included under one legal authority, often against their will, was a recipe for feuding that required the colonial master's continuing involvement and intervention to help maintain order. In other words, Britain and France extended the 'civilising benefits' of the nation state to the Middle East as a cover for their own economic interests, just as decades later the US would try to spread 'democracy' to the region as a cover for its own economic and imperial interests.

Israel, however, had scant interest in applying that 'strongman' model to the occupied territories, where ethnic and sectarian differences between the Palestinians were far weaker, and had been further diminished by the spurt of Palestinian nationalism that was the inevitable response to Israel's own aggressive and land-hungry Jewish nationalism. Installing a Palestinian dictator would only have encouraged even greater Palestinian nationalism and set up a potential challenger to Israeli rule, as well as being an implicit admission that Israel had established itself on the Palestinian homeland. Also, Israel was not running its colonial project at arm's length as Britain and France had mainly done. It was settling the occupied territories with its own citizens, its frontiers slowly but inexorably expanding on to more Palestinian land to incorporate them. To achieve this end, Israel preferred that the Palestinians remain weak and divided so that they would be in no position to resist the occupation, and would be vulnerable to Israel's schemes, under the banner of security, of removing sections of the Palestinian population from the newly settled areas. Much later, the Israeli sociologist Baruch Kimmerling coined a term for this policy: 'politicide'.

Therefore the first task following the 1967 war, when Israel captured the West Bank and Gaza, was to expel or imprison what was left of the Palestinian national leadership that had been dispersed into these territories by the war in Palestine two decades earlier. In the wake of the 1967 war, Israel prevented the emergence of new leaders in the West Bank and Gaza. Instead it first tried 'managing' the local population by co-opting its leaders, along family and communal lines, just as it had already done more successfully among the remnants of the Palestinian population inside Israel after the 1948 war.[17] By 1981 Sharon had refined the system into what was known as the Village Leagues, local anti-PLO militias that were nurtured by Israel and supposed to represent their regions. The system had to be aborted, however, after the Palestinians rebelled against their collaborating leaders.[18]

Israel experimented with other approaches, the most important of which was encouraging the emergence in the occupied territories of the Muslim Brotherhood, an offshoot of the Islamic movement for social and moral reform born in Egypt in the late 1920s. The Brotherhood had established branches in both Gaza and the West Bank after 1948, when the territories fell respectively under Egyptian and Jordanian rule. In 1973, six years after the occupation began, Israel licensed the Brotherhood and allowed it to set up a network of charities and welfare societies, funded by the Gulf states. Israel was hopeful that the Muslim Brotherhood would dissipate Palestinian nationalism and support for the PLO among the local population and encourage a social and moral conservatism that would make the Palestinians more 'moderate'. Israel's thinking at that time was explained by Kimmerling: 'Israelis administering the occupied territories and acting on the advice of orientalist experts supported traditional Islamic elements because they were considered more easily managed and submissive to the Israelis than the PLO nationalists.'[19] In an early example of 'blowback', however, the local Brotherhood under the leadership of Sheikh Ahmed Yassin quickly metamorphosed into Hamas when the first intifada erupted in late 1987, joining the resistance to the occupation alongside Fatah.

With this policy failing too, and faced with stiff pressure from a White House under the more liberal leadership of Bill Clinton, Israel's doves relented for the first time and risked creating a strongman in the occupied territories in the shape of Yasser Arafat. Allowed back to the occupied territories to run the new Palestinian Authority under the Oslo process, Arafat's role was clear: he was supposed to enforce Israel's security in the West Bank and Gaza, just as dozens of other Arab rulers had done before him in their own territories on behalf of Western colonial powers.

What is often overlooked is that many in the Israeli security establishment, if not most, deeply opposed the Oslo accords. Sharon was the most high-profile opponent, but he had backing from the then Chief of Staff, Ehud Barak, who would become the next Labor leader and Sharon's political rival. Barak's successors, Shaul Mofaz and Moshe Ya'alon, also publicly opposed Oslo. That meant that following Yitzhak Rabin's assassination in late 1995, the most significant figures in Israel's political and security establishments, apart from Shimon Peres, were agreed that Oslo had been a dangerous mistake, giving Arafat an international platform from which he could encourage Palestinian nationalism and seek to undermine Israel, both militarily and demographically.[20] It is not surprising, therefore, that the spirit of the Oslo accords – not peace, but developing Arafat as Israel's security contractor – quickly died after Rabin's assassination. Instead the Palestinian president found himself increasingly isolated, and spent much of the second intifada holed up as a prisoner in his compound in Ramallah, while Israel began yet another approach for dissolving Palestinian nationalism: physically carving up the West Bank and Gaza into a series of cantons or ghettoes, from which organised resistance would be impossible.[21] That project, which started with checkpoints and curfews, culminated in the severance of all physical connection between the West Bank and Gaza following the 2005 disengagement and in the building of a 700km wall that snaked through the West Bank. A map produced by the United Nations Office for the Coordination of Humanitarian Affairs in spring 2007 showed in detail the 'fragmentation' of the West Bank into a series of ghettoes, each sealed off from the next by a combination of wall building, land confiscations, settlements, bypass roads and checkpoints.[22]

After Arafat's mysterious death in late 2004,[23] Israel encouraged a new compliant leader, Mahmoud Abbas, to head the Palestinian Authority, ensuring that he was weak and ineffective. Palestinians, aware of the larger processes shaping their lives, voted Abbas' Fatah party out of government in the early 2006 general elections and installed Hamas, which had until then refused to compromise with Israel. Hamas had grown increasingly strong militarily and in terms of its popularity during the latter stages of Oslo when Israeli bad faith in the peace process was becoming more apparent, and during the second intifada when it was seen to be leading resistance to the occupation. Israel, therefore, began reversing its policy of the 1980s: first, it sought to weaken Hamas by publicly holding it accountable for the international sanctions that were starving the Palestinian population of money and food; and second, it began slowly to build up Fatah's forces so that Hamas could be challenged in a power struggle. Israel also arrested Hamas legislators in the West Bank, including some well-known moderates. In late 2006, the occupied territories finally sank into feuding and fighting of a kind that seemed to have been Israel's goal for several decades. The danger was briefly averted in early 2007 when the Arab states intervened to help the rival factions create a national unity government. Israel and the US made little effort to conceal their hostility to this new arrangement, seeking to disrupt it early on by bolstering Abbas loyalists in Gaza with training and weapons in an attempt to undermine Hamas.[24] A leaked report from Alvaro de Soto, the retiring UN envoy for the Middle East peace process, noted the American response as Hamas and Fatah prepared to meet in Mecca over forging a national unity government:

> The US clearly pushed for a confrontation between Fatah and Hamas, so much so that, a week before Mecca, the US envoy [David Welch] declared twice in an envoys meeting in Washington how much 'I like this violence',

referring to the near-civil war that was erupting in Gaza in which civilians were being regularly killed and injured because 'it means that other Palestinians are resisting Hamas'.[25]

The US was keen to bolster Abbas, or his possible successor Mohammed Dahlan, by training and arming the Presidential Guard,[26] though Israel was reported to have blocked some shipments, possibly fearful that they might accidentally create another Arafat. In June 2007, Hamas finally launched an all-out confrontation in Gaza against elements within Fatah it accused of plotting, with outside help, to overthrow the Hamas-led Palestinian Authority.[27] Jonathan Steele, writing in the *Guardian*, noted that Hamas turned on Dahlan loyalists when they realised that the Fatah group was plotting with the US to repeat Israel's round-up of Hamas legislators – this time in Gaza. The man behind the plan was said to be Elliott Abrams, Bush's Deputy National Security Adviser and one of the more durable neocons in the Administration.[28] Abrams could draw on previous experience. During the Reagan years, he had been one of the key players in the Iran-Contra Affair, when the US secretly funnelled weapons to the Contras to overthrow the elected, and left-wing, Nicaraguan government.

Abbas responded to the Hamas triumph in Gaza by creating a rival government in the West Bank. The US and Israel appeared to agree this division offered a further opportunity to entrench the de facto separation between Gaza and the West Bank – or, as the Israeli Foreign Minister, Tzipi Livini, observed: 'We should take advantage of this split to the end. It differentiates between the moderates and the extremists.'[29] The US approved lifting the economic blockade of Abbas' government in the West Bank, while Israel declared that Hamas-controlled Gaza would be treated as a 'terror entity'.[30] One of the most influential Israeli commentators, Akiva Eldar, noted that Ariel Sharon had long dreamt of a 'Hamastan' in Gaza: 'In his house, they called it a bantustan, after the South African protectorates [for the black population] designed to perpetuate apartheid.' Eldar noted that Massimo D'Alema, a few years before he was elected Italy's prime minister, had recalled a meeting at which Sharon confided that the bantustan model was the right one for the Palestinians. Eldar added that the project for cantonising the Palestinians was well advanced:

> Alongside the severance of Gaza from the West Bank, a policy now called 'isolation,' the Sharon-Peres government and the Olmert-Peres government that succeeded it carried out the bantustan program in the West Bank. The Jordan Valley was separated from the rest of the West Bank; the south was severed from the north; and all three areas were severed from East Jerusalem. The 'two states for two peoples' plan gave way to a 'five states for two peoples' plan: one contiguous state, surrounded by settlement blocs, for Israel, and four isolated enclaves for the Palestinians. This plan was implemented on the ground via the intrusive route of the separation fence, a network of roadblocks deep inside the West Bank, settlement expansion and arbitrary orders by military commanders.[31]

Eldar's assessment accorded with that of the World Bank, which in a report published in May 2007 noted that restrictions on movement imposed by Israel meant that 50 per cent of the West Bank was off limits to the Palestinians.[32]

The lesson Israel's commanders had learnt from their occupation of the West Bank and Gaza, or thought they had learnt, was that the most effective way to weaken Palestinian nationalism and maintain control of the occupied territories was to keep the Palestinians factionalised and fighting. The fact that Israel had achieved these goals in spite of the cohesiveness of Palestinian society doubtless made them confident that the lessons could be applied to the rest of the Middle East with even greater success.

OVER THE PRECIPICE AND INTO CIVIL WAR

One of the more surprising assumptions of liberal Western observers was that the US 'war on terror' – even if it was profoundly wrong-headed – was at least well intentioned. On this view, Washington really was trying to improve the lot of the Middle East, and hoping to spread democracy,[33] even if it was at the same time trying to secure control of the region's oil. Thus, the eminent revisionist Israeli historian, Avi Shlaim, who had long been in academic exile in Britain, commented that the neoconservatives had pushed for the invasion of Iraq because they were interested 'in overthrowing Saddam Hussein and in nothing else'.[34] Ibrahim Warde, a professor of law and diplomacy at Tufts University, Massachusetts, observed in *Le Monde diplomatique* that the neocons had indulged in a 'fantasy':

> The general public, eager for miracle solutions, believed their chain of reasoning: the war would be a piece of cake; US troops would be welcomed as liberators; a liberal and secular democracy would emerge in Iraq; the Iraqi government would sign a peace treaty with Israel; through a domino effect, regime change would sweep the region; free elections would crush extremists; the Arab-Israeli conflict would be resolved.[35]

Similarly, Jonathan Steele writing in the *Guardian* in early 2007 concluded: 'The only certainty is that Bush's strategy of calling for democratisation in the Middle East is over. Washington has had to abandon the neocon dream of turning Iraq into a beacon of secular liberal democracy. It is no longer pressing for reform in other Arab states.'[36]

Reassuring as the idea was that these were the intended consequences of invasion, there was little evidence that the ideological sponsors of the Iraq war – both in Israel and in Washington – ever believed such results would be forthcoming. In fact, as Noam Chomsky has pointed out, it would have been 'incomprehensible stupidity' for them to have promoted meaningful democracy in Iraq. An independent Iraq would almost certainly have tried to make an alliance with Iran, giving the pair effective control over the region's oil, recover its role as leader of the Arab world and, as a result, re-arm to confront the regional enemy, Israel.

> We are therefore being asked to believe that the United States will stand by quietly watching a serious challenge to Israel, its primary regional client, as well as the takeover of the world's major energy bloc free from US control, and the displacement of the Saudi royal family, long allied with the United States in opposing secular Arab nationalism. Those who have jumped

enthusiastically on the 'democratization bandwagon' are suggesting that Washington would politely observe such not unlikely developments.[37]

There are far stronger grounds, as we have seen, for supposing that Israel and the neocons knew from the outset that invading Iraq and overthrowing its dictator would unleash sectarian violence on an unprecedented scale – and that they wanted this outcome. In a policy paper in late 1996, shortly after the publication of *A Clean Break*, the key neocon architects of the occupation of Iraq – David Wurmser, Richard Perle and Douglas Feith – predicted the chaos that would follow an invasion. 'The residual unity of the [Iraqi] nation is an illusion projected by the extreme repression of the state', they advised. After Saddam Hussein's fall, Iraq would 'be ripped apart by the politics of warlords, tribes, clans, sects, and key families. Underneath facades of unity enforced by state repression, [Iraq's] politics is defined primarily by tribalism, sectarianism, and gang/clan-like competition.'[38] Interestingly, nowhere in this early neocon document on Iraq is there mention of WMD or terrorist threats. Instead the authors express the concern that, given Iraq's increasing isolation and weakness following the West's sanctions regime, Iran or Syria might try to take over the country. 'Iraq, a nation of 18 million [*sic*], occupies some of the most strategically important and well-endowed territories of the Middle East ... Thus, whoever inherits Iraq dominates the entire Levant strategically.'

A leading Palestinian intellectual and former Israeli Knesset member, Azmi Bishara, pointed out how implausible it was that democracy could emerge from the dissolution of a state:

Democracy cannot come into effect by manacling the sovereignty of a nation and dismantling a country as is currently taking place in Iraq ... The commonly held impression is that society without government is civil society. The notion has become something of a fad. But it is an illusion and a dangerous one at that. Society without government is a society at war, a society in which everyone is at the throats of everyone else. With the collapse of the state in Iraq the fires from 'society's hell' flared out of control. The dual collapse of the dictatorship of Baghdad and the myth of building democracy on the ruins gave rise to the current Iraqi nightmare.[39]

That impending nightmare was understood by the officials preparing the attack on Baghdad, in both the US and Britain. A report published by the US Senate Intelligence Committee in May 2007 revealed that many of the country's intelligence documents had warned of the chaos that would be unleashed in occupying Baghdad. The committee concluded that two classified documents produced by the National Intelligence Council in January 2003, shortly before the attack on Iraq, suggested an 'American invasion would bring about instability in Iraq that would be exploited by Iran and al-Qaida'. Among the warnings contained in the documents were that:

- Al-Qaeda would use the invasion as an opportunity to increase attacks on Western targets, and that the connections between al-Qaeda and other terror groups would become blurred.
- Domestic groups in Iraq's deeply divided society would become violent and the settling of scores would be common.
- Iraq's neighbours, especially Tehran, would jockey for influence after the invasion. The less Iran felt threatened by US actions, the analysts noted, the more chance that it would agree to cooperate in the post-invasion period.[40]

These assessments accorded with revelations that had already been made by senior intelligence officials. In early 2006 Paul Pillar, a veteran of the CIA who had served as the US intelligence community's chief Middle East analyst, wrote in *Foreign Affairs*:

If the entire body of official intelligence analysis on Iraq had a policy implication, it was to avoid war – or, if war was going to be launched, to prepare for a messy aftermath. What is most remarkable about prewar US intelligence on Iraq is not that it got things wrong and thereby misled policymakers; it is that it played so small a role in one of the most important US policy decisions in recent decades.[41]

That view was backed by a senior British diplomat closely involved with the build-up to war. In written testimony to the 2004 Butler inquiry, Carne Ross, who negotiated several UN Security Council resolutions on Iraq, admitted that British and US officials were well aware that Saddam Hussein had no WMDs and that bringing him down would lead to chaos.

> It was the commonly-held view among the officials dealing with Iraq that any threat had been effectively contained. I remember on several occasions the UK team stating this view in terms during our discussions with the US (who agreed). At the same time, we would frequently argue, when the US raised the subject, that 'regime change' was inadvisable, primarily on the grounds that Iraq would collapse into chaos.[42]

Ross' account confirmed earlier reports, based on leaked Downing Street memos, that the British prime minister Tony Blair had been given forecasts by officials of the 'mess post-war Iraq would become'.[43] British warnings about the destabilising effect of an invasion were also reported in the memoirs of Tyler Drumheller, the CIA's head of clandestine operations in Europe until 2005. He noted that a few days after 9/11 a group of British diplomats and MI6 officers met their US counterparts at the British embassy and advised them off what they feared was the likely American response: an attack on Iraq. 'Aren't you concerned about the potential destabilising effect on Middle Eastern countries?' Drumheller recalled one MI6 officer saying.[44]

One of the reasons Pillar, Ross, the wider intelligence community and the neocons had reached this conclusion was that Iraq was one of the least cohesive states in the Middle East, embracing three distinct and rival communities: the Sunnis, Shia and Kurds. The Kurds, who like the Palestinians had been overlooked by the European colonial powers when they were drawing borders across the Middle East, had long-standing ambitions for independence and statehood. The Shia, the largest population in Iraq, belonged to a dissident branch of Islam that had a history of suffering under the dominant Islamic sect of the Sunnis. Iraq's Arab Shia also had close, if difficult, relations with the neighbouring regime in Iran, which had been run by Persian Shia clerics since the revolution in 1979. The minority Sunnis, meanwhile, dominated the army and had ruled the country through a series of autocratic generals for several decades. As in Syria, the secular Ba'athism of the Iraqi regime[45] – along with the iron hand of a brutal dictator like Saddam Hussein – had been successful in holding the country together and dissipating sectarian tensions. It was for this very reason that Israel had long regarded Iraq, as well as Syria and Iran, to be its prime enemies and had made them the targets of its venom: the Arab nationalism of the first two, and a similar Persian chauvinism in Iran, had proven relatively immune to Israeli intrigues.

Imposing democracy overnight on Iraq, even supposing it were intended or possible, would undoubtedly have been a recipe for feuding and the settling of historic scores. But Washington opted for another course. Rather than instituting 'regime change', which would have required the rapid installation of a new, more compliant dictator to hold Iraq together, Washington engineered 'regime overthrow', styling it as 'democracy'. The power vacuum that followed encouraged growing sectarian rifts as groups jostled for influence. This was no cause for concern, according to a prominent neocon intellectual, Daniel Pipes, writing three years after the invasion.

> The time has come to acknowledge that the coalition's achievement will be limited to destroying tyranny, not sponsoring its replacement. There is nothing ignoble about this limited achievement, which remains a landmark of international sanitation ... The benefits of eliminating Saddam's rule must not be forgotten in the distress of not creating a successful new Iraq. Fixing Iraq is neither the coalition's responsibility nor its burden.

Nonetheless, there were benefits for the West to be derived from the civil war in Iraq, according to Pipes, though he did not mention the most obvious one: oil. First, in an echo of the previously noted comments of the former Israeli military intelligence officer Daniel Leshem in the early 1990s, Pipes believed civil war would invite 'Syrian and Iranian participation, hastening the possibility of an American confrontation with those two states'. And second, 'When Sunni terrorists target Shiites and vice-versa, non-Muslims are less likely to be hurt. Civil war in Iraq, in short, would be a humanitarian tragedy but not a strategic one.'[46] In other words, civil war in Iraq offered the benefit that it might give the US the pretext it needed to expand its 'war on terror' to neighbouring states that could be implicated, while it did not risk large US casualties because in a civil war – as opposed to an insurgency – the natives would concentrate on killing each other.

Managing the mess, and milking the benefits, appeared to the neocon vision. The Sunnis were the most powerful constituency in Iraq, given their decades of running the army and the regime, and they were the backbone of the insurgency that was taking its toll on US forces. Their strength could be counteracted, at least in the short term, if the US occupation allowed effective control of the government to pass to the larger Shia population (with the advantage that this could be sold to outside observers as the first shoots of a democratic revolution). Shia leaders were soon running militias and death squads from several key ministries, stoking the sectarian killing. One commentator noted: 'Pentagon financing of these myriad militias and the active involvement of [the US-installed prime minister of the time, Iyad] Allawi in all these operations suggest that the Pentagon itself is destabilizing the country it is supposed to control.'[47]

A longer term solution, however, was needed and looked like it would be realised by carving up Iraq into three statelets: a Kurdish partition in the north, a Shia one in the south and a Sunni one between them.[48] The partition of Iraq had been advocated by Israeli leaders for decades, and was the post-occupation solution suggested by Ariel Sharon to Bush during their meetings in the lead up to war, according to Danny Ayalon, then the Israeli ambassador to the US.[49] There were also leaks that partition had been an option considered by the Iraq Study Group, which in late 2006 had sought ways to salvage the occupation of Iraq – although its final report in December 2006 insisted on preserving the country's territorial integrity. A source in the group told the London *Times*: 'The Kurds already effectively have their own area. The federalisation of Iraq is going to take place one way or another. The challenge for the Iraqis is how to work that through.'[50] The apparent inevitability of the Kurds breaking away to take charge of their own province explained the regular reports of Israeli agents in Kurdish areas offering advice.[51] By January 2007, one of the Bush Administration's former architects of the Iraq invasion, John Bolton, observed that there were no strategic benefits to the US in keeping Iraq united. 'The United States has no strategic interest in the fact that there's one Iraq, or three Iraqs', he told a French newspaper. 'We have a strategic interest in the fact of ensuring that what emerges is not a state in complete collapse, which could become a refuge for terrorists or a terrorist state.'[52] By summer 2007 the Brookings Institution's influential Saban Center, which has close ties to the Israeli security establishment, had produced an analysis paper advocating what it called the 'soft partition' of Iraq: the international community would assist Iraqi communities in separating from each other. 'Each would assume primary responsibility for its own security and governance, as Iraqi Kurdistan already does ... soft partition in many ways simply responds to current realities on the ground.'[53]

The much-delayed Oil Law also seemed to be the key to financing and managing the country's partition. Washington insisted that all regions would receive their fair share of oil revenues (after a large slice of the profits had been taken by private Western corporations), but, as we have already seen, the formula for deciding how to apportion the revenues had yet to be decided. More likely the Bush Administration was intending to use the country's oil wealth to bribe and bully the respective communities, in a pattern of patronage and divide and rule familiar from the days of European colonialism.

Middle East experts, however, pointed out that partition based on sectarian divisions would be fraught with difficulties because the country's largest cities, where most of Iraq's population is to be found, are mixed. The mass displacement of Iraqis through sectarian fighting, which had made refugees of at least four million people by 2007, appeared to be part of the answer. Another indication of how the US might solve this problem in the heart of the occupation zone, in Baghdad, emerged in April 2007. Robert Fisk reported that two of the US military's most senior commanders, David Petraeus and James Amos, had drawn up a lengthy document proposing sealing off occupied areas in Baghdad, enclosing neighbourhoods with barricades and allowing only Iraqis with special ID cards to enter. 'There are likely to be pass systems, "visitor" registration and restrictions on movement outside the "gated communities". Civilians may find themselves inside a "controlled population" prison.'[54] Later the same month US forces started constructing the first wall around the Sunni neighbourhood of Adhamiya.[55]

Fisk noted that at least four Israeli officers had been involved in the debates at Fort Leavenworth in Kansas that had produced the document. That might explain why it sounded much like Israel's own system for separating Palestinians from Jewish settlers in the most difficult area under its occupation, East Jerusalem. Israel had been refining for nearly two decades the mechanics of separating population groups in the West Bank, using a complex system of walls, gates, checkpoints and permits to limit movement among the Palestinian population while allowing Jewish settlers to roam freely through the occupied areas. This now seemed to be the model being pursued by the Bush Administration in Iraq. As with the Palestinian territories, the ultimate goal of this policy may yet be to encourage the forced migration of the Iraqi population into separate ethnic partitions.

IRAQ: A MODEL FOR THE REGION?

A Middle East analyst, Chris Toensing, defined US policy in the Middle East thus: 'For decades, Republican and Democratic administrations alike had pursued three fundamental goals in the region – the security of Israel, the westward flow of cheap oil, and the stability of cooperative regimes.'[56] Had that policy changed? Addressing an audience at the American University in Cairo in summer 2005, the US Secretary of State, Condoleezza Rice, gave the answer: 'For 60 years, my country, the United States, pursued stability at the expense of democracy in this region here in the Middle East – and we achieved neither. Now, we are taking a different course.'[57] In Washington's new language, regional stability was being replaced by a series of democratic revolutions. That was the message required to legitimise to Western publics Bush's goals in the war on terror, but in truth the results of ending enforced stability in the Middle East were far more prosaic and predictable: civil war and sectarian violence.

The other early Middle East battleground was Lebanon, where, as in Iraq, a large Shia population had been marginalised, in Lebanon's case by a system of rule bequeathed by Europe that gave disproportionate power to the Christian and Sunni minorities. Lebanon was also home to a large population of Palestinian refugees, displaced by the war that founded Israel in 1948. A civil war had raged between these various communities from 1975 until 1990, when Syria agreed to send in its forces to guarantee stability. Syria, however, was not the only external actor meddling in Lebanon's affairs. Israel mounted an invasion in 1978, and again in 1982, designed to expel the Palestinian leadership from Lebanon and install a sympathetic Christian government, that led to a two-decade occupation of the country's south. Unlike the Shia in Iraq, the Shia in Lebanon had come to exercise considerable muscle through a militia, Hizbullah, supported by Iran. Emerging in response to Israel's occupation of Lebanon, Hizbullah swiftly became the most effective resistance group, forcing Israeli troops out in 2000. Syria's continuing presence in Lebanon after the Israeli exit deeply irked both Israel and the US. Their pretext for ejecting Syrian forces arrived in February 2005. It was then that a former Sunni prime minister, Rafik Hariri, was assassinated by a bomb in Beirut, one of a spate of car explosions. Widely blamed, Syrian forces were forced to exit the country under the terms of a UN resolution two months later. At the same time the US stepped up attempts at promoting a Cedar Revolution – following similar US-inspired 'democratic' revolutions in Eastern Europe – to strengthen the Lebanese government against Hizbullah. Rival popular demonstrations in favour of the government and in favour of Hizbullah rapidly stirred up sectarian tensions that lay just below the surface.

The Cedar Revolution, however, failed to rein in Hizbullah, and Washington began visibly backing the government of Fuad Siniora and the Lebanese army[58] while covertly directing funds to rival militias, though it claimed these were for 'non-lethal' purposes when the operation became public. Hizbullah's deputy leader Sheikh Naim Qassem suggested otherwise, claiming that the US was arming the other groups in an attempt 'to tie Lebanon into negotiations that benefit Israel and their plan for a new Middle East'.[59] The manipulation of rival militias so that they would deplete each other's energies had strong echoes of Israel's treatment of Palestinian groups in the occupied territories. Washington – as well as Israel, which had predicted civil war as the outcome of its aerial onslaught on Lebanon in summer 2006 – appeared to believe that, by reigniting a sectarian war, Lebanon's neighbour Syria could be dragged into the fray. That, as Daniel Pipes had publicly hoped for in a different context, might justify expanding the 'war on terror' to Damascus.

With the machinations of the US, Israel, Syria, Iran, the Lebanese government, Hizbullah, groups allied to the Hariri family, and others to take into account, making sense of events unfolding in Lebanon was often near-impossible. Most international coverage, however, ignored these complex interactions to present a simple story of US efforts at promoting democracy in Lebanon that were being stymied by Syria and Hizbullah. In this spirit, a UN investigation was established with the barely concealed intent of proving that Syria was responsible for Hariri's assassination. Similarly, the sudden emergence of militant Sunni groups such as Fatah al-Islam in Lebanon was blamed on Syria too. However, there were indications that the US and Israel may have had a hand in these developments – if not directly, at least through allies and proxies. In June 2006, for example, the Lebanese army uncovered several networks of Arab mercenaries who they believed had been sponsored by Israel's Mossad intelligence agency to conduct a recent wave of car bombings and assassinations in Lebanon. Israel had a history of such interference in Lebanon during its long occupation, using a proxy militia – the South Lebanon Army – to wage war against Hizbullah. It had also been blamed for a spy ring broken in 2004 that had plotted to kill Hizbullah's leader, Hassan Nasrallah.[60] The Lebanese Foreign Minister,

Fawzi Salloukh, prepared a file of evidence for the UN Security Council to 'present Israel's nakedness before the international community', but was forced to drop the matter when the US threatened 'grave consequences', including an end to military aid, if Lebanon registered a formal complaint.[61]

Others, however, confirmed his suspicions. Fred Burton, a former counter-terrorism expert with the US State Department who had investigated attacks around the world, noted that the technology used in Lebanon's spate of assassinations was available to only a few countries: the US, Britain, France, Israel and Russia. Burton observed: 'Suppose that these bombings were "merely collateral"? That the true target in the plot is the Syrian regime itself? If Damascus were being framed, who then would be the likely suspect?'[62] Even stronger evidence of Israeli interference emerged soon afterwards when Mahmoud Rafeh, a former South Lebanon Army officer, was caught on camera setting a bomb that killed two members of Islamic Jihad in the city of Sidon. Rafeh later confessed to having been recruited by Mossad.[63]

If Israel was trying to destabilise Lebanon through covert 'black operations', there was growing evidence that the Pentagon and CIA were involved in similar actions there and elsewhere. An ABC News report in early 2007 revealed that the CIA was running what sources characterised as an 'information war', including the use of black propaganda, against Iran, Syria and Hizbullah. One CIA source said Iran was being targeted with a 'pro-democracy' message, and the agency was supporting 'pro-democracy' groups – a reference, it can be assumed, to attempts to stir up ethnic and sectarian tensions in parts of Iran. The CIA operation also involved 'potential allies' outside the region, again a reference, it can be assumed, to enlisting groups in exile to foment tension in Iran – much as the Iraqi exile and convicted criminal Ahmed Chalabi had been recruited by the Bush Administration before the invasion of Iraq. Covert operations by the Pentagon, which, unlike the CIA, is not subject to Congressional oversight, were being run out of the Vice-President's office and the National Security Council, according to the investigative journalist Larisa Alexandrovna. The Pentagon was said to have been resorting since

2003 to 'black' operations involving terrorist groups working on behalf of the US – much as Tehran had been claiming. One group, the Mujahedeen-e Khalq, was reported to be operating in southern areas of Iran, including a Shia region where a series of bomb blasts in 2006 left many dead and hundreds injured.[64]

Seymour Hersh quoted a government consultant explaining the White House's logic in seeking to weaken Iran: 'The minute the aura of invincibility which the mullahs enjoy is shattered, and with it the ability to hoodwink the West, the Iranian regime will collapse.'[65] As in Iraq, regime overthrow seemed preferable to regime change. A Defense Department official added that Bush's staff believed 'a sustained bombing campaign in Iran will humiliate the religious leadership and lead the public to rise up and overthrow the government' – just as Israel's aerial assault was supposed to do in Lebanon. And a Pentagon consultant told Hersh they were working with an array of minority groups in Iran, including the Azeris in the north, the Baluchis in the south-east, and the Kurds in the north-east, minorities who make up 40 per cent of the country's population. The aim was to 'encourage ethnic tensions' and undermine the regime.[66] A former Bush National Security Council official, Flynt Leverett, observed: 'This is all part of the campaign of provocative steps to increase the pressure on Iran. The idea is that at some point the Iranians will respond and then the Administration will have an open door to strike at them.'[67]

But Iraq and Lebanon, and the sustained campaign against Iran, were not isolated incidents of US and Israeli involvement in the Middle East. They fitted into a much larger picture of meddling in the region whose goal became clearer through 2007. As Sheikh Qassem of Hizbullah had suggested, Washington's new game was to deepen the existing fault lines between the Shia and Sunni communities, by backing 'moderate' Sunnis against the 'extremist' Shia in Iran and allies such as Hizbullah. Hersh characterised this policy as a 'redirection', since it meant Washington was now supporting the same sectarian community from which most of the insurgents in Iraq were drawn as well as al-Qaeda's jihadis – the very people the 'war on terror' had been designed to crush.

Instead, Bush and his officials inverted reality by claiming that the insurgency in Iraq was being directed by Iran. 'The White House goal is to build a case that the Iranians have been fomenting the insurgency and they've been doing it all along – that Iran is, in fact, supporting the killing of Americans', a Pentagon consultant said.[68] After six years of the 'war on terror', Bush appeared to be committed to persuading the world that the main threat to global order was not al-Qaeda, the wayward offspring of Saudi Arabia's long indulgence of Islamic extremism, but the Shia minority dispersed across the Middle East. Or as Hersh characterised it during one interview: 'We're in the business now of supporting the Sunnis anywhere we can against the Shia ... Civil war. We're in the business of creating in some places – Lebanon in particular – a sectarian violence.'[69]

According to Hersh, the US was leaving some clandestine operations – possibly the most unpalatable – to the Saudi regime, which had a long history of promoting fundamentalist Sunni Islam and extremist groups. Riyadh was keen to get involved in these anti-Shia machinations, its fear driven by the thought that a stronger Iran, possibly one possessing nuclear weapons, might take control of Iraq and empower the Shia in Saudi Arabia's eastern province, where its major oilfields are located. Iran would then be able to supplant Saudi Arabia's control of OPEC. The Saudi Foreign Minister, Saud al-Faisal, had given vent to these fears in September 2005 when he warned American policy makers at the Council on Foreign Relations: 'If you allow ... for a civil war to happen between the Shiites and the Sunnis, Iraq is finished for ever. It will be dismembered. It will not only be dismembered, it will cause so many conflicts in the region that it will bring the whole region into a turmoil that will be hard to resolve.' He added that US behaviour appeared to be 'handing over the country to Iran without reason. It seems out of this world that you do this.'[70] When Iraq continued sinking deeper into civil war, Saudi Arabia's King Abdullah offered a stark warning to Dick Cheney. During a meeting in Riyadh in December 2006, the king told his American visitor that the kingdom would give money and arms to Iraq's Sunni militias – presumably including those leading the insurgency against US forces – if America withdrew. The king's comments clarified an earlier statement from the Saudi ambassador to Washington, Prince Turki al-Faisal, that 'since America came into Iraq uninvited, it should not leave Iraq uninvited'.[71]

The repressive Arab Sunni monarchical regimes of Saudi Arabia and Jordan, and the Arab Sunni 'presidential monarchy' of Egypt, were, in the language of Washington, 'moderates' because they backed US policy, publicly opposing Shia Iran. The same states were also ready to denounce the Arab Shia militia Hizbullah's inspiring resistance to Israel in the 2006 war. These 'moderate' states' motivation had its roots in their own insecurities, as two Middle East analysts noted: 'By acting to aid an Arab cause, rather than simply talking about doing so, Hizballah exposed the hollowness of the Arab regimes' own promises.'[72] Vali Nasr, a senior fellow at the Council on Foreign Relations and an expert on the Shia in Iran and Iraq, explained Washington's thinking in these terms:

It seems there has been a debate inside the government over what's the biggest danger – Iran or Sunni radicals. The Saudis and some in the Administration have been arguing that the biggest threat is Iran and the Sunni radicals are the lesser enemies. This is a victory for the Saudi line ... The Saudis have considerable financial means, and have deep relations with the Muslim Brotherhood and the Salafis [Sunni extremists]. The last time Iran was a threat, the Saudis were able to mobilize the worst kinds of Islamic radicals. Once you get them out of the box, you can't put them back.[73]

There were signs by summer 2007 that Saudi Arabia may have been overplaying its hand, upsetting the White House by working not only to destabilise and weaken official enemies like Iran and Hizbullah but also to bring down the Shia regime in Baghdad. It emerged that Riyadh had in all probability been behind forged documents circulating in Iraq designed to undermine the country's Shia prime minister, Nuri al-Maliki, by suggesting he was an Iranian agent who had tipped off Moqtada al-Sadr, an Iraqi Shia cleric hostile to the US occupation, about an imminent American crackdown on his militia forces. Zalmay Khalilzad, a neocon who had held a series of key Administration positions, including

US ambassador to Afghanistan, Iraq and the United Nations, wrote in the *New York Times*: 'Several of Iraq's neighbours – not only Syria and Iran but also some friends of the United States – are pursuing destabilising policies.'[74] (It can be assumed that Khalilzad was using the language of 'stability' so frowned on by some of his colleagues in the traditional sense of promoting US interests.) In addition, it was reported that the White House was angry that Saudi Arabia was funding Sunni groups in Iraq and allowing jihadis to cross the border to join the insurgency, often as suicide bombers. According to US estimates, 40 per cent of the 70 or so foreign fighters entering Iraq each month were from Saudi Arabia. Ahead of a high-level meeting in Jedda, a State Department spokesman warned that the US was expecting from Saudi Arabia 'more active, positive support for Iraq and the Iraqi people'.[75] The White House was also known to be unhappy about Saudi support for Hamas and its continuing attempts to promote its peace plan over Bush's own regional peace conference, due to be held in late 2007.

In yet another twist in the White House's approach to the chaos unfolding in Iraq, it was reported in summer 2007 that the US military was arming Sunni tribal groups in the hope that they could be encouraged to turn their weapons on militants allied to al-Qaeda. The tribes were being made to promise that they would use the arms, ammunition, body armour, pick-up trucks and fuel they had been given only against al-Qaeda and not American troops. The US said it would use fingerprinting, retinal scans and other tests to establish whether insurgents had been involved in fighting against its soldiers.[76] The new policy was characterised by a commentator in the *Guardian* newspaper in this way: 'In the medium term, it can only fuel the civil war that most observers expect to erupt with full fury as American and British forces pull back. And that's in addition to arming the largely Shia forces of the Iraqi army. One way or another, Americans are giving Iraqis more weapons with which they can kill each other.'[77] Another commentator, who had worked with the US Marines in Iraq and supported the US policy, pointed out nonetheless that it would negatively encourage further division of Iraq into sectarian communities:

> The United States would be tacitly permitting Sunnis to field militias and defend themselves. This would be one more step toward the fragmentation of Iraq into Sunni, Shia and Kurdish areas ... Ultimately, the United States faces a choice. It can continue to push a national and unified state, and risk letting hard-core insurgents and terrorists go unchallenged. Or the ties that bind the state can be loosened to counter al-Qaida in Iraq with tribal police forces, but at the cost of formalizing sectarian divisions and weakening democratization.[78]

Some observers believed this strategy signalled a return by Washington to the familiar colonial game of 'divide and rule', playing the Sunni and Shia off against each other. That was the view of a long-time Lebanese analyst, Michael Young, who argued that the US was again pursuing 'political "realism" based on imposing a balance of power. Much like the US did during the 1980s when it supported Iraq in its war against Iran, the Bush administration is today using Sunnis against Shiites (though in Iraq it is mainly using Shiites against Sunnis).'[79] But that seemed to be a misreading of the Bush Administration's goals – assuming, as seemed likely, that the neocons were still in control but chastened.[80] Divide and rule – with its traditional tools of containing, bullying and bribing – had been shown to be ineffective with many of today's key actors in the Middle East, including with the jihadis of al-Qaeda and with Hizbullah. This was a lesson Israel had already learnt in its dealings with Hamas.

So if these groups could not be bought or brow-beaten, as states and their armies usually could be, what was the Israeli-neocon future for the Middle East? One of the more astute new players in the region's power game, Hassan Nasrallah, leader of Hizbullah, set out his understanding of their plans in early 2007. He argued that Israel and the neocons wanted to bring about the partition of Iraq, Lebanon and Syria. In Syria, the result would be to push the country 'into chaos and internal battles like in Iraq'. In Lebanon, 'There will be a Sunni state, an Alawi state, a Christian state, and a Druze state', but he added that he did not know 'if there will be a Shiite state'. He suspected that one of the aims of Israel's cluster bombing of south Lebanon the previous summer was 'the destruction of Shiite areas and the displacement of Shiites from Lebanon. The idea was to have the Shiites of Lebanon and Syria flee to southern Iraq.' Partition, he said, would leave Israel surrounded by

> small tranquil states. I can assure you that the Saudi kingdom will also be divided, and the issue will reach to North African states. There will be small ethnic and confessional states. In other words, Israel will be the most important and the strongest state in a region that has been partitioned into ethnic and confessional states that are in agreement with each other. This is the new Middle East.[81]

Nasrallah seemed to understand Yinon's vision of the region very clearly.

If Nasrallah was right, Israel was determined to unravel the legacy of the colonial European powers that had carved out states in the Middle East to suit their own economic goals but which conflicted with Israel's ambition of becoming a regional empire. While the Israeli vision of the Middle East's future looked not only improbable but little more than a deluded fantasy, it echoed the consistent vision set out by the neocons and Israeli hawks. In April 2007 Caroline Glick of the *Jerusalem Post* wrote about the 'next pre-emptive war' Israel (as opposed to the US) should wage. Damascus would be the target, she suggested, and the war's main goal would the destruction of Syria's central authority. The need for such action, reasoned Glick, was clear:

> Centralized governments throughout the Arab world are the primary fulminators of Arab hatred of Israel. These regimes require a constant drumbeat of incitement against Israel to deflect their people's attention from their failure to provide basic services. Decentralized governments would have difficulty blaming the Jews for their failures.

One of the keys to 'decentralizing' Syria – or destroying its Ba'ath regime – and possibly saving Israel the trouble of waging a war, would be a disruptive alliance by Israel with the fifth of the Syrian population who are Kurdish, similar to the clandestine Israeli support already being offered to Iraq's Kurds. Glick recommended aiding the 'restive' Kurds so that they could seek autonomy in a 'federated democracy'. Insisting Syria would remain a single state under her plan, Glick suggested that it could be presented as bringing freedom to Syrians and 'protecting minority rights'. And the benefit to Israel? 'Arming the Kurds would likely muddy the waters in a manner that would cause serious harm to Syria's war-making capacity. How well would Syria contend with the IDF [Israeli army] if it were simultaneously trying to put down a popular rebellion?'[82]

The analysis that Israel needed to break apart Syria just as Iraq had already been effectively dissolved by the US invasion perfectly encapsulated the vision of Oded Yinon a quarter of a century after he articulated it. Glick's argument reflected the current consensus among Israel's General Staff as well as tapping into ideas that had their source in a Zionist tradition dating back to David Ben Gurion and Moshe Dayan. The ingenuity of the promise that, following the collapse of the Soviet Union, the Middle East could be remade to suit US and Israeli interests by spreading instability and inter-communal strife had captivated a generation of rightwing Washington policy makers. The most likely outcome, however, was the forging of new political, religious and social alliances across the Middle East whose effects it was almost impossible to predict or imagine. The only certainty was that, if the West carried on with its 'war on terror', there would be no victory – only 'war without end'.

NOTES

PREFACE, pp. x–xix

1. 'Partition may be the only solution', *Guardian*, 23 June 2007.
2. Excerpt from the introduction to *Overthrow*, available at: www. npr.org/templates/story/story.php?storyId=5325069
3. See, for example, an accurate prediction of what would unfold in Iraq by Uri Avnery, a former Israeli Knesset member and veteran peace activist, in 'The war drummers', *Counterpunch*, 10 September 2002.
4. Chomsky, *Failed States*, pp. 147–8.
5. Confirmation of American covert attempts to assassinate Cuba's Fidel Castro, for example, recently came to light. See 'CIA conspired with mafia to kill Castro', *Guardian*, 27 June 2007.
6. For a rare insight into the views of the insurgents, in an article in which they are allowed to speak for themselves, see 'Out of the shadows', *Guardian*, 19 July 2007.

CHAPTER 1   REGIME OVERTHROW IN IRAQ, pp. 1–35

1. The Sunni and Shia are divided on matters of doctrine, ritual, law, theology and religious organisation. Most of these differences relate to an early break between the two sects over the issue of whom to follow after the Prophet Mohammed's death in 632AD. The Shia advocate strict adherence to the Koran and sunna in accordance with the teachings of the Prophet's cousin and son-in-law, Ali. The Sunnis regard the first four caliphs, disciples of the Prophet, as 'rightly guided', meaning in practice that Sunnis accept the caliphs' innovations and the later interpretations of the Koran by jurists. The Kurds, although mostly Sunni, regard themselves as a distinct ethnic and national group, though they were not given a nation when the European powers divided up the Middle East in the early twentieth century. Significant Kurdish populations exist in Iraq, Iran, Syria and Turkey.
2. Fisk, *The Great War for Civilisation*, pp. 262–3.
3. Ibid., Chapters 6 and 7.
4. 'Why Saddam will never disarm', *Observer*, 23 February 2003.

5. Quoted in Friel and Falk, *The Record of the Paper*, pp. 24–31.
6. 'The defector's secrets', *Newsweek*, 3 March 2003.
7. 'Is Iraq a true threat to the US?', *Boston Globe*, 20 July 2002.
8. 'Final report: Iraq had no WMDs', *USA Today*, 6 October 2004.
9. That was the opinion of the then UN Secretary General, Kofi Annan ('Iraq war illegal, says Annan', *BBC Online*, 16 September 2004). Even Britain's chief legal adviser to the government, Lord Goldsmith, who had publicly backed the lawfulness of a pre-emptive war in 2003, was revealed to have expressed serious doubts in private about its legality at the time ('Lord Goldsmith's legal advice and the Iraq war', *Guardian*, 27 April 2005).
10. Bush's speech is available at: www.whitehouse.gov/news/releases /2003/02/20030226-11.html
11. David Ignatius, 'A war of choice, and one who chose it', 2 November 2003.
12. 'US death toll in Iraq passes 3,500', *Guardian*, 8 June 2007.
13. Figures available at: http://icasualties.org/oif/Civ.aspx
14. 'A very private war', *Guardian*, 1 August 2007. Two-thirds of the contractors, presumably those on the lowest rungs doing jobs like cooking and cleaning, were reported to be Iraqis.
15. 'Bush acknowledges about 30,000 Iraqis have died', *Financial Times*, 12 December 2005.
16. www.iraqbodycount.org
17. 'Iraqi deaths', 29 May 2007, available at: http://lefti.blogspot. com/2007_05_01_archive.html#8981304890241682546.
    An email sent in October 2006 by the bureau chief of a major Western news agency in Iraq – and leaked to the Media Lens website – took a similar view: 'iraq body count is i think a very misleading exercise. we know they must have been undercounting for at least the first two years because we know that we did not report anything like all the deaths we were aware of ... we are also well aware that we are not aware of many deaths on any given day' (Quoted in a letter from Media Lens to the reader's editor of the *Guardian*, dated 20 July 2007).
18. Anderson wrote: 'The study design is robust and employs methods that are regarded as close to "best practice" in this area, given the difficulties of data collection and verification in the present circumstances in Iraq' ('Iraqi deaths survey "was robust"', *BBC Online*, 26 March 2007).
19. UPI, 'Plans for UN meeting on Iraqi refugees', 10 April 2007.
20. 'Children hardest hit by humanitarian crisis in Iraq', *Guardian*, 31 July 2007.

21. 'Out of the shadows', *Guardian*, 19 July 2007.
22. 'Report on Haditha condemns marines; signs of misconduct were ignored, U.S. General says', *Washington Post*, 21 April 2007.
23. Toby Dodge, 'Staticide in Iraq', *Le Monde diplomatique*, February 2007.
24. *The Iraq Study Group Report*, 6 December 2006, available at: www.usip.org/isg/iraq_study_group_report/ report/1206/iraq_study_group_report.pdf
25. 'The last thing the Middle East's main players want is US troops to leave Iraq', *Guardian*, 25 April 2007.
26. Quoted in John Pilger, 'The war on children', *New Statesman*, 19 June 2006.
27. 'Most Iraqis favor immediate U.S. pullout, polls show', *Washington Post*, 27 September 2006.
28. 'Skepticism about U.S. deep, Iraq poll shows', *Washington Post*, 12 November 2003.
29. 'Poll of Iraqis: public wants timetable for US withdrawal, but thinks US plans permanent bases in Iraq', 31 January 2006, available at: www.worldpublicopinion.org/pipa/articles/brmiddleeastnafricara/165.php?nid=&id=&pnt=165&lb=brme
30. 'Most Iraqis want U.S. troops out within a year', 27 September 2006, available at: www.worldpublicopinion.org/pipa/articles/brmiddleeastnafricara/250.php?nid=&id=&pnt=250&lb=brme
31. 'Bush steps up battle for Baghdad', *BBC Online*, 11 January 2007.
32. 'We could be in Iraq for 50 years, says US defence chief', *The Times*, 1 June 2007.
33. Reuters, 'Bush envisions U.S. presence in Iraq like S. Korea', 30 May 2007. A former president, Jimmy Carter, had suspected as much in 2006. 'There are people in Washington ... who never intend to withdraw military forces from Iraq and they're looking for 10, 20, 50 years in the future ... the reason that we went into Iraq was to establish a permanent military base in the Gulf region' ('Why there was no exit plan', *San Francisco Chronicle*, 30 April 2007).
34. 'Withdrawal won't happen', *Guardian*, 9 June 2007.
35. *Foreign Relations of the United States* (Washington: Government Printing Office, 1945), vol. 8, p. 45, cited in Sheldon L Richman, '"Ancient history": U.S. conduct in the Middle East since World War II and the folly of intervention', *Cato Policy Analysis*, No. 159, 16 August 1991.
36. Noam Chomsky, 'On the US and the Middle East', *Komal Newspaper*, 2 January 2004.

37. Pollack, *The Threatening Storm* (New York: Random House, 2002), p. 15, cited in '"The Israel Lobby" in Perspective', *Middle East Report*, No. 243, Summer 2007.
38. Center for Defense Information, *Defense Monitor*, January 1980, cited by Noam Chomsky, *Failed States*, p. 106.
39. Huntington, *International Security*, Summer 1981, cited in Chomsky, *Failed States*, p. 103.
40. *Access to Oil – The United States Relationship with Saudi Arabia and Iran* (Washington: Government Printing Office, 1977), p. 84, cited in Sheldon L Richman, '"Ancient history": U.S. conduct in the Middle East since World War II and the folly of intervention', *Cato Policy Analysis*, No. 159, 16 August 1991.
41. Chomsky, *Failed States*, p. 120.
42. Roger Morris, 'A tyrant 40 years in the making', *New York Times*, 14 March 2003.
43. According to one of the few genuinely critical US representatives, Congressman Dennis Kucinich, the law was effectively drafted in February 2006 by BearingPoint, an American management consultancy firm that was one of the main companies profiteering from the Iraq war. Shell, BP, ExxonMobil, ChevronTexaco and ConocoPhillips were then invited to offer their comments on the draft (Gary Leupp, 'The Iraqis' failure to pass the U.S.-authored Oil Law', *Dissident Voice*, 27 July 2007).
44. 'Our man in Iraq', *The American Lawyer*, 25 April 2007.
45. 'Iraqi unions vs. Big Oil', *Middle East Report*, No. 243, Summer 2007.
46. 'Iraq imposes "Saddam style" ban on oil union', *Observer*, 5 August 2007.
47. 'Good news from Baghdad at last: the oil law has stalled', *Guardian*, 3 August 2007.
48. Munir Chalabi, 'Political comments on the draft of the Iraqi oil law', *Znet*, 15 March 2007.
49. '"Clock is ticking" on U.S. patience', *San Francisco Chronicle*, 20 April 2007.
50. 'While Washington sleeps, effort to privatize Iraq's oil continues', *Common Dreams*, 18 May 2007.
51. Available at: www.saudiembassy.net/Publications/MagFall01/SA-US-Relations.htm
52. Just such a price-fixing cartel was established by the oil companies in 1928, when Shell, BP and Esso met in Scotland to end competition, set quotas and avoid surplus supplies to 'stabilise' the market and maximise their profits. OPEC effectively superseded that agreement.

53. OPEC was the brainchild of two oil ministers, Juan Pablo Perez Alfonzo of Venezuela and Sheikh Abdullah Tariki of Saudi Arabia. A private agreement between the two countries in 1958 quickly expanded to encompass the other biggest oil producers: Iran, Iraq and Kuwait.

54. 'Saudi government provided aid to 9/11 hijackers, sources say', *Los Angeles Times*, 2 August 2003. A 2004 US inquiry let Saudi Arabia off the hook for the attacks, though it failed to address many key questions about Saudi funding to groups allied with the hijackers ('9/11 probe clears Saudi Arabia', *BBC Online*, 17 June 2004).

55. Curtis, *Web of Deceit*, pp. 254–7.

56. Available at: http://usa.usembassy.de/etexts/speeches/rhetoric/rmnvietn.htm

57. Available at: www.jimmycarterlibrary.org/documents/speeches/su80jec.phtml

58. Zunes, *Tinderbox*, p. 68.

59. In 1941 a similar goal was desired by Harry Truman, then a Senator: 'If we see that Germany is winning we ought to help Russia and if Russia is winning we ought to help Germany and that way let them kill as many as possible' (quoted in Chomsky, *Failed States*, p. 122).

60. Ibid., pp. 69–75.

61. Pollack, *The Threatening Storm*, p. 36, cited in 'The strategic logic of the Iraq blunder', *Middle East Report*, No. 239, Summer 2006.

62. Zunes, *Tinderbox*, p. 80.

63. Howard Fineman, 'The Bushes' Saddam drama', *Newsweek*, 8 January 2007.

64. 'While we slept', *The Nation*, 11 May 2007.

65. Friedman, 'News of the week in review', *New York Times*, 7 July 1991, cited in Noam Chomsky, 'The Gulf embargo', *Lies of Our Times*, September 1991.

66. 'The war economy of Iraq', *Middle East Report*, No. 243, Summer 2007.

67. 'How to rebuild Iraq', *Time*, 18 April 2003.

68. Quoted in John Pilger, 'Squeezed to death', *Guardian*, 4 March 2000.

69. Ibid.

70. *Philadelphia Enquirer*, 1 April 1999, cited in Edwards and Cromwell, *Guardians of Power*, p. 19.

71. Speech available at: www.fas.org/news/iraq/1997/03/bmd970327b.htm

72. One hagiographic account of Wolfowitz noted coyly his ties to Israel: 'You hear from some of Wolfowitz's critics, always off the record, that Israel exercises a powerful gravitational pull on the man. They may not know that as a teenager he spent his father's sabbatical semester in Israel or that his sister is married to an Israeli, but they certainly know that he is friendly with Israel's generals and diplomats' ('The sunshine warrior', *New York Times*, 22 September 2002).

73. Kissinger's allegations against Perle echoed the claim made years later by two AIPAC officials on trial for receiving classified documents that senior Bush officials were regularly passing secrets about Iran to the Israel lobby (see Chapter 2). *The Price of Power: Kissinger in the Nixon White House* (New York: Summit Books, 1983), p. 322, cited in Hirst, *The Gun and the Olive Branch*, p. 49.

74. 'Bush and Sharon nearly identical on Mideast policy', 9 February 2003.

75. Ibid.

76. Quoted in Kathleen Christison, 'The Siren Song of Elliott Abrams', *Counterpunch*, 26 July 2007.

77. 'Bush and Sharon nearly identical on Mideast policy', 9 February 2003.

78. '"All the dreams we had are now gone"', *Ha'aretz*, 21 July 2007.

79. 'Without a doubt', *New York Times*, 17 October 2004.

80. Anatol Lieven, 'The push for war', *London Review of Books*, 3 October 2002.

81. Israel had stuck to a policy of 'nuclear ambiguity', claiming disingenuously that it would not be the first country to introduce nuclear weapons to the Middle East. It had to maintain this pretence not least because an admission that it possessed nuclear arms and a refusal to sign up to the Non-Proliferation Treaty would have made it impossible for the US Congress to continue passing billions of dollars of aid to Israel annually. However, Ehud Olmert broke with this policy, intentionally or not, in alluding during an interview to Israel's nuclear arsenal: 'Iran, openly, explicitly and publicly threatens to wipe Israel off the map. Can you say that this is the same level, when they are aspiring to have nuclear weapons, as America, France, Israel, Russia?' ('Olmert's nuclear remark spurs damage control bid', *Ha'aretz*, 12 December 2006).

82. *A Clean Break* is available at: www.iasps.org/strat1.htm

83. Available at: www.newamericancentury.org/iraqclintonletter.htm

84. Available at: www.newamericancentury.org/iraqletter1998.htm

85. Available at: www.newamericancentury.org/RebuildingAmericas-Defenses.pdf

86. In June 2007 Libby was jailed on four charges, including obstruction of justice and perjury, in what became known as the 'Plame affair', concerning leaks from the White House that named a CIA agent, Valerie Plame, thereby endangering her. The leak was in retaliation for her husband, Joseph Wilson, a former ambassador, criticising the White House in the US media and his refutation of Bush's claims that Saddam Hussein had tried to buy enriched uranium from Niger. It later emerged that the leak had come from Richard Armitage, then the Deputy Secretary of State ('"Scooter" Libby gets 2½ years in jail for perjury', *Guardian*, 6 June 2007). The sentence was commuted by President Bush a few weeks later ('Saved from prison by Bush's favour: the White House aide who lied to a grand jury', *Guardian*, 3 July 2007).

87. James Mann, *Rise of the Vulcans* (New York: Viking, 2004), p. 211, cited in '"The Israel lobby" in perspective', *Middle East Report*, No. 243, Summer 2007.

88. 'Bush: "We're smoking them out"', *CNN Online*, 26 November 2001.

89. This book does not analyse events in Afghanistan in any detail in the belief that the US occupation there was more marginal to Israel and the neocons' plans to remake the Middle East, though undoubtedly the creation of a permanent US military base next to resource-rich Iran and Central Asia may have had its own attractions. From the neocon point of view, the main goals in attacking Afghanistan, a state which even under the Taliban had almost no central authority, were to provide legitimacy for the 'war on terror' against Islamic extremism and a dry run for the invasion of Iraq. The US installed a weak puppet leader, Hamid Karzai, who nominally ruled over the provinces but the warlords quickly reasserted their power, as did the Taliban. After the occupation, the production of opium, which financed and fuelled the competition between the warlords, reached new heights. It is possible, though beyond the scope of this book, that US intelligence agencies and organised American crime did have an interest in securing Afghanistan's lucrative drugs trade for their own ends, just as the oil industry wanted Iraq's oil. For more on this, see Michel Chossudovsky, 'Who benefits from the Afghan Opium Trade?', 21 September 2006, available at: www.globalresearch.ca/index.php?context=viewArticle&code=CHO2 0060921&articleId=3294

90. The speech, in January 2002, is available at: www.whitehouse.gov/news/releases/2002/01/20020129-11.html

91. A critic listed the key neocons of the time: Paul Wolfowitz, the Deputy Secretary of Defense; Douglas Feith, number three at the Pentagon; Lewis 'Scooter' Libby, Cheney's chief of staff; John Bolton, in the State Department 'to keep Colin Powell in check'; and Elliott Abrams, head of Middle East policy at the National Security Council (Michael Lind, 'How neoconservatives conquered Washington – and launched a war', *Antiwar.com*, 10 April 2003).

92. The most notorious example was Judith Miller, a correspondent for the *New York Times* who 'broke' many of the stories that built the case for an attack on Iraq. Miller had close connections to a neocon think-tank, the Middle East Forum. Miller resigned from the newspaper a few months after it ran an editorial acknowledging flaws in its reporting on Iraq; ten of the twelve reports discussed by the editorial had been authored by Miller. But the *Times* appeared to have learnt little from the experience, with a close colleague of Miller's, reporter Michael Gordon, preparing a similar case for war against Iran. There were much wider failings by the US media too, as was finally admitted by some senior TV and newspaper journalists in a PBS documentary, *Buying the War*, broadcast on 25 April 2007. For example, Bob Simon of CBS's *60 Minutes* says White House claims that one of the 9/11 hijackers had met an Iraqi official in Prague were proven false by the programme with a few phone calls. 'If we had combed Prague, and found out that there was absolutely no evidence for a meeting between Mohammad Atta and the Iraqi intelligence figure; if we knew that, you had to figure the administration knew it.' Nonetheless, Simon did not refer to this finding in the show. The *Washington Post* editorialised in favour of attacking Iraq 27 times, and published about 1,000 articles and columns on the war in 2002. A huge anti-war march in the US was given a total coverage of 36 words ('Record of Iraq war lies to air April 25 on PBS', *Truthout*, 12 April 2007).

93. One infamous document, a forgery, purported to show that Iraq had been buying uranium from Niger. Much overlooked at the time was the fact that the same document also suggested, again implausibly, that Iraq was collaborating with Iran on building nuclear weapons. Professor Juan Cole and others have linked several key neocons to this episode, suggesting that the Niger forgery was designed to line up Iran for the next attack. See: www.juancole.com/2004/08/pentagonisrael-spying-case-expands.html

94. These kinds of improbable collaborations between regional enemies were an enduring element of White House claims in the 'war on terror'. As well as Iran and Iraq collaborating on the development

of nuclear weapons (see previous note), the Shia regime of Iran was also later accused of supplying weapons to Sunni insurgents in Iraq and of aiding the Taliban in Afghanistan.

95. 'Pentagon probe fills in blanks on Iraq war groundwork', *Los Angeles Times*, 6 April 2007.

96. 'Pentagon report debunks prewar Iraq–Al Qaeda connection', *Christian Science Monitor*, 6 April 2006.

97. Despite the Pentagon inquiry findings, Cheney continued to claim a link between Saddam Hussein's Iraq and al-Qaeda ('Cheney defiant over al-Qaida link to Iraq', *Guardian*, 7 April 2007).

98. Bob Woodward, *Bush at War* (New York: Simon & Schuster, 2002), p. 49, cited in Friel and Falk *The Record of the Paper*, p. 116.

99. 'What Tenet knew', *New York Review of Books*, 19 July 2007.

100. 'Bush decided to remove Saddam "on day one"', *Guardian*, 12 January 2004. This account was confirmed in an interview in 2007 with former NATO commander General Wesley Clark, who recounted meeting a general in the Pentagon shortly after 9/11: 'He says, "We've made the decision we're going to war with Iraq." This was on or about the 20th of September [2001]. I said, "We're going to war with Iraq? Why?" He said, "I don't know." He said, "I guess they don't know what else to do." So I said, "Well, did they find some information connecting Saddam to al-Qaeda?" He said, "No, no ... I guess it's like we don't know what to do about terrorists, but we've got a good military and we can take down governments." And he said, "I guess if the only tool you have is a hammer, every problem has to look like a nail."' ('Gen Wesley Clark weighs presidential bid: "I think about it every day"', *Democracy Now*, 2 March 2007).

101. This document and related ones are available at: www.judicialwatch. org/iraqi-oil-maps.shtml

102. *The Economist* noted: 'UN sanctions forbid foreigners from investing in the oilfields. But that has not stopped firms rushing to sign contracts in the hope of exploiting fields when sanctions are lifted ... All this must be bad news for those excluded from the party: the Americans' ('Saddam more than doubles exports of oil in charm offensive', 15 October 2002).

103. Palast, *Armed Madhouse*, p. 121.

104. Ibid., p. 53.

105. Ibid., p. 60.

106. Ibid., Chapter 2.

107. 'Bush and Sharon nearly identical on Mideast policy', *Washington Post*, 9 February 2003.

108. 'Sharon promises to help Bush if he attacks Saddam', *Daily Telegraph*, 8 February 2002.
109. Michael Smith, 'The real news in the Downing Street memos', *Los Angeles Times*, 23 June 2005.
110. 'Israelis watch the street, not the skies', *Guardian*, 17 August 2002.
111. Robert Novak, 'Sharon's war?' *CNN Online*, 26 December 2002.
112. 'Israel to US: don't delay Iraq attack', *CBS News Online*, 16 August 2002.
113. From a report in the *Daily Star* newspaper (Beirut), 2 October 2002, cited in Hirst, *The Gun and the Olive Branch*, pp. 114–15.
114. According to *Ha'aretz*: 'The [Israeli] ministers left the cabinet session with the feeling that the IDF [Israeli military] is well able to track activities in western Iraq and that this area is now devoid of missile launchers and operating airfields. They concluded that the only way left for Iraq to attack Israel with chemical or biological weapons is to try to deliver them by plane' ('Who would give the go-ahead?', 22 March 2003).
115. 'Peace Index / Most Israelis support the attack on Iraq', *Ha'aretz*, 6 March 2003.
116. 'Sharon warned Bush of Saddam threat', *Jerusalem Post*, 11 January 2007; and 'Sharon warned Bush', *Forward*, 12 January 2007. Yossi Alpher, the author of one of these articles, felt the need to underscore the implications of Ayalon's observation: 'Certainly [Sharon] would have poured cold water on the postwar assertions of critics, like professors Stephen Walt and John Mearsheimer, who have fingered Israel, the American Israel Public Affairs Committee and pro-Israelis in the administration for instigating the war.' Nonetheless, the connection stuck, as one Israeli foreign ministry official complained to *Ha'aretz*: 'To this day we cannot shake the linkage between Israel and the Iraq war' ('Israel's NIS 500m insurance policy', 6 July 2007).
117. 'Enthusiastic IDF awaits war in Iraq', *Ha'aretz*, 17 February 2003.

CHAPTER 2   THE LONG CAMPAIGN AGAINST IRAN, pp. 36–78

1. Information about the 7th Herzliya conference is available from an official website: www.herzliyaconference.org/Eng/_Articles/Article.asp?CategoryID=33&ArticleID=1596
2. For more on the early conferences, see my book *Blood and Religion*, pp. 116–17.

3. Sharon's address is available at: www.haaretz.com/hasen/pages/
   ShArt.jhtml?itemNo=373673

4. A short history of Woolsey's more extreme positions can be found
   in Stanley Heller, 'The Ravings of James Woolsey', *Counterpunch*,
   2 April 2007.

5. Mendel, 'Diary', *London Review of Books*, 22 February 2007.

6. An official in Tehran noted in summer 2007, 'We can exit from the
   non-proliferation treaty, but we can never exit from a fatwa' ('Iran
   raises stakes in war of nerves over enriching uranium', *Guardian*,
   25 July 2007).

7. 'The riddle of Iran', *Economist*, 19 July 2007.

8. The White House plan violated the 1972 Anti-Ballistic Missile
   Treaty. There were grounds for fearing that the US scheme, to
   locate missile sites in the UK, Poland and the Czech Republic, was
   far from defensive. As one observer pointed out: 'Russia has around
   5,700 active nuclear warheads. The silos in Poland will contain just
   10 interceptor missiles. The most likely strategic purpose of the
   missile defence programme is to mop up any Russian or Chinese
   missiles that had not been destroyed during a pre-emptive US
   attack' (George Monbiot, 'Brown's contempt for democracy has
   dragged Britain into a new cold war', *Guardian*, 31 July 2007).

9. 'Antimissile plan by U.S. strains ties with Russia', *Washington
   Post*, 21 February 2007.

10. 'Nuclear weapons programs are about regime survival', *Znet*, 10
    June 2007.

11. 'Sharon on the warpath: Is Israel planning to attack Iran?',
    International Herald Tribune, 21 August 2004.

12. Mendel, 'Diary', *London Review of Books*.

13. Quoted in Shahak, *Open Secrets*, pp. 54–5.

14. Quoted in ibid., p. 82.

15. Quoted in ibid., pp. 90–1.

16. Quoted in ibid., p. 83.

17. Quoted in ibid., p. 36.

18. The nuclear arming of any Arab state had been a red line in Israeli
    military thinking for some time. Israel Shahak quotes comments by
    General Amnon Shahak-Lipkin, then Deputy Chief of Staff, made
    in an interview in April 1992: 'I believe that the State of Israel
    should from now on use all its power and direct all its efforts to
    preventing nuclear developments in any Arab state whatsoever'
    (*Open Secrets*, p. 34).

19. 'Israel worried Iran could benefit from Iraq war', *Ha'aretz*, 18
    February 2003.

20. 'Sharon says U.S. should also disarm Iran, Libya and Syria', *Ha'aretz*, 18 February 2003.
21. 'Sharon promises to help Bush if he attacks Saddam', *Daily Telegraph*, 8 February 2002.
22. 'Attack Iran the day Iraq war ends, demands Israel', *The Times*, 5 November 2002.
23. 'Sharon says U.S. should also disarm Iran, Libya and Syria', *Ha'aretz*.
24. 'Israel thrusts Iran in line of US fire', *Guardian*, 2 February 2002.
25. 'Who would give the go-ahead?', *Ha'aretz*, 22 March 2003.
26. 'Israel to US: now deal with Syria and Iran', *Ha'aretz*, 13 April 2003.
27. 'Israel thrusts Iran in line of US fire', *Guardian*.
28. Israel's obsession with remaining undisputed military top dog in the region included lobbying against US weapons sales even to weak Arab nations. An arms deal with the Persian Gulf states, for example, was threatened in April 2007 after Israel objected that it would damage Israel's military deterrent in the Middle East. According to a report in *Ha'aretz*: 'The United States has made few, if any, sales of satellite-guided ordnance to gulf countries, several officials said. Israel has been supplied with such weapons since the 1990s and used them extensively against Hezbollah in the Second Lebanon War' ('Report: Israeli objections delaying U.S. arms sale to Arab countries', 5 April 2007).
29. 'A Conversation with Zbigniew Brzezinski', *The American Prospect*, 20 May 2007.
30. 'UN: Iran has only 100s of centrifuges', *Jerusalem Post*, 13 April 2007.
31. 'Sanctions are not working', *Guardian*, 11 April 2007.
32. 'Pentagon analyst gets 12 years for disclosing data', *New York Times*, 20 January 2006.
33. 'Trial of ex-AIPAC staffers postponed', *The Jewish Week*, 28 April 2006.
34. 'New front sets sights on toppling Iran regime', 16 May 2003.
35. Jim Lobe, 'Shadowy neo-con adviser moves on Iran', Inter-Press News Agency, 24 June 2003.
36. See, for example, 'The jihad on Iraq', *National Review*, 26 January 2004.
37. 'The riddle of Iran', *Economist*, 19 July 2007.
38. 'Israel targets Iran nuclear plant', *Sunday Times*, 18 July 2004.

39. 'Cheney says Israel might "act first" on Iran', *New York Times*, 21 January 2005.
40. See, for example, 'Dagan: one nuke not enough for Iran', *Jerusalem Post*, 27 December 2005; 'Military Intelligence: Iran will cross nuclear threshold by 2009', *Ha'aretz*, 11 July 2007.
41. 'Iran is judged 10 years from nuclear bomb', *Washington Post*, 2 August 2005.
42. Available at: www.acronym.org.uk/docs/0509/doc14.htm
43. 'The US and the Iranian nuclear impasse', *Middle East Report*, No. 241, Winter 2006.
44. Available at: www.un.org/News/Press/docs/2006/sc8792.doc.htm
45. Available at: www.un.org/News/Press/docs/2006/sc8928.doc.htm
46. *Democracy Now*, 21 October 2005. A transcript is available at: www.democracynow.org/article.pl?sid=05/10/21/144258
47. 'The coming wars', *New Yorker*, 24 January 2005.
48. 'The Iran plans', *New Yorker*, 17 April 2006.
49. 'The redirection', *New Yorker*, 5 March 2007.
50. For details of the incentive scheme, see the translation of a *Ma'ariv* article from 8 July 2007, 'Israel to Iranian Jews: immigration at any price', available at: www.cjp.org/page.html?ArticleID=148952

    In consequence, Israel had a very real interest in finding other ways to encourage these Jews to leave Iran. Certainly there is evidence of previous Israeli intrigues to force Jews to leave other Middle East states and come to Israel. Israel may have hoped that, in addition to the obvious benefits of the spying operations, such espionage would create a climate in which Iranians started to distrust their Jewish neighbours and that it might lead to a popular backlash against them. That would 'prove' Israel's claims of rampant anti-Semitism in the Middle East and, in line with Israeli goals, force Iran's Jews to flee to Israel.
51. Hersh, 'Last stand', *New Yorker*, 10 July 2006. See also: 'Plan B', *New Yorker*, 28 June 2004; and 'The next act', *New Yorker*, 27 November 2006.
52. Available at: www.mfa.gov.il/MFA/Government/Speeches+by+Israeli+leaders/2006/Address+by+PM+Olmert+to+a+joint+meeting+of+US+Congress+24-May-2006.htm
53. For example, in his speech to the Herzliya conference, former Democratic Senator John Edwards observed: 'The war in Lebanon had Iranian fingerprints all over it. I was in Israel in June, and I took a helicopter trip over the Lebanese border. I saw the Hezbollah rockets, and the havoc wreaked by the extremism on Israel's border.

Hezbollah is an instrument of the Iranian government, and Iranian rockets allowed Hezbollah to attack and wage war against Israel.' Available at: www.rawstory.com/news/2007/Edwards_Iran_must_know_world_wont_0123.html.

Edwards, like most observers, ignored the fact that Hizbullah, though clearly supported financially and militarily by Iran, had its own local agenda (particularly in relation to the Shebaa Farms and a prisoner swap) and its own domestic concerns, not least the need, as a political party as well as a militia, not to lose the support of Lebanese Shia voters and political allies such as Michel Aoun's Christian faction, the Free Patriotic Movement. It is also worth noting that the Shia of Hizbullah identify as Arabs whereas the Shia of Iran identify as Persians.

54. Hersh, 'Watching Lebanon', *New Yorker*, 21 August 2006.
55. 'IDF retrieves bodies of four tank soldiers killed in south Lebanon', *Ha'aretz*, 14 July 2006.
56. 'Islamic Jihad leader killed in Lebanon', *Washington Post*, 26 May 2006; 'Lebanese man confesses to killings on behalf of Israel', *Ha'aretz*, 13 June 2006.
57. UNIFIL's reports are available online at: www.un.org/Depts/dpko/missions/unifil/unifilDrp.htm
58. The UN quietly changed its view in summer 2007 and agreed that the territory was in fact Lebanese after all ('UN tells Israel: Place Shaba Farms in hands of UNIFIL', *Ha'aretz*, 11 July 2007).
59. In October 2005, Nasrallah had observed: 'We do not need a regional war to regain occupied land; we just need to liberate Lebanese occupied land [the Shebaa Farms] and free our remaining prisoners of war ... If this could be accomplished by recourse to the international community and international relations, then we would welcome that' (quoted in 'Hizballah after the Syrian withdrawal', *Middle East Report*, No. 237, Winter 2005).
60. For more on Facility 1391, see 'Inside Israel's secret prison', *Ha'aretz*, 10 July 2003, and my article 'Facility 1391: Israel's Guantanamo', *Le Monde diplomatique*, November 2003.
61. 'Nasrallah: "mistake" led to deaths of 3 IDF soldiers', *Ha'aretz*, 25 June 2004.
62. 'Middle East foes swap prisoners', *BBC Online*, 29 January 2004.
63. 'Kidnap of soldiers in July was Hezbollah's fifth attempt', *Ha'aretz*, 19 September 2006.
64. '"No" to Lebanon War II', *Ha'aretz*, 13 July 2006.
65. 'Hezbollah warns Israel over raids', *BBC Online*, 12 July 2006.

66. Perhaps disingenuously, Nasrallah later observed: 'We did not think that the capture [of the two Israeli soldiers] would lead to a war at this time and of this magnitude. You ask me if I had known on July 11 ... that the operation would lead to such a war, would I do it? I say no, absolutely not' ('Nasrallah: We wouldn't have snatched soldiers if we thought it would spark war', *Ha'aretz*, 28 August 2006).

67. 'Top IDF officer: we knew war would not get abducted soldiers back', *Ha'aretz*, 25 April 2007. According to Major General Gadi Eisenkott, the war was supposed to 'launch a massive strike on Hezbollah targets, and return the territory in which the group was operating to Lebanese sovereignty'.

68. 'Capture of soldiers was "act of war" says Israel', *Guardian*, 13 July 2007.

69. 'Deadly Hezbollah attack on Haifa', *BBC Online*, 16 July 2006.

70. 'IDF commander: we fired more than a million cluster bombs in Lebanon', *Ha'aretz*, 12 September 2006.

71. Human Rights Watch, *First Look at Israel's Use of Cluster Munitions in Lebanon in July–August 2006*, 30 August 2006.

72. 'Israel attacks Beirut airport and sets up naval blockade', *New York Times*, 13 July 2006.

73. 'Iran and Syria helping Hizballah rearm', *Time*, 24 November 2006.

74. 'Israel strikes back after Haifa attacked', *CNN Online*, 17 July 2006.

75. 'IAF foils rocket transports from Syria', *Ynet*, 17 July 2006.

76. Binyamin Netanyahu, 'No cease-fire', *Wall Street Journal*, 23 July 2006. The same line was widely promoted by pro-Israel organisations. See, for example, 'Proportionality in the war in Lebanon' by the head of the Anti-Defamation League, Abraham Foxman, published in *Ha'aretz* on 23 July 2006.

77. The media emphasised Nasrallah's warmongering rather than his calls for an end to the fighting ('Pushing for a ceasefire from behind a barrage of Katyushas', *Guardian*, 28 July 2006).

78. 'Israel carries out airstrikes in Lebanon despite 48-hour halt', *USA Today*, 31 July 2006.

79. This apparently did not go entirely unnoticed by some Washington officials. 'The most important story in the Middle East is the growth of Nasrallah from a street guy to a leader – from a terrorist to a statesman,' said Robert Baer, a former CIA agent in Lebanon and long-time critic of Nasrallah, following the month-long war. Richard Armitage, the former Deputy Secretary of State, called

Nasrallah 'the smartest man in the Middle East' (quoted in 'The Redirection', *The New Yorker*, 5 March 2007).

80. For example, Israeli spokesman Mark Regev declared: 'Our operation in Lebanon is designed to neutralize one of the long arms of Iran – Hezbollah. Hezbollah is their proxy, being used as an instrument of Teheran to advance their extremist agenda and the blow to Hezbollah is a blow to Iranian interests and a blow to all extremist jihadist forces in the region' ('Ahmadinejad: destroy Israel, end crisis', *Washington Post*, 3 August 2006).

81. Again a double standard was applied to Hizbullah during the fighting. Israeli officials, backed by the international community, claimed that the Shia militia had been putting Lebanese civilians in harm's way by hiding their fighters and arms inside local communities. Jan Egeland, the UN's head of humanitarian affairs, called this 'cowardly blending'. In fact, there was little evidence for this claim, as was pointed out by a Human Rights Watch investigation at the time (*Fatal Strikes*, August 2006). A year later a report by UNIFIL noted that Hizbullah was moving its rockets from their original rural firing sites, in what were called 'nature reserves', into Shia villages in order to hide them from UN inspectors. The only reasonable conclusion to draw was that they had been kept well away from the villages during the war a year earlier ('Hezbollah hides rockets from UN in S. Lebanon villages', *Ha'aretz*, 22 July 2007). In contrast to Hizbullah, Israel had committed the offence of 'cowardly blending' during the war in at least two respects: first, Israeli soldiers had been found, as they usually are, in public places, queuing alongside Israeli civilians at bus stops and in bank lines, and sitting in cafes and restaurants; and second, Israel had chosen to build many of its military sites, including army bases and weapons factories, inside or next to civilian communities. Apart from in my own reports, these aspects of the war went entirely unremarked. See, for example, my articles 'The human shields of Nazareth', *Anti-war.com*, 19 July 2006; 'Israel, not Hizbullah, is putting civilians in danger', *Counterpunch*, 3 August 2006; and 'Hypocrisy and the clamor against Hizbullah', *Counterpunch*, 9 August 2006.

82. This error was made, for example, by the BBC's reporter Matthew Price, who appeared to be repeating Israeli government misinformation. See my 'The human shields of Nazareth', *Anti-war.com*, 19 July 2006.

83. 'Firefighters battle blaze at munitions warehouse in Nazareth', *Ha'aretz*, 18 May 2007.

84. I was given access to the HRA's field research before publication. The final report was due in autumn 2007, if the military censor passed it.

85. 'Katyusha rocket hit Haifa oil refineries complex during Second Lebanon War', *Ha'aretz*, 22 March 2007.

86. 'Report: Iran admits to supplying Hezbollah with drones', *Ha'aretz*, 10 November 2004; 'Hizbullah flies drone over Israel', *Ynet*, 11 April 2005. In the latter report, a Hizbullah spokesman said the drone would be used 'each time enemy [Israeli] aircrafts violate Lebanese sovereignty'.

87. 'Hizbollah's response reveals months of planning', *Independent*, 16 July, 2006. Schiff admitted that Hizbullah knew of the Miron base and had the ability to hit it in 'There should have been a preventive strike', *Ha'aretz*, 13 April 2007.

88. 'Siniora admits weakness of state's authority', *Daily Star* (Beirut), 28 August 2006.

89. Seymour Hersh, 'Watching Lebanon', *New Yorker*, 21 August 2006.

90. Ibid.

91. *Democracy Now*, 14 August 2006. A transcript is available at: www.democracynow.org/article.pl?sid=06/08/14/1358255

92. Hersh, 'Watching Lebanon'.

93. *Democracy Now*, 14 August 2006.

94. 'The Gray Zone', *New Yorker*, 6 August 2006.

95. 'Israel set war plan more than a year ago', *San Francisco Chronicle*, 21 July 2006.

96. 'PM: war in Lebanon was planned months in advance', *Ha'aretz*, 9 March 2007.

97. 'Senior IDF officer to Haaretz: PM did not order us to prepare for war', *Ha'aretz*, 12 March 2007.

98. 'Reservists called up for Lebanon strike', 12 July 2006.

99. 'Wagged by the military tail', *Ha'aretz*, 29 March 2007.

100. '"Army misled Olmert," Ben-Eliezer tells Winograd panel', *Israel News*, 18 June 2007.

101. 'In the shadow of the army', *Ha'aretz*, 11 May 2007.

102. 'A very, very painful response', *Ha'aretz*, 4 May 2007.

103. Ibid.

104. 'Senior IDF officer to Haaretz: PM did not order us to prepare for war', *Ha'aretz*.

105. In hindsight, it is possible to interpret UN Resolution 1559, passed in September 2005 after it was pushed heavily by the US, as seeking to establish the optimum conditions for an attack on Hizbullah. The resolution was designed to make Hizbullah more vulnerable

to Israel, first by ousting its local patron, Syria, from Lebanon and then by demanding the Shia militia disarm. It succeeded in achieving the first goal but not the second.

106. 'Lebanese hate Israel, upset at Nasrallah', *Ynet*, 15 July 2006.

107. 'Neocons: we expected Israel to attack Syria', *Ynet*, 16 December 2006.

108. 'Secretary Rice holds a news conference', *Washington Post*, 21 July 2006.

109. 'IDF prepared for attack by Syria', *Jerusalem Post*, 30 July 2006.

110. 'Bush caught off-guard in chat with Blair', *CNN Online*, 17 July 2006.

111. Available at: www.whitehouse.gov/news/releases/2006/07/20060 721-5.html
    The Max Boot article was published in the *Los Angeles Times* on 19 July 2006.

112. 'Bolton admits Lebanon truce block', *BBC Online*, 22 March 2007.

113. 'Pines-Paz: We expected the int'l community to end the war for us', *Ha'aretz*, 25 June 2007.

114. 'A war in the summer?', *Ha'aretz*, 23 April 2007; and 'IDF predicts possible conflict with Lebanon, Syria in 2007', *Ha'aretz*, 10 January 2007.

115. 'Mossad chief warned: Home front isn't ready', *Ha'aretz*, 30 March 2007.

116. 'A home front, but no command', *Ha'aretz*, 31 July 2006; 'Israel seeks operational link with U.S. missile defense system', *Ha'aretz*, 3 January 2007; 'U.S., IDF hold joint exercise on response to nukes', *Ha'aretz*, 18 March 2007; and 'Gov't may resurrect laser-based missile protection system', *Ha'aretz*, 2 August 2007.

117. 'War clouds gather over the Golan', *Forward*, 9 March 2007.

118. In fact, Syria became so convinced it was facing an imminent attack from Israel that Olmert used his Passover interviews in April 2007 to reassure Damascus that the Israeli army was not planning to strike. The reports suggested that Olmert was concerned that a 'miscalculation' by Damascus might lead to an overreaction and start an early war. Possibly, assuming the neocons still wanted Israel to attack Syria at some point, Olmert hoped to avoid hostilities with Syria before the army had recovered from its Lebanon failure and the 'home front' was better prepared for rocket attacks ('Israel seeks to reassure Syria: no summer attack', *Ha'aretz*, 2 April 2007; 'PMO DG Dinur says home front not ready for war', *Ha'aretz*, 12 July 2007).

119. 'Make a deal with Syria and weaken the Iran-Hezbollah axis', *Forward*, 26 January 2007. This position concurred with that of Israel's head of military intelligence, Amos Yadlin, who, according to *Ha'aretz*, believed that Syria's instincts were 'to respond, not initiate military procedures against Israel'. He told the government: 'Syria is building its military strength, but the likelihood of an all out-war at Syria's initiative is low' ('MI chief: chances of Syria starting a war against Israel are low', *Ha'aretz*, 26 February 2007).

120. 'Secret understandings reached between representatives from Israel and Syria' and 'How the covert contacts transpired', *Ha'aretz*, 16 January 2007.

121. 'NSC chief: Syrian bid for talks with Israel is genuine', *Ha'aretz*, 8 May 2007; 'Foreign Ministry memo: Assad sincere', *Jerusalem Post*, 10 May 2007.

122. Olmert found the leaks so embarrassing that in their immediate wake he tried to deny that the contacts had ever taken place ('Assassination of a peace initiative', *Ha'aretz*, 17 January 2007).

123. 'New forum to call for Syria talks', *Ha'aretz*, 28 January 2007.

124. 'Bush assails Pelosi's trip to Syria', *International Herald Tribune*, 3 April 2007.

125. 'U.S. official: Peace effort aimed at lessening Arab, EU pressure', *Ha'aretz*, 11 May 2007. See also 'Israel, U.S. views on Syria talks unchanged', *Ha'aretz*, 25 May 2007.

126. 'War clouds gather over the Golan', *Forward*.

127. The Baker-Hamilton report is available at: www.usip.org/isg/iraq_study_group_report/report/1206/

128. 'In Iraq, stay the course – but change it', *New York Sun*, 24 October 2006.

129. 'Deadly triggers', *Newsweek*, 24 January 2007; 'US warns Iran over Iraqi insurgency', *Guardian*, 1 February 2007; and 'U.S. to reveal Tehran's link to Iraq insurgency', *Washington Times*, 11 February 2007.

130. 'US commander accuses Iran of aiding Iraqi Shi'ite insurgency', *Voice of America Online*, 22 June 2006.

131. 'Top General casts doubt on Tehran's link to Iraq militias', *CNN Online*, 14 February 2007. See also: 'Doubts about Iran', *Newsweek*, 8 February 2007.

132. 'US accuses Iran of supplying arms to Taliban insurgents', *Guardian*, 19 April 2007.

133. 'Iran's secret plan for summer offensive to force US out of Iraq', *Guardian*, 22 May 2007.

134. Bush's speech is available at: www.whitehouse.gov/news/releases /2007/01/20070110-7.html

135. 'Chomsky on why Bush does diplomacy mafia-style', *Alternet*, 26 February 2006.

136. 'The war of humiliation', *Independent*, 2 April 2007.

137. 'UN Security Council unanimously approves tighter Iran sanctions', *Ha'aretz*, 24 March 2007.

138. 'American armada prepares to take on Iran', *Daily Telegraph*, 25 February 2007.

139. Olmert's speech is available at: www.pmo.gov.il/PMOEng/ Communication/PMSpeaks/speechher240107.htm

140. 'Former Mossad chief: Iran cannot destroy Israel', *Jerusalem Post*, 19 November 2006. A month later, his successor, Meir Dagan, observed that the West had plenty of time to engage in diplomatic negotiations with Tehran ('Israeli official: we have time to block Iran nuclear program', *Ha'aretz*, 19 December 2006).

141. 'Blowback', *Jerusalem Post*, 6 July 2007.

142. 'Iranian threat exaggerated, expert says', *Ynet*, 17 April 2007.

143. 'West "humiliating" Iran, says Hans Blix', *Ynet*, 26 February 2007.

144. 'So who's going to destroy Iran's nuclear reactor?', *Ha'aretz*, 7 March 2007. Strangely, this solid support among Israelis for an attack appeared not to be dented by the many reports in the local media of the horrifying array of chemical and biological weapons Iran supposedly had ready to launch against Israel. See, for example, 'Blowback', *Jerusalem Post*, 6 July 2007.

145. See, for example, 'Iran can also be wiped off the map', *Jerusalem Post*, 8 May 2006.

146. 'Netanyahu: It's 1938 and Iran is Germany; Ahmadinejad is preparing another Holocaust', *Ha'aretz*, 14 November 2006.

147. Ibid.

148. 'PM: Israel won't let world sink into apathy over Iran', *Jerusalem Post*, 29 January 2007.

149. For example, Khamenei said: 'We will never start a war. We have no intention of going to war with any state' ('Khamenei speech: excerpts', *BBC Online*, 4 June 2006).

150. See Informed Comment, from 3 May 2006: www.juancole. com/2006/05/hitchens-hacker-and-hitchens.html

151. '"Israel must be wiped off the map": the rumor of the century', *Anti-war.com*, 26 May 2007.

152. A few months earlier, these two issues had been directly linked when an Iranian newspaper arranged a Holocaust International

Cartoon Contest ('In Tehran, a riposte to the Danish cartoons', *International Herald Tribune*, 24 August 2006).

153. 'Britons to attend Iran's Holocaust conference', *Guardian*, 6 December 2006.

154. 'Tehran faces backlash over conference to question Holocaust', *Guardian*, 16 January 2006.

CHAPTER 3   END OF THE STRONGMEN, pp. 79–115

1. One Washington insider, Steven C. Clemons, noted that as Bush fell increasingly under the influence of Rice and Gates, Cheney started bypassing the White House. 'The thinking on Cheney's team is to collude with Israel, nudging Israel at some key moment in the ongoing standoff between Iran's nuclear activities and international frustration over this to mount a small-scale conventional strike against Natanz using cruise missiles. This strategy could be expected to trigger a sufficient Iranian counter-strike against US forces in the Gulf as to compel Bush to forgo the diplomatic track that the administration realists are advocating and engage in another war' (quoted in Gary Leupp, 'Cheney, Israel and Iran', *Counterpunch*, 26 May 2007).

2. Quoted in Seymour Hersh, 'Watching Lebanon', *New Yorker*, 21 August 2006.

3. 'Bush "would understand" attack on Iran', *Jerusalem Post*, 2 November 2006; and 'Bush: I would understand if Israel chose to attack Iran', *Ha'aretz*, 20 November 2006.

4. 'Iran forces Israeli rethink', *Guardian*, 2 April 2007.

5. 'Revealed: Israel plans nuclear strike on Iran', *The Times*, 7 January 2007.

6. 'If Israel had tactical nukes, would it use them against Iran?', *Jerusalem Post*, 8 January 2007.

7. 'Former Mossad chief not against taking out Ahmadinejad', *Ynet*, 18 April 2007.

8. 'The push for war', *London Review of Books*, 3 October 2002.

9. 'As US power fades, it can't find friends to take on Iran', *Guardian*, 2 February 2007.

10. See, for example, Robert Fisk, 'Lebanon slides towards civil war as anniversary of Hariri's murder looms', *Independent*, 14 February 2007.

11. See, for example, 'Interview: As'ad Abukhalil on the Nahr al-Bared siege', *Electronic Intifada*, 24 May 2007; Jim Quilty, 'The Collateral Damage of Lebanese Sovereignty', *Middle East Report Online*, 18 June 2007; and the transcript, dated 22 May 2007, of

an interview with Seymour Hersh broadcast on CNN that can be found at: http://rawstory.com/news/2007/Hersh_Bush_arranged_support_for_militants_0522.html.

Danny Rubinstein, a veteran *Ha'aretz* correspondent with excellent contacts in the Arab world, reported unsympathetically comments from his Palestinian informants that Fatah al-Islam was funded by Saudi Arabia. 'The idea was to develop a fanatical Sunni Muslim force in Lebanon that would effectively act as a counterweight to the Shi'ite Hezbollah zealots' ('In the name of Islam?', *Ha'aretz*, 12 June 2007).

12. 'Olmert: new Palestinian gov't must abide by Quartet demands', *Ha'aretz*, 11 February 2007.

13. 'U.S. pressing Israel to bolster pro-Abbas forces in Gaza', *Ha'aretz*, 20 May 2007.

14. Available at: www.congress.gov/cgi-bin/query/D?c108:6:./temp/ ~c108fpK2Jj::

15. Quoted by Seymour Hersh, 'The Syrian bet', *New Yorker*, 28 July 2003. Stephen Zunes points out that President Clinton offered to remove Syria from the US list of 'sponsors of terrorism' during Israeli-Syrian peace talks in the 1990s. According to US State Department reports, Damascus has not been directly implicated in an act of terror since 1986. However, Clinton conditioned such a removal on Damascus accepting Israel's terms for peace ('Washington takes aim at Syria', *Foreign Policy in Focus*, 2 May 2007).

16. Kaveh Bayat, 'The ethnic question in Iran', *Middle East Report*, No. 237, Winter 2005.

17. 'The botched US raid that led to the hostage crisis', *Independent*, 3 April 2007.

18. 'The secret war against Iran', 3 April 2007. Details of the programme are available at: http://blogs.abcnews.com/theblotter/2007/04/abc_news_exclus.html

19. Interestingly, this was exactly how the international policy was seen by Iranian officials. Alireza Zaker Esfahani, head of the Strategic Research Centre, a think-tank closely allied to Ahmadinejad, observed that the US goal was to provoke 'psychological distress' among Iranians in an attempt to 'undermine the unity and solidarity of the people' ('Iran's "security outlook"', *Middle East Report Online*, 9 July 2007).

20. 'Livni: Israel cannot accept Arab peace initiative in current form', *Ha'aretz*, March 2007; 'Livni, Jordanian FM to meet Sunday on Saudi initiative', *Ha'aretz*, 14 April 2007.

21. 'Sharon tells cabinet: Saudi plan threatens Israel's security', *Ha'aretz*, 4 March 2002; 'Government unimpressed by the latest version of Saudi peace proposal', *Ha'aretz*, 20 April 2002. The draft text of the 2002 plan is available at: www.haaretz.com/hasen/pages/ShArt.jhtml?itemNo=145479&contrassID=3&subContrassID=0&sbSubContrassID=0

22. 'Israel doesn't want peace', *Ha'aretz*, 8 April 2007.

23. Leader, *Financial Times*, 5 March 2005, cited in Chomsky, *Failed States*, p. 160.

24. A lone dissenting voice in this divisive debate on the left was Gabriel Ash. See his 'AIPAC and the anti-war movement: missing in action?', *Dissident Voice*, 21 April 2007. He critiqued the Mearsheimer and Walt thesis in 'Why oppose the Israel lobby?', *Dissident Voice*, 18 April 2006.

25. 'Bush says U.S. pullout would let Iraq radicals use oil as a weapon', *Washington Post*, 5 November 2006.

26. 'Chomsky on why Bush does diplomacy mafia-style', *Alternet*, 26 February 2006. An outspoken neocon, Michael Ledeen, reportedly made much the same point in the early 1990s: 'Every ten years or so, the United States needs to pick up some small crappy little country and throw it against the wall, just to show the world we mean business' (quoted in Jonah Goldberg, 'Baghdad delenda est, part two', *National Review*, 23 April 2002).

27. 'In 2003, U.S. spurned Iran's offer of dialogue', *Washington Post*, 18 June 2006.

28. 'Rice denies seeing Iranian proposal in '03', *Washington Post*, 8 February 2007.

29. The pair did not remain entirely alone in the mainstream. George Soros, a billionaire businessman and Holocaust survivor, wrote in the *New York Review of Books*: 'Aipac under its current leadership has clearly exceeded its mission, and far from guaranteeing Israel's existence, has endangered it' ('On Israel, America and AIPAC', vol. 54, no. 6, 12 April 2007). Pulitzer prize-winning columnist Nicholas Kristof also accused American politicians of muzzling themselves when it came to Israel's actions ('Talking about Israel', *New York Times*, 18 March 2007). On the margins was to be found a wealth of argument that Israel was shaping, or dictating, US foreign policy. Key texts include: Stephen Green, *Talking Sides: America's Secret Relations with a Militant Israel* (1984); Edward Tivnan, *The Lobby* (1988); Paul Findley, *They Dare to Speak Out* (2003); J.J. Goldberg, *Jewish Power* (2005); and Jim Petras, *The Power of Israel in the US* (2006).

30. 'The Israel lobby', *London Review of Books*, 23 March 2006.

31. Analyses that focused exclusively on the pro-Israel lobby to explain US Middle East policy also failed to take into account other relevant factors, particularly Washington's growing confidence in its own military invincibility following the collapse of the Soviet Union. Hubris seemed to be a reasonable part of the diagnosis for the Bush Administration's excesses and miscalculations.

32. I first proposed this model in an article entitled 'End of the strongmen', *Counterpunch*, 19 December 2006. The Syrian ambassador to London, Sami Khiyami, proposed something similar in the *Guardian* a few weeks later: 'Such objectives can only be achieved if the coherence of Middle Eastern societies is undermined. So the aim is not confined to toppling regimes, but extends to questioning the foundations of nation states. A policy has been designed to encourage sectarianism, ethnic divides, regional xenophobia, and the eventual Balkanisation of the Arab Middle East. Sadly, the outcome may be the partition of several states, producing smaller entities, regarded as easier to manage and dominate' ('The threat of Balkanisation', 13 March 2007).

33. Quote from Ledeen's book, *The War Against the Terror Masters*, cited in 'Flirting with Fascism', *The American Conservative*, 30 June 2003.

34. 'Cheney's grim vision: decades of war', *San Francisco Chronicle*, 15 January 2004.

35. The determination of many on the left to take a stand on one side or the other in this debate of who was driving US and Israeli policy led to some unfortunate special pleading. In an otherwise clear-sighted analysis of the 2006 Lebanon war, for example, Stephen Zunes tried to characterise Israel as a 'victim' of neocon policy ('U.S. role in Lebanon debacle', *Foreign Policy in Focus*, 18 May 2007).

36. The 'science' of understanding the Arab mind is well entrenched in the Israeli academy, with well-known exponents including Arnon Sofer, Raphael Israeli and David Bukay. Israeli, of Hebrew University, who was called to give 'expert' testimony on behalf of the state in a trial in 2004, observed that the Arab mentality was composed of 'a sense of victimization', 'pathological anti-Semitism' and 'a tendency to live in a world of illusions' (Sultany, *Israel and the Palestinian Minority: 2004*, p. 102).

37. Seymour Hersh, 'The Gray Zone', *New Yorker*, 24 May 2004, and 'The General's Report', *New Yorker*, 25 June 2007.

38. Israel Shahak revealed that on the third day of the Suez war, Prime Minister David Ben Gurion told the Knesset that the job of Israel's soldiers was 'to re-establish the kingdom of David and Solomon'

by annexing the Sinai. Shahak records that at that point the whole Knesset, apart from four Communist MKs, stood and sang the national anthem (*Open Secrets*, p. 44).

39. See, for example: 'Israel reveals secrets of how it gained bomb', *Daily Telegraph*, 22 December 2001; 'How the UK gave Israel the bomb' and 'US kept in the dark as secret nuclear deal was struck', *Guardian*, 4 August 2005; 'Papers reveal UK's nuclear aid to Israel', *Guardian*, 10 December 2005.

40. Cohen, *Whistleblowers and the Bomb*, pp. 12–13.

41. This revelation was made in the Hebrew edition, published in 2005, of a book on the 1967 war by Segev. Rather than destroying all copies of the book, Israel's military censor agreed to the line about nuclear weapons being covered with correction fluid ('How Israel's nuclear secret just slipped out', *The Age*, 23 July 2005). The book was published in English in May 2007 under the title *1967: Israel, the War, and the Year that Transformed the Middle East*. Segev made the point again, this time uncensored, in *Ha'aretz* in summer 2007, when he noted that Shimon Peres had done his best to prevent Israel from launching the Six-Day War. 'A few days before [the war] began he proposed that it be averted by means of a nuclear test: The Arabs would be frightened off, Israeli deterrence would be rehabilitated, there would be no need to attack Egypt. [Prime minister] Levi Eshkol and [defence minister] Moshe Dayan rejected the idea' ('Dreaming with Shimon', 19 July 2007).

42. Stephen Green, *Taking Sides: America's Secret Relations with a Militant Israel, 1948–1967* (London: Faber and Faber, 1984), p. 20, cited in Hirst, *The Gun and the Olive Branch*, p. 107.

43. The strategic relationship probably grew following the Suez crisis, with both countries seeing it as in their interests to contain Egypt's Nasser. In 1965 the US lent Israel $13 million for military purposes; by 1966, the year before the Six-Day War, the aid had jumped to $90 million (Clyde R. Mark, 'Israel–U.S. foreign assistance facts', *Congressional Record*, 1 May 1990, pp. 5420–3, cited in Sheldon L. Richman, '"Ancient history": U.S. conduct in the Middle East since World War II and the folly of intervention', *Cato Policy Analysis*, no. 159, 16 August 1991).

44. 'Senator Fulbright, 1967: The trouble is that the Jews think they have control of the Senate', *Ha'aretz*, 11 April 2007.

45. See 'The tentacles of a porcupine' and 'What price friendship?', *Ha'aretz*, 13 April 2007.

46. *US News and World Report*, 19 June 1967, cited in '"The Israel lobby" in perspective', *Middle East Report*, no. 243, Summer 2007.

47. The same transcripts of the Senate Foreign Relations Committee (see notes 44 and 45) show several Senators in awe of Israel's performance on the battlefield. On 7 June 1967, Senator Stuart Symington observed: 'In the last 12 hours, in 12 hours, I think it is fair to say ... General Dayan has really accomplished more against three or four countries ... than we have in two years in Vietnam.' Senator Gordon Allott added: 'Fortunately for the United States, a courageous people, with guts and foresight, have saved our bacon ... in the eyes of the world.'

48. Honore Catudal, *Israel's Nuclear Weaponry: A New Arms race in the Middle East* (London: Grey Seal, 1991), pp.13–42, cited in Hirst, *The Gun and the Olive Branch*, p. 119.

49. George Ball and Douglas Ball, *The Passionate Attachment*, p. 201.

50. Today, the Christian Zionists are reported to number in the tens of millions in the US. They believe that the Jews must return to the land promised them by God to bring about the Second Coming. Any Jews who have not converted to Christianity before the Messiah's arrival will perish in the Battle of Armageddon. Bush draws significant support from the Christian Zionists and this has been cited as one of the reasons for his strong support of Israel. See Gershom Gorenberg, *The End of Days*.

51. *The Passionate Attachment*, p. 212.

52. See Finkelstein, *Beyond Chutzpah*, Part One.

53. 'Economist tallies swelling cost of Israel to US', *Christian Science Monitor*, 9 December 2002. The same economist, Thomas Stauffer, who had originally made the calculations for the US army, believed that the cost doubled if the price of instability in the region caused by the Israeli-Palestinian conflict was included ('The costs to American taxpayers of the Israeli-Palestinian conflict: $3 trillion', *Washington Report on Middle East Affairs*, June 2003).

54. Mitchell Plitnick and Chris Toensing, '"The Israel lobby" in perspective', *Middle East Report*, no. 243, Summer 2007.

55. Many theories have been advanced for not only why Israel not only attacked the *Liberty* but also sought to sink it, and why Washington has never held an inquiry or released key documents relating to the event. One intriguing possibility is that Israel hoped that, if there were no survivors of the *Liberty*, it could be made to look as if Egypt attacked the ship and the US would be drawn into attacking Cairo. In fact, the available evidence suggests that the US very nearly did attack Egypt, only calling back its warplanes at the last moment. A BBC documentary on this subject, *Dead*

in the Water, can be viewed at: www.informationclearinghouse. info/article5073.htm

56. *The Passionate Attachment*, p. 58.

57. Ibid., pp. 105–7.

58. *Tinderbox*, p. 40. Zunes rather simplifies this relationship. Israel used its influence in Washington to try to prevent US arms sales to the Arab regimes, including Bush's $33 billion spending bonanza in summer 2007 ('U.S. Congressmen say will try to block proposed Saudi arms deal', *Ha'aretz*, 30 July 2007). Israel also damaged the interests of US arms manufacturers over many decades by secretly selling components of US military technology in its possession. Recent covert arms sales to China led to a rare show of US hostility towards Israel ('US acts over Israeli arms sales to China', *Guardian*, 13 June 2005).

59. 'US accused of fuelling arms race with $20bn Arab weapons sale', *Guardian*, 30 July 2007.

60. Israel Shahak notes, for example, that Jordan's peace treaty with Israel in 1994 offered strategic advantages to the Israeli air force, opening a direct route to Iraq and Iran. Or as the veteran military correspondent Amir Oren revealed shortly before the signing ceremony: 'The agreement is intended to establish a military alliance between Israel and Jordan and thus extend the boundary of Israel's military presence to the eastern tip of the Jordanian desert ... Israel's undisguised military presence there, right on the border of Iraq, means that the route of its war planes to Iran will be hundreds of kilometres shorter.' Oren noted that, with Jordan expected to grant Israel the right to overfly its territory in 'emergency situations', the air force could undertake bombing missions without refuelling stops (quoted in Shahak, *Open Secrets*, pp. 78–9).

61. George Ball notes that Ben Gurion made this comment in a diary entry for 24 May 1948 and that Moshe Sharrett reported a similar comment from Ben Gurion in his own diary on 27 February 1954 (*The Passionate Attachment*, p. 120). Michael Bar-Zohar, Ben Gurion's biographer, reports the Israeli leader making much the same observation in 1956 (*Ben-Gurion*, p. 236).

62. *The Passionate Attachment*, p. 121.

63. The English translation is taken from 'From the Israeli press', *Journal of Palestine Studies*, vol. 11, no. 3 (Spring, 1982), p. 169.

64. Ibid., pp. 169–70.

65. Ibid., pp. 171–2.

66. See, for example, Reinhart, *Israel/Palestine*, Chapter 4.

67. In 2002 the Middle East Studies Association allowed Gazit to 'review' Shahak's book. Although Shahak translated the article by Gazit cited here from Hebrew, Gazit makes no claim in the review that his opinions have been misrepresented and produces no evidence to dispute Shahak's argument. Instead, he simply ignores the evidence of his own writings and states: 'I have known Israel intimately for the past seventy years ... Upon reading *Open Secrets*, I asked myself if the two of us had been living in the same country.' The review is available at: http://fp.arizona.edu/mesassoc/ Bulletin/36-1/36-1Israel-ArabWorld.htm#Shahak

68. *Open Secrets*, p. 41.

69. Ibid., p. 42.

70. Ibid., p. 43.

71. 'For Israel, September 11 was a Hanukkah miracle', *Ha'aretz*, 18 December 2001.

72. 'The stale myth of battlefield bravado', *Ha'aretz*, 13 April 2007.

73. Richard Sale, UPI, 1 March 2001, cited in Reinhart, *Israel/Palestine*, p. 199.

74. *Ha'aretz*, 19 October 2001, cited in ibid., p. 202.

75. *Yed'iot Aharonot*, 7 November 2000, cited in ibid., p. 200.

76. 'Surprising conversations', *Ha'aretz*, 1 June 2007.

77. *Open Secrets*, p. 43.

78. *Journal of Palestine Studies*, vol. 11, no. 3 (Spring, 1982), p. 168.

79. The first use of this phrase is usually attributed to the influential neocon thinker Bernard Lewis in an article entitled 'The roots of Muslim rage', published in the *Atlantic Monthly* in September 1990. Similar ideas, however, have popular and deep roots in Israeli thinking, where for decades generals, politicians, academics and journalists have characterised Israel as an outpost of Western civilisation in a hostile Arab and Muslim world.

80. See 'From the Israeli press', *Journal of Palestine Studies*, vol. 11, no. 4 (Summer–Autumn, 1982), pp. 209–14; Israel Shahak's version, which was translated at the request of the Association of Arab American University Graduates following immediately in the wake of Israel's invasion of Lebanon, is available online at: http://the-unjustmedia.com/the%20zionist_plan_for_the_middle_east.htm

81. 'Egypt and the Zionist plan of division', *Al-Ahram Weekly*, 12–18 July 2007. This article was one of four in which Nafaa examined Yinon's approach to the Middle East, warning readers that Yinon's essay encapsulated decades of Zionist thinking towards the Arab world.

82. The quotes used here are from the *Journal of Palestine Studies* translation; p. 210.
83. Ibid., p. 209.
84. Ibid., p. 210.
85. Ibid., p. 211.
86. Ibid., p. 212.
87. Ibid., p. 213–4.
88. Bar-Zohar, *Ben-Gurion*, p. 236.
89. Abba Eban, *Personal Witness: Israel Through My Eyes* (New York: 1992), p. 92, cited in Shlaim, *The Iron Wall*, p. 178.
90. Shlaim, *The Iron Wall*, p. 185.
91. 'Israel: the ultimate winner', *Al-Ahram Weekly*, 17–23 April 2003.
92. Bar-Zohar, *Ben-Gurion*, p. 260.
93. Ibid., p. 262.
94. Hersh, 'Plan B', *New Yorker*, 28 June 2004; 'Israelis "train Kurdish forces"', *BBC Online*, 20 September 2006.
95. Israel Shahak noted that, in the last days before the Shah's fall, Ariel Sharon had prepared to send elite units of the Israeli army to Tehran to help Iran's generals, but the plan was overruled at the last minute by Menachem Begin (*Open Secrets*, p. 44).
96. David Nyhan, *Boston Globe*, 21 October 1982, cited in Chomsky, *The Fateful Triangle*, p. 457.
97. Ibid., pp. x–xi.
98. Ibid., p. 463.
99. Ibid., p. 455.
100. 'Castle of sand', *Yed'iot Aharonot*, 9 August 1982, cited in ibid., p. 459.
101. 'Egypt and the Zionist plan of division', *Al-Ahram Weekly*. Similar plans for the Sinai have been intermittently resurrected. In late 2005 Uzi Arad, a former head of Mossad intelligence and the organiser of the Herzliya conferences – and probably one of the most influential Israeli thinkers behind the scenes – promoted a scheme put forward by Yehoshua Ben Arieh, the former rector of Hebrew University. In it, Israel would give Egypt a corridor of land in the Negev while Cairo would donate part of the northern Sinai to Gaza's Palestinians. In return, Israel would receive large areas of the West Bank from the Palestinians ('Trading land for peace', *New Republic*, 28 November 2005).
102. *Journal of Palestine Studies*, vol. 11, no. 4, p. 214.

CHAPTER 4   REMAKING THE MIDDLE EAST, pp. 116–149

1. For a useful overview of the al-Qaeda phenomenon, see Jason Burke's *Al-Qaeda*.
2. The idea of 'permanent war' had been articulated by an Israeli general, Yitzhak Rabin, back in 1991, according to Israel Shahak. Rabin told his Labor Knesset faction that Israel was doomed to live forever in war, or under the threat of war, from the entire Arab world. He also argued that Israel 'must assume an essentially aggressive role, so as to be in the position to dictate the terms of a conclusion', and that any attack on Israeli soil would incur the following response: 'They will be destroyed root and branch'. Shahak believed Rabin was referring to using tactical nuclear weapons against such enemies (*Open Secrets*, p. 46).
3. 'The war on terror won't end in Baghdad', *Wall Street Journal*, 4 September 2002.
4. 'The war drummers', *Counterpunch*, 10 September 2002.
5. Similar contempt for the oil industry and its allies' obsession with stability was shown in late 2002 by David Frum, a former editor at the *Wall Street Journal*, speechwriter for President Bush and a resident fellow of the American Enterprise Institute, part of the neocon establishment: 'Listen to the retired officials and distinguished public servants who have criticised President Bush's Iraq policy – the Brent Scowcrofts and the James Bakers, the Anthony Zinnis and the Laurence Eagleburgers – and you will hear that word "stability" over and over again. "Stability" means oil.' Interestingly, Frum pointed this out as he tried to make the following revealing argument: Bush, he said, wanted to bring democracy to Iraq but the oil industry opposed democratisation, believing it would provoke a civil war that would be bad for business. Therefore, according to Frum, a war against Iraq could not be about oil ('America in the dock', *Daily Telegraph*, 21 October 2002).
6. 'James Baker's disciples', *Jerusalem Post*, 7 June 2007.
7. One minor theory worth noting was that, in occupying Iraq, the US would have control of the country's extensive water system that feeds the rivers of neighbouring states. On this view, Washington may have seen such control as leverage it could use to pressure states and groups in the region (Stephen Pelletiere, 'A war crime or an act of war?', *New York Times*, 31 January 2003).
8. The article is available at: www.palestinecenter.org/cpap/pubs/20020418ftr.html
9. 'The push for war', *London Review of Books*, 3 October 2002.

10. Mike Whitney, 'Putin's censored press conference', *Signs of the Times*, 10 June 2007, available at: www.signs-of-the-times.org/ articles/show/134240-Putin's+Censored+Press+Conference:+The +transcript+you+weren't+supposed+to+see+

11. Reuters, 'China weighs Iran and Iraq risks for oil prize', 27 November 2006.

12. Chomsky, 'Beyond the ballot', *Khaleej Times*, 6 January 2006.

13. Quoted in Shahak's online foreword to Yinon's article, dated 13 June 1982.

14. There were plenty of reports of Israel using experimental weapons in the occupied territories during the second intifada and before. See, for example, my article 'Vale of tears', *Al-Ahram Weekly*, 5 April 2001; 'Italian probe: Israel used new weapon prototype in Gaza Strip', *Ha'aretz*, 11 October 2006; 'Gaza doctors say patients suffering mystery injuries after Israeli attacks', *Guardian*, 17 October 2006. Israel also admitted using phosphorus bombs in Lebanon in 2006: 'Israel admits it used phosphorus weapons', *Guardian*, 23 October 2006. There was evidence Israel had used enriched uranium devices there too: 'An enigma that only the Israelis can fully explain', *Independent*, 28 October 2006.

15. 'Laboratory for a fortressed world', *The Nation*, 14 June 2007.

16. An interesting sidenote concerns the background of the head of the Homeland Security Department, Michael Chertoff. His father, an American rabbi, married Livia Eisen, who lived in Israel for many years and was an air hostess for the country's national carrier El Al in the 1950s. There are reports that she was involved in Operation Magic Carpet, which brought Jews to Israel from Yemen. It therefore seems possible that Livia Eisen was an Israeli national, and one with possible links to the Mossad. Unusually, Chertoff was not questioned about his background or his connections to Israel during the US Senate hearing in 2005 into his appointment.

17. These practices were honed during the first 20 years of the state, when Israel's Palestinian citizens lived under martial law, and are discussed in my book *Blood and Religion*. For an insight into how similar practices continue to this day, see 'Nobody has forgotten about October', *Ha'aretz*, 1 June 2007.

18. Hirst, *The Gun and the Olive Branch*, pp. 520–6.

19. Kimmerling, *Politicide*, p. 76.

20. For more on this opposition, see my book *Blood and Religion*, especially Chapter 1.

21. For the evolution of this policy, see my book *Blood and Religion*, Chapter 4.

22. Map available at: www.reliefweb.int/rw/fullMaps_Sa.nsf/ luFullMap/2E4FB73CC49B3CD9C12572F30041476A/$File/ ocha_ACC_opt070507.pdf?OpenElement

23. There is evidence that Sharon and the army wanted to kill Arafat much earlier but were prevented by Washington from doing so while the coalition against Iraq was being built. According to a Sharon confidant, the journalist Uri Dan, Bush eventually gave permission for Israel to kill Arafat so long as it was done in a way that could not be detected (Uri Avnery, 'If Arafat were still alive', *Guardian*, 31 January 2007).

24. Israel and the US tried various ways to strengthen Fatah against Hamas. In November 2006, a US general admitted that Washington was building up Fatah's forces to give them the edge against Hamas (Reuters, 'U.S. general says building up Abbas's guard', 24 November 2006). In December, US and European officials visited a training base for Fatah's Badr Brigade in Jordan to discuss deploying its 1,000 members in Gaza and the West Bank ('PA official: Haniyeh, Abbas will meet in Jordan later this week', *Ha'aretz*, 25 December 2006). Then Egypt sent a shipment of arms to forces loyal to Abbas in Gaza ('Israel confirms arms shipment sent to aid Abbas', *New York Times*, 28 December 2006). Plans to step up this aid emerged in spring 2007 ('Israel backs U.S. plan to arm pro-Abbas forces', *Ha'aretz*, 16 April 2007).

25. The 53-page leaked report can be viewed at: http://image.guardian. co.uk/sys-files/Guardian/documents/2007/06/12/DeSotoReport. pdf

26. 'U.S. pressing Israel to bolster pro-Abbas forces in Gaza', *Ha'aretz*, 20 May 2007; 'Israel agrees to allow Abbas-controlled Presidential Guard to train near Jericho', *Ha'aretz*, 24 May 2007.

27. 'Fatah defiant on West Bank as Hamas takes Gaza', *Guardian*, 15 June 2007.

28. 'Hamas acted on a very real fear of a US-sponsored coup', *Guardian*, 22 June 2007.

29. 'Washington rallies behind Abbas with end to Palestinian boycott', *Guardian*, 19 June 2007.

30. 'Abbas wins US backing as Fatah stages revenge raids', *Independent*, 17 June 2007.

31. 'Sharon's dream', *Ha'aretz*, 18 June 2007.

32. 'World Bank scolds Israel for impeding travel in West Bank', *Ha'aretz*, 9 May 2007.

33. In this mythologised view of US foreign policy, Paul Wolfowitz was often cited as the chief proponent of the democratisation model. His sudden interest in democracy for the Middle East was,

however, hard to reconcile with his earlier career, including his time as US ambassador to Indonesia in the late 1980s when he was fiercely loyal to the country's dictator, General Suharto. When later, in 1999, the US promoted Indonesia's withdrawal from occupied East Timor, Wolfowitz objected, in the words of one reporter, on the grounds that, 'due to tribal and clan-based tensions, [East Timor] would descend into civil war. Only the TNI [Indonesian army] had prevented such an outcome, according to Wolfowitz' ('Wolfowitz visited Indonesia for closer military ties, not tsunami relief', Pacific News Service, 19 January 2005).

34. 'It is not only God that will be Blair's judge over Iraq', *Guardian*, 14 May 2007.
35. 'US: can Congress defy Bush?', March 2007.
36. 'As US power fades, it can't find friends to take on Iran', *Guardian*, 2 February 2007.
37. Chomsky, *Failed States*, p. 147.
38. *Coping with Crumbling States: A Western and Israeli Balance of Power Strategy for the Levant*, Institute for Advanced Strategic and Political Studies, December 1996. Available at: www.iasps. org/strat2.htm
39. 'Shattered illusions', *Al-Ahram Weekly*, 19 April 2007.
40. 'U.S. intelligence agencies predicted problems U.S. now facing in Iraq', *Ha'aretz*, 26 May 2007.
41. 'Intelligence, policy, and the war in Iraq', *Foreign Affairs*, March/April 2006.
42. 'The full transcript of evidence given to the Butler inquiry', *Independent*, 15 December 2006.
43. 'The real news in the Downing Street memos', *Los Angeles Times*, 23 June 2005.
44. 'The calamity of disregard', *Guardian*, 4 August 2007.
45. The ideology of Ba'athism emerged in 1950s Damascus. Its core belief was that the Arab nation had a special mission to end colonial interference and promote humanitarianism through becoming a mass socialist movement. Ba'athism concentrated on land reform and public ownership of natural resources.
46. Pipes, 'Civil war in Iraq?', *New York Sun*, 28 February 2006.
47. Pepe Escobar, 'Exit strategy: civil war', *Asia Times*, 10 June 2005.
48. This was also the diagnosis of Iraq's future made by Hizbullah leader Sheikh Hassan Nasrallah: 'The daily killing and displacement which is taking place in Iraq aims at achieving three Iraqi parts, which will be sectarian and ethnically pure as a prelude to the partition of Iraq. Within one or two years at the most, there will

be total Sunni areas, total Shiite areas, and total Kurdish areas. Even in Baghdad, there is a fear that it might be divided into two areas, one Sunni and one Shiite ... A day will come when [Bush] will say, "I cannot do anything, since the Iraqis want the partition of their country and I honor the wishes of the people of Iraq"' (quoted in 'The redirection', *New Yorker*, 5 March 2007).

49. 'Sharon warned Bush', *Forward*, 12 January 2007.

50. 'America ponders cutting Iraq in three', *The Times*, 8 October 2006.

51. 'Kurdistan's covert back-channels', *Mother Jones*, 11 April 2007.

52. 'French report: former U.N. envoy Bolton says U.S. has "no strategic interest" in united Iraq', *International Herald Tribune*, 29 January 2007.

53. *The Case for Soft Partition in Iraq*, Saban Center analysis, no. 12, June 2007, available at: http://www.brook.edu/fp/saban/analysis/june2007iraq_partition.htm

54. 'Divide and rule – America's plan for Baghdad', *Independent*, 11 April 2007.

55. 'Latest US solution to Iraq's civil war: a three-mile wall', *Guardian*, 21 April 2007.

56. 'Regional implications of the Iraq War', *Foreign Policy in Focus*, 27 March 2007.

57. The speech is available at: www.state.gov/secretary/rm/2005/48328.htm

58. See for example, Reuters, 'U.S. sends more arms to Lebanon', 26 May 2007. Robert Fisk noted, however, that the weapons being sent by the US to the Lebanese army had been doctored, at the request of Israel, so that they could not be used to defend the country in case of war between the two. 'The Gazelles [helicopters] have no rockets – courtesy of the United States, because Israel fears they will be used against its own forces. The Belgians even offered Leopard tanks – again vetoed by the United States – in case the Lebanese used them against the Israelis. So the Lebanese are armed sufficiently to fight Palestinians, but not enough to fight their enemies on their southern frontier' ('Can the Lebanese army fight America's war against terror?', *Independent*, 3 June 2007).

59. 'Hizbullah accuses US of secret war and arming opponents', *Guardian*, 11 April 2007.

60. 'Lebanon "smashes Israel spy ring"', *BBC Online*, 18 May 2004.

61. 'Beirut to complain to UN about "Israeli" hand in assassinations', *Ha'aretz*, 17 June 2006.

62. UPI, 'Terror in Beirut', 26 June 2005.
63. 'Beirut to complain to UN about "Israeli" hand in assassinations', *Ha'aretz*.
64. 'CIA running black propaganda operation against Iran, Syria and Lebanon, officials say', *Raw Story*, 4 June 2007.
65. 'The coming wars', *New Yorker*, 24 January 2005.
66. 'The Iran plans', *New Yorker*, 17 April 2006.
67. 'The redirection', *New Yorker*, 5 March 2007.
68. Ibid.
69. A transcript, dated 22 May 2007, of the interview, with CNN, can be found at: http://rawstory.com/news/2007/Hersh_Bush_arranged_support_for_militants_0522.html
70. Toby Jones, 'The Iraq effect in Saudi Arabia', *Middle East Report*, no. 237, Winter 2005.
71. 'If US leaves Iraq we will arm Sunni militias, Saudis say', *Guardian*, 14 December 2006.
72. Morten Valbjorn and Andre Bank, 'Signs of a new Arab cold war', *Middle East Report*, no. 242, Spring 2007.
73. Ibid.
74. 'Why the United Nations belongs in Iraq', 20 July 2007.
75. 'US accuses Saudis of telling lies about Iraq', 28 July 2007.
76. 'US arms Sunni dissidents in risky bid to contain al-Qaida fighters in Iraq', *Guardian*, 12 June 2007.
77. Timothy Garton Ash, 'Faced with the tragedy of Iraq, the US must rethink its whole foreign policy', *Guardian*, 14 June 2007. Shortly afterwards American inspectors discovered that 190,000 weapons – 110,000 AK-47s and 80,000 pistols – given to the Iraqi security forces by the US army had gone missing, and presumably ended up in the hands of the insurgents or criminals ('US "loses track" of Iraq weapons', *BBC Online*, 6 August 2007).
78. Carter Malkasian, 'America's tribal strategy for Iraq', Comment is Free, *Guardian*, 15 June 2007.
79. 'Seymour Hersh and Iran', *Counterpunch*, 5 March 2007.
80. Such a view was supported by a report in the *Guardian* in summer 2007 which argued that Vice-President Dick Cheney was again gaining the upper hand against Rice and Gates on a showdown with Iran. A Washington source reportedly observed that 'Mr Bush and Mr Cheney did not trust any potential successors in the White House, Republican or Democratic, to deal with Iran decisively. They are also reluctant for Israel to carry out any strikes because the US would get the blame in the region anyway.' Patrick Cronin, a director at the UK-based International Institute of Strategic Studies, added: 'The red line is not in Iran. The red line is in Israel. If Israel

is adamant it will attack, the US will have to take decisive action. The choices are: tell Israel no, let Israel do the job, or do the job yourself' ('Cheney pushes Bush to act on Iran', *Guardian*, 16 July 2007).

81. Quoted in 'The redirection', *New Yorker*, 5 March 2007.
82. 'Fighting the next war', *Jerusalem Post*, 19 April 2007.

SELECT BIBLIOGRAPHY

Abunimah, Ali, *One Country: A Bold Proposal to End the Israeli-Palestinian Impasse* (New York: Metropolitan Books, 2006)

Aburish, Said, *Arafat: From Defender to Dictator* (London: Bloomsbury, 1998)

Ball, George, and Douglas Ball, *The Passionate Attachment: America's Involvement with Israel, 1947 to the Present* (New York: W. W. Norton, 1992)

Bar-Zohar, Michael, *Ben-Gurion* (Tel Aviv: Magal Books, 2003)

Ben-Ami, Shlomo, *Scars of War, Wounds of Peace: The Israeli–Arab Tragedy* (London: Phoenix, 2006)

Benvenisti, Meron, *Sacred Landscape: The Buried History of the Holy Land since 1948* (Berkeley: University of California Press, 2000)

Burke, Jason, *Al-Qaeda: The True Story of Radical Islam* (London: Penguin, 2004)

Carey, Roane (ed.), *The New Intifada: Resisting Israel's Apartheid* (London: Verso, 2001)

Chomsky, Noam, *The Fateful Triangle: The United States, Israel and the Palestinians* (London: Pluto Press, 1999)

—— *Understanding Power* (London: Vintage, 2003)

—— *Failed States: The Abuse of Power and the Assault on Democracy* (New York: Owl Books, 2006)

Cohen, Yoel, *Whistleblowers and the Bomb: Vanunu, Israel and Nuclear Secrecy* (London: Pluto Press, 2005)

Cook, Jonathan, *Blood and Religion: The Unmasking of the Jewish and Democratic State* (London: Pluto Press, 2006)

Curtis, Mark, *Web of Deceit: Britain's Real Role in the World* (London: Vintage, 2003)

Edwards, David, and David Cromwell, *Guardians of Power: The Myth of the Liberal Media* (London: Pluto Press, 2006)

Elon, Amos, *A Blood-Dimmed Tide* (London: Allen Lane, 2000)

Ezrahi, Yaron, *Rubber Bullets: Power and Conscience in Modern Israel* (Berkeley: University of California Press, 1998)

Finkelstein, Norman, *Image and Reality of the Israel-Palestine Conflict* (London: Verso, 2001)

—— *The Holocaust Industry: Reflections on the Exploitation of Jewish Suffering* (London: Verso, 2000)

—— *Beyond Chutzpah: On the Misuse of Anti-Semitism and the Abuse of History* (Berkeley: University of California Press, 2005)

Fisk, Robert, *Pity the Nation: The Abduction of Lebanon* (New York: Nation Books, 2002)

—— *The Great War for Civilisation: The Conquest of the Middle East* (London: Fourth Estate, 2005)

Friel, Howard, and Richard Falk, *The Record of the Paper: How the New York Times Misreports US Foreign Policy* (London: Verso, 2007)

Gorenberg, Gershom, *The End of Days: Fundamentalism and the Struggle for the Temple Mount* (New York: Oxford University Press, 2002)

—— *The Accidental Empire: Israel and the Birth of the Settlements, 1967–1977* (New York: Times Books, 2006)

Hirst, David, *The Gun and the Olive Branch* (London: Faber, 2003)

Huntington, Samuel, *The Clash of Civilizations and the Remaking of World Order* (New York: Free Press, 2002)

Khalidi, Rashid, *Palestinian Identity: The Construction of Modern National Consciousness* (New York: Columbia University Press, 1997)

Kimmerling, Baruch, and Joel Migdal, *The Palestinian People: A History* (Cambridge, MA: Harvard University Press, 2003)

Kimmerling, Baruch, *Politicide: Ariel Sharon's War against the Palestinians* (London: Verso, 2003)

—— *The Invention and Decline of Israeliness: State, Society and the Military* (Berkeley: University of California Press, 2005)

Kinzer, Stephen, *Overthrow: America's Century of Regime Change from Hawaii to Iraq* (New York: Times Books, 2006).

Kretzmer, David, *The Occupation of Justice: The Supreme Court of Israel and the Occupied Territories* (New York: SUNY, 2002)

Laqueur, Walter, and Barry Rubin (eds), *The Israel–Arab Reader* (New York: Penguin Books, 2001)

Masalha, Nur, *A Land Without a People: Israel, Transfer and the Palestinians, 1949–96* (London: Faber, 1997)

—— *Imperial Israel and the Palestinians: The Politics of Expulsion* (London: Pluto Press, 2000)

—— *The Politics of Denial: Israel and the Palestinian Refugee Problem* (London: Pluto Press, 2003)

Massad, Joseph, *The Persistence of the Palestinian Question: Essays on Zionism and the Palestinians* (London: Routledge, 2006)

Morris, Benny, *The Birth of the Palestinian Refugee Problem Revisited* (New York: Cambridge University Press, 2004)

—— *Righteous Victims: A History of the Zionist–Arab Conflict, 1881–2001* (New York: Vintage, 2001)

Neumann, Michael, *The Case Against Israel* (California: Counterpunch, 2005)

Palast, Greg, *Armed Madhouse* (New York: Plume, 2007)

Pappe, Ilan, *A History of Modern Palestine: One Land, Two Peoples* (Cambridge: Cambridge University Press, 2004)

—— *The Ethnic Cleansing of Palestine* (Oxford: One World, 2006)

Prior, Michael, *Zionism and the State of Israel* (London: Routledge, 1999)

Reinhart, Tanya, *Israel/Palestine: How to End the War of 1948* (New York: Seven Stories Press, 2002)

—— *The Road Map to Nowhere: Israel/Palestine since 2003* (London: Verso, 2006)

Rogan, Eugene, and Avi Shlaim (eds), *The War for Palestine: Rewriting the History of 1948* (Cambridge: Cambridge University Press, 2001)

Roy, Sara, *Failing Peace: Gaza and the Palestinian–Israeli Conflict* (London: Pluto Press, 2007)

Said, Edward, *Peace and its Discontents: Essays on Palestine in the Middle East Peace Process* (New York: Vintage, 1996)

—— *The End of the Peace Process: Oslo and After* (London: Granta, 2001)

Shahak, Israel, *Jewish History, Jewish Religion: The Weight of Three Thousand Years* (London: Pluto Press, 1994)

—— *Open Secrets: Israeli Nuclear and Foreign Policies* (London: Pluto Press, 1997)

Shahak, Israel, and Norton Mezvinsky, *Jewish Fundamentalism in Israel* (London: Pluto Press, 1999)

Shlaim, Avi, *The Iron Wall: Israel and the Arab World* (London: Penguin Books, 2000)

Sternhell, Zeev, *The Founding Myths of Israel* (New Jersey: Princeton University Press, 1999)

Sultany, Nimr (ed.), *Israel and the Palestinian Minority: 2004* (Haifa: Mada, 2005)

Swisher, Clayton E., *The Truth About Camp David* (New York: Nation Books, 2004)

Thomas, Gideon, *Gideon's Spies: Mossad's Secret Warriors* (New York: Pan Books, 1999)

Tilley, Virginia, *The One-State Solution: A Breakthrough for Peace in the Israeli–Palestinian Deadlock* (Michigan: University of Michigan Press, 2005)

Van Creveld, Martin, *Moshe Dayan* (London: Weidenfeld and Nicolson, 2004)

Wasserstein, Bernard, *Divided Jerusalem* (London: Profile Books, 2002)

Zunes, Stephen, *Tinderbox: US Middle East Policy and the Roots of Terrorism* (London: Zed Books, 2003)

INDEX

Abbas, Mahmoud, 83, 129–30, 181n
ABC News, 84, 142
Abdel Jawwad, Saleh, 110–12
Abdul Ahad, Ghaith, x–xi
Abdullah, king of Saudi Arabia, 144–5
Abrams, Elliott, 24, 26, 31, 47, 60, 70, 88, 130, 157n
Abu Ghraib prison, 94
Adhamiya, 139
Afghanistan,
  and al-Qaeda, 28
  and sectarian tensions, 109
  and the Taliban, 17, 117, 156n
  as a US base, 39
  Iranian involvement, claims of, 72, 158n
  Soviet invasion of, 18
  US attack on, xii, xvii, 43, 117, 156n
Agha, Hussein, 7
Ahmadinejad, Mahmoud
  and nuclear programme, 46
  and Syria, 65, 69
  Hitler, comparison with, 40, 75–6
  Holocaust, denial of, 77–8
  threat of assassination, 80
  'wipe Israel off the map', 57, 74, 75–7
Aiken, George, 96
al-Faisal, Prince Turki, 145
al-Faisal, Saud, 144
al-Hamishmar, 41, 102
al-Maliki, Nuri, 12, 13, 145
al-Qaeda, 179n
  and Iran, 72

  and Iraq, 7, 29–30, 72, 134, 146–7
  and Saudi Arabia, 119
  and Syria, 84
  and Afghanistan, xvii, 28
  and the 'war on terror', 40, 85, 92–3, 143, 144, 147
  rise of, 17, 116–17
al-Sadr, Moqtada, 145
al-Watan, 65
Alawis, 44, 108, 109
Albright, Madeleine, 23
Alexandrovna, Larisa, 142
Alfonzo, Juan Pablo Perez, 154n
Algeria, 12
Aljibury, Falah, 31
Allawi, Iyad, 137
Allott, Gordon, 175n
Alpher, Yossi, 159n
American Enterprise Institute, 23, 47, 84, 118, 179n
American Israel Public Affairs Committee (AIPAC), 23, 47, 48, 89–90, 121, 155n, 159n, 172n
American University, 139
Amit, Meir, 80
Amitay, Morris, 48
Amos, General James, 139
an-Nahar, 59
Annan, Kofi, 151n
Anderson, Sir Roy, 5, 151n
Anti-Ballistic Missile Treaty (1972), 160n
anti-Semitism, 32, 35, 52, 98, 162n, 173n
Aoun, Michel, 163n

Arab Association for Human
    Rights (Nazareth), 58
Arab League, 19, 20, 84
Arab nationalism, threat of, 10–11,
    18, 94, 100, 110, 111, 132,
    136
Arad, Uzi, 60, 79, 178n
Arafat, Yasser, 26, 35, 128, 129,
    181n
Arens, Moshe, 112
Armitage, Richard, 156n, 164n
arms deals, 24, 48, 68, 97, 98,
    99–100, 111, 112, 125, 144,
    146, 161n, 176n, 181n, 183n
Arrow missiles, 68
Ash, Gabriel, 172n
Assad, Bashar, 35, 65, 69, 70, 83
Association of Arab American
    University Graduates, 177n
Atta, Mohammad, 157n
Atlantic Monthly, 177n
Avnery, Uri, 119, 150n
AWACS, 19, 98
Ayalon, Danny, 34–5, 137, 159n
Azeris, 84, 143

Ba'ath party, 11, 18, 29, 31, 136,
    148, 182n
Badr Brigade, 181n
Baer, Robert, 164n
Baghdad, 139, *see also* Iraq
Bahrain, 109
Baker, James, 7, 16, 21, 71, 119–20
Baker-Hamilton Report, 72
Bali, Asli U, 50
Ball, George, 97, 99, 176n
Baluchis, 84, 143
bantustans, 130–1
Bar-Zohar, Michael, 110–11, 176n
Barak, Ehud, 42, 102, 106, 128
Bargewell, Eldon, 6
Barnea, Nahum, 44
Basra, 110
Bay of Pigs, 88
BBC, 67, 175n

BearingPoint, 153n
Bechor, Guy, 105
Begin, Menachem, 99, 178n
Beirut, *see* Lebanon
Belgium, 48
Ben Arieh, Yehoshua, 178n
Ben Eliezer, Binyamin, 33–4, 43, 63
Ben Gurion, David, 63, 100–1,
    110–11, 149, 173n, 176n
Benn, Aluf, 35, 41, 42, 64
Benvenisti, Meron, 104
Benziman, Uzi, 45
Bir Zeit University, 110
Bishara, Azmi, 133
Blair, Tony, 66, 135
Blix, Hans, 75
Bloomberg School of Public Health,
    5
'blowback', xii, 17, 28, 127
Bolton, John, 26, 44, 67, 90, 138,
    157n
Boot, Max, 67
Boston Globe, 112
Bremer, Paul, xi, 31
Britain,
    and arms sales, 125
    and Iran, 73, 112
    and Iraq, 4, 5, 8, 33, 134, 135,
        146
    and Israel, 76, 94–5
    and Lebanon, 142
    and Russia, 160n
    and the Suez War (1956), 94,
        110
    and Zionism, 95
    colonial role, 9, 11, 14, 16, 22,
        108, 123, 126
British Petroleum (BP), 153n
Brookings Institution, 138
Brzezinski, Zbigniew, 46
Bubiyan island, 20
Budapest, 74
Bukay, David, 173n
Burghardt, Jutta, 23
Burns, Nicholas, 37
Burns, William, 47

Burton, Fred, 142
Bush Administration, *see* United States
Bush, George H.W. (Bush Snr), 21, 90, 98
Bush, George W. (Bush Jnr), *see also* United States
  and Christian Zionists, 175n
  and diplomacy, 170n
  and Iran, 52, 144, 184n
  and Iraq, 3–4, 8, 9, 45, 72
  and Jacques Chirac, 79
  and Lebanon, 60
  and the Libby trial, 156n
  and the neocons, 23–4, 25, 27, 132
  and the regional conference (2007), 99–100, 146
  and Saudi/oil links, 16, 119
  and Sharon, 33, 34, 43–4, 137
  and Syria, 69
  at the G8 summit, 66
  axis of evil speech, 28
  criticism of, 14
  on oil 'blackmail', 86
  on the Shia threat, 144
Bush at War, 29
Bushehr reactor, 49
Butler inquiry, 135

Cairo, 139
Camp David (1978), 106
Carter Doctrine, 18–19, 92
Carter, Jimmy, 18, 46, 92, 99, 152n
Case, Clifford, 96
Casey, General George, 72
Castro, Fidel, 150n
Cedar Revolution, 140
Centcom, 18, 51
Center for Security Policy, 23
Central Intelligence Agency (CIA), 2, 11, 14, 17, 20, 29, 37, 82, 84, 95, 112, 142
Chalabi, Ahmed, 31, 142
Chandrasekaran, Rajiv, x–xi

Cheney, Dick
  and Iran, 49, 79, 87, 142, 170n, 184n
  and Iraq, 14, 30, 158n
  and the Lebanon War (2006), 60
  and the neocons, 25, 27, 90
  and the Saudis, 144
  and Syria, 69
  on permanent war, 92–3, 104, 117
Chertoff, Michael, 180n
ChevronTexaco, 153n
Chile, xii
China,
  and arms sales, 98, 176n
  and Iran, 50, 52
  and the neocons, 27
  and oil, 30, 124
  US, threat to, 28, 123, 124, 160n
Chirac, Jacques, 79
Chomsky, Noam,
  on democracy promotion, 132–3
  on Iraq and Vietnam, xii–xiii
  on Ottomanisation, 113–14
  on a possible Shia alliance, 124
  on the 'surge', 73
  on US control of oil, 9–11
  on US foreign policy, 86–8
Christian Zionism, 97, 175n
Clark, General Wesley, 158n
'clash of civilisations', theory of, xv, 10, 26, 106, 108, 111, 177n, *see also* neocons *and* Israel
Clawson, Patrick, 52
Clean Break, A, 26, 66, 133
Clemens, Steven C., 170n
Clinton, Bill, 21, 23, 25, 26, 90, 123, 128, 171n
Coalition for Democracy in Iran, 48
Coalition Provisional Authority, 31
Cohen, Ariel, 118, 120
Cold War, 17, 26, 96, 97, 114
Cole, Juan, 76, 157n
Communist influence, 11, 40, 108, 123

Conference of Presidents of Major American Jewish Organizations, 23
Congress (US), 23, 53, 96, 98
ConocoPhillips, 153n
Council on Foreign Relations, 31, 144
Cronin, Patrick, 184n
Cuba, xii, 87–8, 150n
Curtis, Mark, 16–17
Czech Republic, 160n

D'Alema, Massimo, 130
Dagan, Meir, 169n
Dahlan, Mohammed, 83, 130
Damascus, see Syria
Dan, Uri, 181n
'Danish cartoons affair', 78
Dayan, Moshe, 101, 102, 149, 174n, 175n
Dayan, Uzi, 103–4, 106
De Soto, Alvaro, 129–30
Defense Policy Board, 25
democracy promotion, claims of, 3–4, 8, 9, 85, 122, 123, 124, 126, 131–2, 133, 136, 139, 141, 142, 179n, 181n
Department of Homeland Security, 125, 180n
Dimona, 94
Disengagement Plan, see Gaza
'Domino theory', 10–11
Downing Street memos, 33, 135
Drumheller, Tyler, 135
Druze, 114, 117, 147

East Jerusalem, 131, 139
East Timor, 182n
Eban, Abba, 110
Economist, 38–9, 48, 158n
Edwards, John, 37, 162–3n
Egeland, Jan, 165n
Egypt,
    and Arab nationalism, 21, 100
    and Iran, 38
    and Israel, 45, 106, 107, 109, 111, 114, 178n
    and the Muslim Brotherhood, 127
    and the Palestinians, 181n
    and the Six-Day War (1967), 96, 175n
    and the Suez War (1956), 94, 110
    and the US, 99, 145, 175n
Eisen, Livia, 180n
Eisenhower Doctrine, 17
Eisenhower, Dwight, 111
Eisenkott, Gadi, 57, 164n
Eitan, Rafael, 102
El Al, 180n
el-Baradei, Muhammad, 46
Eldar, Akiva, 130–1
Energy Task Force, 30
England, Gordon, 37
Esfahani, Alireza Zaker, 171n
Eshkol, Levy, 105, 174n
Esso, see ExxonMobil
Ethiopia, 111
Europe,
    and the Holocaust, 78
    and Iran, 41, 44, 48, 51, 52, 76, 124
    colonial role, 108, 110, 113, 126, 138, 140, 148
    protests over Iraq, 34
European Union, 70
Evron, Boaz, 114
ExxonMobil, 153n

Facility 1391 (prison), 54
Fahd, king of Saudi Arabia, 15
Faisal, king of Iraq, 11, 14
Faisal al-Saud, king of Saudi Arabia, 15
Farsi, 76–7
Fatah, 83, 128, 129–30, 181n
Fatah al-Islam, 82, 141, 171n
Feith, Douglas, 24, 26, 29, 47, 51, 133, 157n

Financial Times, 85
Fisk, Robert, 58–9, 73, 138–9, 183n
Foreign Affairs, 106, 134
Foreign Suitors for Iraqi Oilfield Contracts, 30–1
Fort Leavenworth, 139
Forward, 47, 68
France
  and Iraq, 20
  and Lebanon
  and the Suez War (1956), 94, 110
  Atomic Agency, 97
  colonial role, 9, 14, 108, 126
  support for Israel, 94
Franklin, Larry, 47
Free Patriotic Movement, 163n
Friedman, Thomas, 21
Frum, David, 179n
Fulbright, J. William, 96

G8 summit, 66
Gaddafi, Colonel Muammar, 35, 43
Galilee, 68
Gallup poll, 8
Gates, Robert, 9, 13, 79, 170n, 184n
Gaza, *see also* Palestinians
  and Sharon, 33
  as a laboratory, 125–31
  civil war, 83, 129–31
  comparison with Iraq, 8, 91
  disengagement, 24, 36, 50, 98, 128
  land swaps, 114, 178n
Gazit, Shlomo, 103, 105–6, 177n
Gemayel, Bashir, 100
Georgia, 124
Germany, 76
Ghilan, Maxim, 122
Gibraltar, 80
Gingrich, Newt, 26
Gissin, Rana'an, 33
Glick, Caroline, 119–20, 148–9

Golan Heights, 54, 69, 101
Gold, Dore, 37, 40
Gordan, Michael, 157n
Grenada, xii
Green Zone, x, 5, *see also* Iraq
Guardian, 46–7, 72, 130, 132, 146, 184n
Guatemala, xii
Gulf War (1991), 2, 13, 16, 19, 21–2, 40, 43, 90, 105, 113

Ha'aretz, 34, 43, 55, 58, 65, 75, 159n, 161n, 174n
Haditha, 6
Hadley, Stephen, 47
Hagel, Chuck, 33
Haifa, 55, 57, 58, 59, 60
Halabja, 1
Halevy, Ephraim, 35, 74, 103–4, 106
Halliday, Denis, 22–3
Halutz, Dan, 55, 63, 64, 65
Hamas, 127, *see also* Palestinians
  and Iran, 41, 74
  and Saudi Arabia, 118, 119, 146
  and unity government, 83
  and the US, 85
  civil war, 129–30
  Islamic radicalism, xv
  Israel's view of, 44, 56, 147
Hamilton, Lee, 71
Hariri, Rafik, 83, 140
Harkabi, Yehoshafat, 102
Hawaii, xii
Hejaz, 123
Heritage Foundation, 118
Hersh, Seymour, 23, 51–2, 53, 60–1, 65, 112, 143, 144
Herzl, Theodor, 36
Herzliya conference (2001), 103–4, 106
Herzliya conference (2003), 36
Herzliya conference (2007), 36–8, 40, 73–4, 75
Hickenlooper, Bourke, 95–6

Hiro, Dilip, 39, 48
Hirst, David, 45
Hizbullah, xvii, *see also* Lebanon
  and covert US operations, 82,
    140–1, 142
  and Iran/Syria axis, 41, 44, 51,
    53, 67, 68, 74, 118, 162–3n,
    165n
  and the neocons, 26
  and rocket attacks, 49, 53, 55,
    56, 57–9, 60, 66
  and sectarian tensions, 82, 140–1
  and Shebaa Farms, 70
  and the 'war on terror', 37, 104,
    145, 147
  Israeli army (2000), ousting of,
    43, 54, 140
  Israeli attack on (2006), 53–65,
    74, 93, 117, 164n, 165n
  popularity of, xv, 140
  prisoners dispute with Israel,
    54–5, 57, 163n
  spy drones, use of, 58
  US army (1983), ousting of, 17
Holocaust Cartoon Contest, 169n
Holocaust Conference, 77–8
Honduras, xii
Hudson Institute, 24
Human Rights Watch, 165n
Huntington, Samuel, 10, 106, 108
Hussein, king of Jordan, 98
Hussein, Saddam, *see* Saddam
  Hussein

Ibn Saud, 123
IDF (Israel Defence Forces), 35, 62,
  65, 149
India, 30, 98, 111, 124
Indonesia, 182n
Institute for Advanced Strategic
  and Political Studies, 25
Institute for Strategic Affairs, 74,
  101
insurgency, *see* Iraq

International Atomic Energy
  Agency, 38, 46–7, 49–50, 75
International Crisis Group, 2
International Institute for Strategic
  Studies, 184n
International Journal of Middle
  East Studies, 77
International Monetary Fund
  (IMF), 13
Iran,
  and Hizbullah, 41, 43, 44, 59,
    140, 165n
  and Iraq, 7, 44, 71–2, 73, 86,
    134, 144, 157n, 158n
  and oil, 121–2, 122, 154n
  and Saudi Arabia, 144–5
  and the Shia alliance, 28, 37, 67,
    120–1, 124, 132, 135
  and Syria, 41, 42, 44, 56–7, 66,
    104
  and the Taliban, 72, 158n
  and the UN, 38, 50, 73
  Hamas, support for, 41
  Iran-Iraq War (1980–88), 1, 19,
    20, 41, 48
  Islamic Revolution of 1979, 14,
    17, 18, 19, 135
  Israel, supposed threat to, 38,
    40, 41, 45, 49, 53, 56, 57,
    74–8, 120
  Jewish citizens of, 51–2, 162n
  nuclear programme, 14, 38–52,
    74–5, 155n
  Persian nationalism, 18, 136
  resistance, exemplar of, 43
  sectarian tensions in, 84, 109
  the Shah, overthrow of (1953),
    xii, 14–15, 87, 112
  the Shah, US support for, 17–18
  US campaign against, 41, 46, 47,
    48–52, 59–61, 73, 84, 88–9,
    93, 100, 142–3, 170n, 184–5n
Iran-Contra scandal, 24, 130
Iraq, *pre-US invasion*:
  and al-Qaeda, 29–30, 72, 158n

and colonial rule, 108
and the Gulf War (1991), 19,
    21–2, 90
and no-fly zones, 22, 41
and oil, 11–14, 118–19, 120,
    138, 154n, 158n
Iran-Iraq War (1980–88), 1, 19,
    20, 41, 48
Israeli promotion of US attack,
    32–5, 44, 159n
sectarian tensions, 1
UN inspections, 1–3
UN sanctions, 2, 3, 22–3, 30, 41,
    158n
welfare system, 22
Iraq, *the US invasion and after:*
and al-Qaeda, 146–7
and 'democracy promotion',
    131–2
and elections, 85
and the Shia alliance, 120–1,
    124, 135
body counts, 4–6
civil war, x–xi, 6–7, 81, 121,
    135, 136–9
ethnic cleansing, 5–6, 138, *see
    also* partition
the Green Zone, x, 5
humanitarian catastrophe, 4–6
the insurgency, xvii, 5, 6–8,
    71–2, 81–2, 121, 137, 146–7,
    150n
the Kurds, 8–9
massacres by US army, 6
opinion polls, 8, 85
partition, x–xi, xiii, 32, 82, 125,
    137–9, 147–8, 182–3n
regime change, xi–xii, xiv, 21–2,
    26–7, 29–32, 122, 136, 179n
Saudi interference, 145–6
WMD, xvii, 1–3, 29, 45, 135
Iraq Body Count, 4–5, 151n
Iraq Study Group, 7, 71, 72, 119,
    137
Iraqi Petroleum Company, 11, 14

Irbil, 84
Iron Dome, 68
Islamic Jihad, 54, 142
Israel, *grand strategy:*
9/11, exploitation of, 103–4
'clash of civilisations', promotion
    of, xv, 35, 42, 51–2, 80,
    103–4, 106, 111, 179n
Hitler/Nazi comparison, abuse
    of, 34, 35, 73–8
reordering of Middle East,
    xiii–xv, 28, 32, 89–90, 91–3,
    101–2, 107–10, 119–20, 122,
    125, 133, 147–9, 173n
Israel, *relations with the US:*
arms deals, 97, 98
early relations, 95–101, 174n,
    175n
Israel lobby, 47–8, 89–90, 95–6,
    97–8, 172n, 173n
military aid, 97, 98, 155n, 174n
the neocons, influence on, 27–8,
    32, 91–4, 118–20
Israel, *domestic policy:*
Arab mind, 'science' of, 93–4,
    173n
Arab nationalism, fear of,
    xiii–xiv, 100
Herzliya conferences, 36–8, 40,
    73–5, 103–4
human shields, use of civilians
    as, 58, 165n
military censor, 58, 174n
military intelligence, advice of,
    34, 40, 42, 62–3, 103, 168n
missile defence systems, 49, 68,
    167n
opinion polls, 34, 75, 169n
rule by army, 62–4, 102–5
Israel, *relations with the
    Palestinians:*
occupied territories, plan to
    annex, 21
Palestinian nationalism,
    destruction of, 126–31, 181n

Israel, *foreign policy:*
  arms sales, 99–100, 125–6, 176n
  early patron in France and
    Britain, 94
  Golan Heights, 54, 69, 101
  Kurds in Iraq, 111–12, 138
  non-Arab pact (1958), 111–12
  nuclear monopoly, 39, 45, 74,
    94–5, 97, 101, 102, 109,
    117–18, 155n, 160n, 174n,
    179n
  OPEC, plan to undermine, xiv,
    92, 118–20, 122
  Shah of Iran, support for, 112,
    178n
Israel, *past relations with region:*
  Six-Day War (1967), 95–7, 99,
    105
  Lebanon, invasions of, 99, 100,
    107, 140
  Lebanon, withdrawal from
    (2000), 43, 54, 140
Israel, *current relations in region:*
  Egypt, 45, 106, 107, 109, 111,
    114, 178n
  Iran, campaign against, 40–5,
    50–1, 53, 73–8, 162n
  Iran, possible first strike against,
    45, 49, 79–80, 170n, 184–5n
  Iran, spies in, 51, 111–12
  Iraq, partition of, 137, 139
  Iraq, promotion of attack, 32–5,
    44, 159n
  Jordan, 45, 98, 176n
  Lebanon, overflights of, 54
  Lebanon War (2006), xiv, xv, 28,
    53–65, 93, 117, 141, 143,
    164n, 180n
  Lebanon War, attempt to widen
    to Syria and Iran, 56–7
  Lebanon War, dry-run for attack
    on Iran, 60
  Lebanon War, use of cluster
    bombs, 56, 148

  Syria, threatened attack on,
    65–70, 167n
  Saudi peace plan, opposition to,
    84–5, 104
Israeli, Raphael, 173n
Italy, 130

Japan, 9
Jedda, 146
Jerusalem, 68, 77, 104
Jerusalem Post, 62, 66, 119, 148
Jewish Institute for National
  Security Affairs, 23, 33
jihadis, 28, *see also* al-Qaeda
Johns Hopkins University, 5
Johnson, Lyndon, 96, 99
Joint Chiefs of Staff, 10
Jordan,
  and Iraq, 19
  and Israel, 45, 98, 176n
  and the neocon vision, 123
  and the oil industry, 12
  and the Palestinians, 114–15,
    125, 127
  and sectarian tension, 108
  and US support, 100, 111, 145
  Ben Gurion's plan for, 110
Jordan River, 115
Jordan Valley, 131
Journal of Palestine Studies, 107

Kadima party, 75
Kalman, Matthew, 61
Kamel, Hussein, 2
Karzai, Hamid, 156n
Kaspi, Yo'av, 41
Katyusha rockets, 53, 59
Katz, Ya'acov, 80
Kennan, George, 10
Khalilzad, Zalmay, 145–6
Khameini, Ayatollah Ali, 76, 169n
Kharg island, 79
Khatami, Mohammed, 84
Khomeini, Ayatollah, 38, 77, 112
Khiyami, Sami, 173n

Khuzestan, 73
Kimmerling, Baruch, 127
Kinzer, Stephen, xi–xii
Kiryat Shmona, 55
Kissinger, Henry, 23–4, 31, 87, 98, 155n
Klein, Naomi, 125
Knesset, 105, 119, 133
Koran, 150n
Kristof, Nicholas, 172n
Kucinich, Dennis, 14, 153n
Kuntar, Samir, 55
Kurds, 150n
  and the Gulf War (1991), 21
  and partition of Iraq, 8–9, 135, 137–8, 147
  gassing in Iraq, 1–2
  in Iran, 84, 143
  in reordered Middle East, 114, 117, 125
  in Syria, 148–9
  links to Israel, 111–12, 138, 149
Kuwait,
  and the oil industry, 11, 154n
  invasion of (1990), 2, 13, 19–20, 41, 113
  power of, 122
  sectarian pressures on, 109

Labor party, 34, 75, 128
Lake, Anthony, 19
Lancet, 5
Le Monde diplomatique, 132
Lebanon,
  civil war (1975–90), 140
  colonial rule, 108
  Israeli invasion (1978), 99, 140
  Israeli invasion (1982), 100, 107, 140
  Israeli overflights, 54
  Israeli plan for a Christian state, 101, 140
  Israeli war on (2006), 28, 53–65, 82, 93, 117, 141, 148, 164n, 180n
  Israeli withdrawal from (2000), 43, 54
  sectarian tension in, 82, 140–2
  Shebaa Farms row, 54, 69–70, 163n
  Syrian influence, 100–1, 140–1
  threat of partition, 147–8
Ledeen, Michael, 47–8, 92, 118, 172n
Leshem, Daniel, 41, 136
Leverett, Flynt, 88, 143
Levy, Gideon, 85
Lewis, Bernard, 37, 177n
Libby, Lewis "Scooter", 27, 156n, 157n
Liberty (US ship), 99, 175n
Libya, 19, 35, 43, 44, 100
Lieven, Anatol, 24–5, 80–1, 122–4
Likud party, 33, 75
Litani River, 100, 110
Livini, Tzipi, 130
London Review of Books, 89
Lord Goldsmith, 151n
Lott, Trent, 26
Lukoil, 31

Ma'ariv, 101, 162n
Malka, General Amos, 62–3, 104
Maronites, 100, 108, 114
Mearsheimer, John, 89–90, 98, 121, 159n, 172n
Mecca, 16, 123, 129
Media Lens, 151n
Medina, 16
Meir, Gideon, 56
Mendel, Yonatan, 37–8, 40
MI5, 73
MI6, 112, 135
Middle East Forum, 157n
Middle East Studies Association, 177n
Miller, Judith, 157n
Mofaz, Shaul, 57, 102, 128
Mohammadi, Manouchehr, 78

Mohammed (Prophet), 78, 108, 150n
Morocco, 82
Morris, Roger, 11
Moscow, 124
Mossad, 54, 56, 74, 80, 107, 111–12, 141–2, 180n
Mossadeq, Mohammed, 14, 112
Mosul, 110
Mount Miron, 59
Mujahedeen e-Khalq, 143
Muslim Brotherhood, 127, 145

Nabulsi, Karma, 8
Nafaa, Hassan, 107, 114, 177n
Nahariya, 55
Nahr al-Bared, 82
Narouzi, Arash, 77
Nasr, Vali, 145
Nasrallah, Hassan, 35, 55, 57, 141, 147–8, 163n, 164–5n, 182–3n, see also Hizbullah
Nasser, Gamal Abdel, 21, 94, 100, 110, 174n
Natanz, 46, 51, 80, 170n
National Intelligence Council, 134
National Intelligence Estimate, 49
National Security Council, 24, 30, 47, 60, 69, 142
NATO, 50, 123, 158n
Nazareth, 58
Nazis, 35, 40, 76–7
Negev, 178n
neocons,
  and Iran, 27, 47–8, 67, 71–2, 84, 133
  and Iraq, 23, 26–7, 28–32, 118, 122, 132, 133, 136, 137
  and Israel, 23, 25–6, 91–4, 118–19, 125, 155n
  and the Israel lobby, 47–8, 89–90, 121–2
  and the Lebanon War (2006), 60, 93
  and Saudi Arabia, 43, 118–19, 122–3
  and Syria, 66–7, 133
  'clash of civilisations', promotion of, 26, 40, 80, 119–20, 122
  influence, apparent waning of, 71, 72, 147
  oil industry, fight with, 31–2, 118–21, 122
  philosophy of power, 24–7, 92, 172n, 181–2n
  strategy for Middle East, xi, xiv, 26–7, 66, 91–3, 118–24, 133, 147–8, 173n
Netanyahu, Binyamin, 25–6, 75–6
Neumann, Thomas, 33
New York, 16
New York Times, 21, 146, 157n
New Yorker, 51
Newsweek, 2
Nicaragua, xii, 24, 130
Niger, 156n, 157n
Nixon Doctrine, 17–18, 98
Nixon, Richard, 15, 17, 23, 98
North Korea, 27, 28, 39, 44, 75
Nuclear Non-Proliferation Treaty, 25, 38, 41, 46, 155n, 160n

O'Neill, Paul, 30
Occupied Territories, see Palestinians, Gaza and West Bank
Office of Special Plans, 29
Olmert, Ehud,
  and the Arab peace plan, 85
  and Iran, 37, 53, 73–4, 75, 80, 100
  and the Lebanon War (2006), 61–5
  and nuclear weapons, 155n
  and the Palestinians, 98, 131
Oman, 11, 109
OPEC,
  and the Gulf War (1991), 20
  and US support, 100
  establishment of, 15, 153–4n

Iran, threat from, 120–1, 144
neocon plan for, xiv, 43, 92,
 118–19, 120–1
oil industry plan for, 32, 120–1
Open Secrets, xviii, 102, 177n
Operation Desert Storm, 21, 41
Operation Magic Carpet, 180n
Oren, Amir, 104, 176n
Osiraq nuclear reactor, 49
Oslo peace process, 25, 128, 129
Ottomanisation, xiii, 109–10,
 113–14
Overthrow, xi–xii
Oxford Research Group, 46

Pace, General Peter, 72
Pakistan, 17, 84, 102, 109
Palast, Greg, 30–1, 118, 120
Palestinians,
 and elections, 85
 and ghettoisation, 128–9, 139
 and the Gulf War (1991), 113
 and intifadas, 128, 129
 and the Iran-Iraq War, 112–13
 and the Muslim Brotherhood,
  127
 and the peace process, 45, 128,
  129
 and sanctions, 83
 and Saudi Arabia, 119, 146
 and Sharon's plans, 105
 and unity government, 129–30
 Arab world, dependence on, 32,
  43, 112–13, 118, 122
 civil war, threat of, 83, 129–31
 ethnic cleansing of, xiii, xiv, 35,
  112–13, 114–15, 125
 Gaza disengagement, 24, 36, 50,
  98, 128
 in Jordan, 98, 108
 in Lebanon, 82, 100, 112, 140
 Iran, links to, 74, 78
 Israeli demographic fears, 36
 Israeli 'divide and rule', 126–31,
  139, 181n

occupied territories as
 laboratory, xv, 125–6, 141,
 180n
occupied territories as template
 for Iraq, xv, 8, 91, 125
Panama, xii
Patai, Raphael, 93–4
Patriot missiles, 68
Pelosi, Nancy, 69
Pentagon, 16
 and Iran, 50–2, 72, 79, 142–3
 and Iraq, 29, 137, 158n
 control by neocons, 31
Peres, Shimon, 34, 42, 75, 95, 106,
 128, 131, 174n
Peretz, Amir, 63
Peri, Yoram, 113
Perle, Richard, 24, 25–6, 30, 133,
 155n
Perrin, Francis, 97
Petraeus, General David, 139
Pilger, John, 23
Pillar, Paul, 134
Pines Paz, Ophir, 67
Pipes, Daniel, 71, 136–7, 141
Plame, Valerie, 156n
PLO, 127
Poland, 160n
Pollack, Kenneth, 10, 20
Powell, Colin, xiii
'pre-emptive' war, xvi, xvii, 3, 25,
 27, 28, 39, 43, 65, 68, 104,
 105, 148, 151n, 160n
preventive war, *see* pre-emptive war
Price, Matthew, 165n
Project for the New American
 Century, 23, 27
Puerto Rica, xii
Putin, Vladimir, 123–4

Qassem, Sheikh Naim, 59, 141, 143
Qatar, 11

Rabin, Yitzhak, 42, 102, 106, 128,
 179n

Rafael Armaments Development
    Authority, 74
Rafeh, Mahmoud, 142
Ramallah, 128
Rapid Deployment Force, *see*
    Centcom
Ravid, Yitzhak, 74
Reagan, Ronald, 25, 31, 98, 130
Rebuilding America's Defenses, 27
Regev, Mark, 165n
Revolutionary Guard, 72, 73
Rice, Condoleezza, 47, 57, 60, 66,
    79, 88–9, 139, 170n, 184n
Ritter, Scott, 3, 50
Riyadh, 144–5
Roosevelt, Franklin D., 15
Rosen, Steve, 47
Ross, Carne, 135
Rove, Karl, 47
Royal Dutch Shell, 31, 153n
Royal Institute of International
    Affairs, 16
Rubin, Uzi, 74
Rubinstein, Danny, 171n
Rumsfeld, Donald, 25, 26, 29, 31,
    90
Rusk, Dean, 96
Russia, *see also* Soviet Union
    and the Gulf War (1991), 20
    and Iran, 49, 50, 52, 124
    and Iraq, 30
    and Lebanon, 142
    and Syria, 68
    and the US, 39, 123–4, 154n,
        160n

Saban Center, 138
Sadat, Anwar, 107
Saddam Hussein *see also* Iraq
    and the Palestinians, 32, 43, 113
    and WMD, 1–2, 33, 34, 50, 135
    comparison with Hitler, 21, 34
    containment of, 20–2, 23, 26, 87
    crushing of dissent, 21
    debts from Gulf War, 13, 14

    hero of Arab world, 21
    Kuwait, invasion of, 19–20
    US backing for, 11, 19
Saguy, General Uri, 42
Salafis, 145
Salloukh, Fawzi, 142
San Francisco, 30
San Francisco Chronicle, 61
Satterfield, David, 47
Saud, House of, 15–16, 18
Saudi Arabia,
    9/11, connection to, 16, 154n
    and arms sales, 18–19, 98, 99,
        119
    and Iraq, 144–6
    and the neocon plan, 122–3, 148
    and US bases, 16, 18, 20
    as US asset, 17–18, 132, 145
    control of OPEC, 15, 20, 21, 32,
        43, 92, 118–19, 120, 124, 144
    Israel and US, threat to, 32, 122
    possible nuclear ambitions, 38
    regional peace plan, 84–5, 104
    Sunni-Shia split, provocation of,
        81, 82, 109, 144–6, 171n
    US elites, links to,15–16
    US, rift with, 85, 144–6
SAVAK, 112
Schiff, Ze'ev, 59, 63, 105, 125
Seale, Patrick, 9
Second World War, 9, 17, 80, 92,
    96, 103, 154n
Security Council (UN), 50, 52
Segev, Tom, 95, 174n
Senate Foreign Relations
    Committee, 7, 95, 175n
Senate Intelligence Committee, 134
Serbia, 124
Shah of Iran, 14, 17–18, 77, 87,
    100, 112–13
Shahak, Israel, xviii, 102, 107,
    160n, 173–4n, 176n, 177n,
    178n, 179n
Shahak-Lipkin, General Amnon,
    160n
Shapir, Yiftah, 74

Sharon, Ariel
  and Iran, 42–5, 49, 178n
  and Iraq, 32–5, 137, 159n
  and Lebanon, 64, 65, 100, 107
  and Ottomanisation, 114
  and the Palestinians, 36, 85, 125,
    127, 128, 130–1, 181n
  and the power of generals, 63,
    102, 105
  doctrine of empire, 101–2, 106,
    117
  in coma, 61
Sharrett, Moshe, 176n
Shawcross, William, 2
Shebaa Farms, 54, 69, 163n
Shell, see Royal Dutch Shell
Shia,
  and blowback, 17
  and the Iran-Iraq War, 19
  and the neocons, 40, 119
  and Oded Yinon, 109–10
  and oil, 120–1
  'arc of extremism', 28, 37, 67,
    69, 81
  colonial policy, 108
  history of, 150n
  in Iraq, 1, 6, 8, 21, 125
  in Lebanon, 26, 82, 140
  in Syria, 44
  Iran's Shia alliance, 43, 67, 68,
    69, 124, 135
  Iranian interference in
    Afghanistan, 72
  Iranian interference in Iraq,
    71–2
  war with Sunnis, US promotion
    of, 80, 81, 136–7, 143–7
Shlaim, Avi, 110, 131
Sidon, 54, 142
Simon, Bob, 157n
Sinai, 94, 107, 110, 114, 174n, 178n
Singh, Anupama Rao, 22
Siniora, Fuad, 60, 82, 140
Sistani, Grand Ayatollah Ali, 85
Six-Day War (1967), 24, 95–7, 99,
    105, 108, 127, 174n

Skyguard, 68
Snow, Tony, 9
Sofer, Arnon, 173n
Soros, George, 172n
South Africa, 130
South Korea, 9, 124
South Lebanon Army, 141, 142
Soviet Union, see also Russia
  Afghanistan, invasion of, 17, 18,
    28
  and Iran, 14
  and the Suez War (1956), 94
  Cold War threat, 25, 96, 97
  empire, collapse of 24, 105–6,
    114, 116, 118, 123, 149, 173n
  influence in Middle East, 10,
    17–18, 98, 101, 106, 116
State Department (US), xiii, xiv, 8,
    30, 31, 88, 95, 118, 146,
    157n, 171n
Stauffer, Thomas, 175n
Steele, Jonathan, 130, 132
Strategic Future for Israel, 49
Strategic Research Centre (Iran),
    171n
Sudan, 19, 111
Suez War, 94, 110, 173n, 174n
Suharto, General, 182n
Sunday Times, 49
Sunnis,
  and blowback, 17
  and the Iran-Iraq War, 19
  and the neocons, 40, 119, 122
  and Oded Yinon, 109–10
  colonial policy, 108
  history of, 150n
  in Iraq, 1, 6, 7, 8, 125, 136
  in Lebanon, 82, 140, 141
  in Syria, 44
  Iranian interference in
    Afghanistan, 72
  Iranian interference in Iraq,
    71–2
  Ottomanisation, 114
  rise of jihadis, 116

Sunnis, *continued*
  US funding of jihadis, 28
  war with the Shia, US promotion
    of, 80, 81, 136–7, 143–7
Symington, Stuart, 96, 175n
Syria,
  and colonialism, 108
  and the Golan, 54, 69, 101
  and Iraq, 72, 83
  and the neocons, 26, 37, 40
  and Shebaa Farms row, 54
  and Six-Day War (1967), 96
  and the US, 84, 171n
  Egypt, union with, 100
  Iran, alleged ties with, 41, 42,
    44, 56–7, 65, 66, 104
  Israel, threat to, 43, 44
  Israeli attack, threat of, 65–70,
    148–9, 167n
  Lebanon, influence in, 100–1,
    140–1, 167n
  partition, threat of, 109, 147,
    148–9
Syria Accountability Act, 83

Taliban, xvii, 17, 72, 84, 117, 118
Tariki, Sheikh Abdullah, 154n
Tehran, *see* Iran
Tel Aviv, 60, *see also* Israel
Tenet, George, 29–30
Tibet, 123
Time magazine, 22
The Times (London), 44, 137
Timur, Zvi, 102
Toensing, Chris, 139
Total Elf Aquitaine, 31
Truman Doctrine, 17
Truman, Harry, 33, 95, 154n
Turkey, 18, 21, 38, 102, 109, 111,
    113, 114

Ukraine, 124
Unicef, 22
United Arab Emirates, 11, 19
United Jewish Appeal, 96

United Kingdom, *see* Britain
United Nations, 79
  and Iran, 38, 50, 52, 73
  and Lebanon, 54, 83, 140, 141,
    142, 163n, 165n, 166n
  and the Palestinians, 128–9
  inspections in Iraq, 1–2
  Oil for Food program, 22
  Resolution 1701, 56
United States, *foreign policy:*
  9/11, exploitation of, 28–9,
    154n, 157n
  and oil, xi, xii, xiv, 9–10, 27,
    30–2, 73, 86, 119, 122, 124,
    179n
  and oil industry, xiv, 30–2, 87–8,
    119–21
  anti-ballistic missiles in Europe,
    39
  'blowback', xii, 17, 28
  civil war, promotion of, 81–5,
    140–3, 146, 147, 184n
  democracy promotion, claims of,
    3–4, 85, 126, 131–3, 136,
    139–40, 142, 181n
  divide and rule, 100, 137, 147–8
  military expansionism, 92–3,
    124
  nuclear states, fear of, 27
  permanent war, 92
  'pre-emptive' war, doctrine of,
    xvi, xvii, 3, 25, 27, 28, 43, 65
  proxies, development of, 17–18
  Sunni-Shia split, accentuation of,
    28, 80, 81–2, 141, 143–8
  'war on terror', exploitation of,
    xv, 137, 156n
United States, *Israel:*
  arms race, fuelling of, 97,
    99–100, 119, 161n, 176n
  lobby, effect of, 47–8, 89–90,
    95–6, 97–8, 161n
  Arab mind, 'science' of, 93–4
  special relationship, 111
  Suez War (1956), 94

Yom Kippur War (1973), 97, 98
Zionism, identification with, 95
United States, *Iraq:*
  al-Qaeda, links to, 29, 146, 147
  containment policy, 20–2, 23,
    87
  the insurgency, 81–2, 146, 184n
  intelligence before invasion,
    134–5
  mercenaries, use of, 4, 6, 151n
  the Oil Law, 12–14, 138, 153n
  partition, 137–8
  permanent bases, 8, 9, 71, 121,
    152n
  regime change, xi–xii, xiv, 21–2,
    26–7, 29–32, 122, 136, 179n
  State Department view, xiii, xiv,
    12, 30–2, 118
  the 'surge', 9, 72–3
  White House split, 71–2
United States, *Iran:*
  campaign against, 41, 46, 47,
    48–52, 88–9, 100, 142–3
  moves in UN, 50, 73
  nuclear strike against, option of,
    51–2
  undercover activities, 51, 84,
    142–3
  military attack preparations,
    50–2, 59–61, 73, 93, 170n,
    184–5n
  Israeli unilateral action, hints of,
    49, 79
United States, *other Middle East
    states:*
  Afghanistan, xii, xvii, 17, 72,
    109, 117, 156n, 158n
  Lebanon, 82, 140–2, 183n
  the Palestinians, 83, 98, 129–30,
    146, 181n
  Russia, 123–4
  Saudi Arabia, 85, 98, 132,
    144–6, 154n
  Syria, 69–70, 83, 86, 142
University of Maryland, 8

Van Creveld, Martin, 39, 68–70
Venezuela, 10
Vietnam War, xii–xiii, 9, 17, 97,
    175n
Vilayat e-Faqih, 40
Village Leagues, 127
Von Sponeck, Hans, 23

Wahhabism, 40, 123
Wall Street Journal, 179n
Walnut Creek, 30
Walt, Stephen, *see* Mearsheimer,
    John
'war on terror', xv, 9, 28–9, 35, 45,
    80, 106, 131, 137, 140, 141,
    143, 144, 149, 156n, 157n
Warba island, 20
Warde, Ibrahim, 132
Washington, *see* United States
Washington Institute for Near East
    Policies, 52
Washington Post, 24, 50, 88, 157n
Weisglass, Dov, 45
Weissman, Keith, 47
Welch, David, 129
West Bank, *see also* Palestinians
  and land swaps, 178n
  and the neocons, 24
  and separation principles, 139
  and Sharon, 85
  and the Six-Day War (1967), 105
  civil war, 83, 125–31
  comparison with Iraq, 8, 91
  ethnic cleansing of, 114–5
Western media, 4–5, 57, 123
White House, *see* United States
Wilson, Joseph, 156n
Winograd Committee, 61–4, 67,
    104
WMD (weapons of mass
    destruction), 1–3, 29, 34, 50,
    133, 135, *see also* Iraq
Wolfensohn, John, 24
Wolfowitz, Paul, 26, 27, 29, 31,
    87, 155n, 157n, 181n

Woodward, Bob, 29
Woolsey, James, 37, 40, 90, 160n
World Bank, 24, 131
World Court, 76
World Food Programme, 23
World Trade Center, 16, 26, 29
World War Two, *see* Second World
    War
World Zionist Organisation, 107
Wurmser, David, 26, 60, 66, 133
Wurmser, Meyrav, 24, 66, 69

Ya'alon, Moshe, 37, 102, 128
Yadlin, Amos, 168n
Yassin, Sheikh Ahmed, 127
Yed'iot Aharonot, 66, 103, 105
Yemen, 20, 82, 109, 180n

Yinon, Oded, 107–10, 114–15,
    116, 117, 124, 148, 149
Yom Kippur War (1973), 15, 97,
    98
Young, Michael, 147

Ze'evi, Rehavam, 102
Zinni, Anthony, 47
Zionism
    and fear of Arabs, 76
    and the neocons, 26
    and reordering of Middle East,
        32, 91, 110–11, 112, 149,
        177n
    and the US, 95
Zunes, Stephen, 20, 99, 171n,
    173n, 176n